THE INFLUENCE OF QUAKER WOMEN ON AMERICAN HISTORY

Biographical Studies

Edited by
Carol and John Stoneburner

Studies in Women and Religion
Volume 21

The Edwin Mellen Press
Lewiston/Queenston

Library of Congress Cataloging-in-Publication Data

The Influence of Quaker women on American history.

(Studies in women and religion ; v. 21)
Includes bibliographies and index.
1. Women, Quaker--Biography. 2. Women, Quaker--
Influence. I. Stoneburner, John. II. Stoneburner, Carol.
III. Series.
BX7793.153 1986 289.6'088042 86-23634
ISBN 0-88946-528-2 (alk. paper)

This is volume 21 in the continuing series
Studies in Women and Religion
Volume 21 ISBN 0-88946-528-2
SWR Series ISBN 0-88946-549-5

The Edwin Mellen Press   The Edwin Mellen Press
Box 450   Box 67
Lewiston, New York   Queenston, Ontario
USA 14092   L0S 1L0 CANADA

Printed in the United States of America

To our parents,
Charlotte Simkin Lewis
Asa Ray Lewis
Margaret Lois Timmons Stoneburner
Charles William Stoneburner
and
our son,
Stephen Jonathan Stoneburner

TABLE OF CONTENTS

ACKNOWLEDGMENTS

This volume is an outgrowth of an Interdisciplinary Symposium on American Quaker Women As Shapers of Human Space which was held at Guilford College in 1979. Most of the articles were originally given at that occasion. We are grateful to the authors of these articles for their significant contributions to this volume. We note that the article by James C. Cooley, Jr., "American Quaker Presence in Late Nineteenth-Century China" first appeared in The Proceedings of the Southwest Conference for Asian Studies, (New Orleans, 1980), and that paper on "Charity Cook" by Algie I. Newlin first appeared in print in The Southern Friend: Journal of the North Carolina Friends Historical Society (Autumn, 1979). The paperr "Lucretia Mott: Holy Obedience and Human Liberation" by Margaret H. Bacon, first appeared in print in the March, 1980 (Vol. 26, No. 5) Friends Journal. Permission to reprint has been granted by Friends Journal.

Both the symposium and this volume have been strongly supported by numerous persons at Guildford College. Presidents Grimsley Hobbs and William Rogers; Assistant to the President, Bruce Stewart; and Deans Catherine Frazer, Sybille Colby and Samuel Schuman have, over time, supported the completion of this work. Colleagues Judith Harvey, Jacquline Ludel, Jane Godard Caris, Jerry Caris Godard, Ann Deagon, O. Theodore Benfey, Treva Mathis and Carole Treadway were all helpful in shaping the symposium. During the symposium the assistance of faculty and staff, Sarah Malino,

Mildred Marlette, Joesephine Moore, James Newlin, Hugh Stohler, Damon Hickey and Henry Hood were very important. The work of Sandra Beer, then a senior religious studies major was essential as Assistant Director. More recently the help gained from Beverley Rogers' careful reading of the entire manuscript is acknowledged with thanks.

During the formative period before the symposium, visits on the Guilford campus by Elise Boulding, Rachel DuBois, Helen Hole and Mary Maples Dunn gave encouragement to invest the time and energy for this study. This was continued by a small group of faculty who met and helped formulate the metaphor, "shaping human space." R. Melvin Keiser assisted the whole process by drafting a pre-symposium paper "On Human Space."

Financial support for the symposium was provided by the J.M. Ward Trust, Guildford's Women's Studies Program and Emmett and Kay Bringle of Greensboro. Support in the form of critical reading and comments on "The Introduction" by Hugh Barbour, Elise Boulding and Tony Stoneburner are gratefully acknowledged. Editors from Edwin Mellen Press, Herbert Richardson and Elizabeth Clark have been encouraging and helpfully critical. We appreciate Liela Johnson's work in typing the final copy.

Of special importance to us has been the constant support and encouragement of colleagues Mel and Beth Keiser. They gave very essential support during the whole process -- from its conceptualization to the tedious work of helping us with some of the editing.

For this we are very grateful. Their children Megan and John Christopher and our son, Stephen Jonathan have lived a good share of their lives with some part of this study on American Quaker women periodically occuring in the background or the foreground. Collectively we are glad to send it out to readers in hopes that the articles gathered here will inform and inspire further exploration, analysis and action in areas of human equality, justice, and freedom.

CONTRIBUTORS

Margaret Hope Bacon is author of recently published, Mothers of Feminism: The Story of Quaker Women in America and Let This Life Speak about Henry J. Cadbury. Earlier books include Valiant Friend: The Life of Lucretta Mott, The Quiet Rebels: The Story of Quakers in America and I Speak for My Slave Sister: The Life of Abby Kelley Foster. Previously a writer for the American Friends Service Committee, she is presently involved in research, writing and lecturing.

Dr. Hugh Barbour is Professor of Religion at Earlham College and Professor of Church History at Earlham School of Religion. His earlier study Quakers In Puritan England has recently been republished and he is working with Jerry Frost on a history of American Quakers. The article in this volume has been revised and expanded and appears in a recent festschrift in honor of Edwin Bronner, Seeking the Light: Essays in Qaker History edited by J.W. Frost and John M. Moore.

Dr. Elise Boulding is Professor Emeritus in Sociology at Dartmouth College. Among her earlier publications are The Underside of History: A View of Women Through Time, From a Monastery Kitchen and The Social System of the Planet Earth with Gay Burgess and Kenneth Boulding. Her most recent book is How to Think About the Planet.

Dr. James C. Cooley, Jr. is Associate Professor of History at the University of North Carolina in Greensboro and author of T.F. Wade in China: Pioneer in Global Diplomacy. He is presently doing research on British Quaker Missionaries in China.

Dr. Susan Forbes is presently Senior Associate at the Refugee Policy Group in Washington, D.C. A recent study "A Special Humanitarian Concern, Refugee Admissions Since Passage of the 1980 Refugee Act" is in Immigration News. Previous work was as Research

Director of Select Commission on Immigration and Refugee Policy and Assistant Professor of American Studies, Brandeis University.

Amelia R. Fry is Project Director on leave from the California Governmental Eras Oral History Series and interview/editor of Suffragists Series at Regional Oral History Office of University of California at Berkeley. Her biography of Alice Paul is forthcoming and she has written several papers and articles on Alice Paul.

Dr. Helen G. Hole (deceased) was Professor Emeritus of English Literature at Earlham College. She was author of Things Civil and Useful: A Personal View of Quaker Education and a history of Westtown Friends Boarding School. She also taught at Earlham School of Religion and Pendle Hill.

Dr. Winthrop Hudson, is Adjunct Professor of Religion at the University of North Carolina at Chapel Hill. The fourth edition of his Religion in America was published recently as well as a book, Walter Rauschenbusch, Selected Writings, which he edited.

Dr. Algie I. Newlin (deceased) was Professor Emeritus of History at Guilford College. He is the author of numerous articles and booklets on Quakerism in North Carolina and author of a book, Charity Cook.

Carol Stoneburner is Director of Faculty Development and Coordinator of Women's Studies at Guilford College. She was the Director of the Symposium on American Quaker Women As Shapers of Human Space, Guilford College.

Dr. John H. Stoneburner is Craven Professor of Religious Studies at Guilford College where he teaches church history, contemporary theology and inter-disciplinary studies and has held administrative positions.

Dr. Barbara Miller Solomon is Senior Lecturer on History and Literature and on The History of American

Civilization at Harvard University. (ret.) She is author of *Ancestors and Immigrants: A Changing New England Tradition*, and numerous articles on women in *Dictionary of Notable American Women*. Her most recent book is *In The Company of Educated Women: A History of Women and Higher Education in America*.

Dr. Margaret Sery Young is Professor of Behavior in the Companion Animal Department, North Carolina State University, School of Veterinary Medicine. As she was earlier interested in and did research on the profession and practice of human medicine, she is now working on the profession and practice of veterinary medicine and human--animal relationships and interactions.

PREFACE

This book is a study of Quaker women as Public Friends. A "Publick Friend," at the very inception of Quakerism in the 1650's, was one (male or female) who expressed his or her faith by preaching to and attempting to convert and reform the larger society. Although this is a very important and continuing dimension of the Religious Society of Friends, not all Quaker men and women have faced outwards towards the world and sought interaction of this kind.

This sub-set of Quaker women, the Public Friends, development was unique in developing an intentional interaction with the larger society which was atypical of Protestant Christian women and which challenged the societal norms of appropriate gender-defined behavior. And they were successful. Quaker women have given important leadership to the movement of women into public space. Of the first 59 Quaker missionaries to the colonies in America ("Publishers of Truth") from 1656 to 1663,[1] 26 were women; of the four Quaker martyrs in the seventeenth American colonies, one was a woman. Of the 1,359 women included in The Dictionary of Notable American Women 1607-1950, 85 were Quakers, or 6.3%. (Where Quakers were less than 1%--50,000--of the population at the end of the Colonial period, the high water mark. The percentage of Quakers in the population has markedly declined--about 125,000 Quakers in 1950).[2] Noting the disproportionate representation by Quaker women reflected in the lists of classification (by activity/profession) of the Dictionary of Notable American Women suggests areas where they left their mark: 48% of the ministers and evangelists, 40% of the abolitionists, 22% of the naturalists, 22% of the physicians, 18% of the prison reformers, and 18% of the feminists, 16% of entrepreneurs, 11% of the political advisers and appointees, and 10% of the college adminis-trators. Female Public Friends continued to have an impact on Quakerism, on issues affecting the American colonies and nation and on other non-Quaker women for over three hundred years.

Three centuries is an unusually long historical span to describe and the period since the mid-seventeenth century is especially difficult given the tremendous changes in the experience of Quakers, Americans, and women. Within this complex intermeshing of experience we tell the story of women and Quakerism from the point of view of this small group of women who have understood themselves as shapers of the world they inhabit. While they taught each other, from generation to generation, they share no common religious vocabul-ary. To tell their story is thus to tell many stories, yet all embody a pattern of action that seeks to persuade the world to be less selfish, more caring, and more open to its underlying relationship to God.

To these many stories, which are fundamentally one story, we bring the questions and insights of scholars from a variety of academic disciplines. Thus we make this study a multi-faceted exploration of women-initiated social change. Perceptions from the fields of theology, religious and social history, sociology, anthropology, and psychology are combined to articulate a description and theory of religious/social interaction more complex than any one disciplinary perspective can provide.

The eleven essays collected here bring into focus in the life-stories of individual women the distinctive qualities of the particular time, place, and way of being and speaking as Quakers. Included in this study are group portraitures of a sample of seventeenth century English and American women who were preachers, prophetesses, writers, spiritual counselors and leaders in the earliest years of the Society of Friends and of twenty-five English Quaker women (seventeenth and eighteenth century) who were included in the fourteen volume Friends Library (published by the Orthodox branch of Quakerism between 1837 and 1850). Also included are studies of the following individual women: eighteenth century North Carolina traveling minister, Charity Cook; nineteenth century preacher-reformer, Lucretia Mott; suffragist-reformer, Susan B. Anthony; educators, Martha Tyson, Prudence Crandall, Maria Mitchell, Emily Howland, Mary Mendenhall Hobbs, Martha Carey Thomas, Jane Rushmore; physician, Ann Preston and medical practitioner Clemence Lozier; and missionaries to China, evangelist Esther Butler, doctor Lucy Gaynor, teacher/ educator Lenna Stanley. Twentieth- century women are lawyer/reformer and Director of the National Consumer's League, Florence Kelley; professor of economics and peace advocate, Emily Greene Balch; and scholar, lawyer and political lobbyist, Alice Paul. The "Introduction" will delineate facets of the Quaker tradition which informed these lives, sketch a collective profile of these women as shapers of human space, and describe ways these female Public Friends interacted with and provided leadership for the larger society.

To have excluded so many other important American female public friends is frustrating. Some of those who are not included and who merit much more serious attention are the earliest traveling ministers in the American colonies, Mary Fisher, Ann Austin, Elizabeth Hooten and martyr, Mary Dyer; Mother Ann Lee and Publick Universal Friend Jemima Wilkinson, both founders of religious utopian communities who had been members of and were influenced by the Society of Friends; founders of early colonial towns and communities, Lady Deborah Moody and Elizabeth Haddon Estaugh; eighteenth century writers/historians, Susanna Wright and Deborah Logan, and diarist Elizabeth Sandwich Drinker. The absence of a paper on Abigail Kelley Foster or Sarah and Angelina Grimke'is a particular lack. Although their preaching /speaking in public to a sexually mixed audience was not new for Quaker women, it seems to have been shocking to the nineteenth century public.

It was difficult to select Florence Kelley as illustrating development of social analysis and action during the first half of the twentieth century and thus not focus on some of her colleagues such as Edith and Grace Abbott, and social workers, Martha Pratt Falconer and Alice Shaffer. Similarly by studying Nobel Peace Prize recipient Emily Green Balch and her work for international peace, we have slighted the similar work of another, and probably better known Nobel Peace Prize recipient, Jane Addams, who manifested many character-istics of her Quaker childhood. Some of the important contributions of these women and others are, however, included in the Appendix in a "Time-Line" of public acts by noted Quaker women from 1650 to 1950. The Appendix also includes a list of 85 Quaker women included in The Dictionary of Notable American Women, 1607-1950 and compares them to a sample of 85 non-Quaker women from that source. These records in the Appendix add important dimensions to the fuller narratives found in the essays on individual women.

Before turning to the Introduction's delineation of facets of the Quaker tradition which informed these lives and of a collective profile of public Quaker women as shapers of human space, it will be useful to explain the selection of the metaphor of "shapers of human space" for American Quaker women. It was first used for a three-day interdisciplinary symposium held at Guilford College in March, 1979. All but two of the essays included here were delivered at that conference. The metaphor itself evolved out of much formal and informal discussion among an interdisciplinary group of faculty at Guilford College. Several steps were considered. First, we tried to listen carefully to a number of contemporary Quaker women speak about their own religious/public/ social experience. Secondly, we listened to scholars of Quaker women. We soon joined them in beginning to have serious questions about intellectual categories being used to describe women's historical experience. In particular, we found that the concepts of public space as male and private domestic space as female, and masculinity as active and femininity as passive, were not only contrary to Quaker women's experience, they were insufficient to capture the wholeness of their lives. Quaker religious experience for both men and women involved receptivity and action, action emerging out of receptivity, and receptivity following action, just as domestic space became public and public space enacted concerns of private space. It is out of this understanding that "shapers" (reflecting being shaped and shaping) was chosen.

"Human" was chosen, even when we were most definitively focusing on the leadership of Quaker women in the women's movement, because the ultimate definition for Quaker women is always for human rights, human needs, human creation. There is implicit in this phrase not just more inclusiveness than one may find in "feminism"--Quaker women also addressed the issues and the rights of Native Americans, slaves, prisoners--but also a focus on "this worldliness." This focus manifests the Quaker conviction that its work is "now" in the historic present. Its work is, however, not merely human energy and power, but transformation by the Spirit. Quakers are very much a part of the religious sub-tradition that sees the divine-human relationship as one of co-workers actively involved in a "New Creation." Hence the choice of the "human" adjective.

"Space" was chosen as an alternative to "spheres," because sphere in women's history has come to mean domesticity as a passive existence delimited by males. It doesn't adequately describe the experience of Quaker women. We needed a metaphor that suggested open interaction between the public-private and active-passive rather than their hierarchical dualistic ordering by the metaphor of spheres. In addition we had a heuristic motive, namely to encourage the persons writing the essays to pay especially close attention to the various spaces in which public Quaker women lived worked, and visited and what they learned from these spaces.

The intentional openness of the metaphor of "space" was seen as consistent with the inherent "openness" of continuing revelation in Quaker belief and action but also gave intellectual "room" for scholars coming from

sociology, literature, history, religious studies, and
anthropology. "Space" gets interpreted in many ways
within this collection of essays. Sometimes space is
literal, speaking of room arrangements and building
architecture, or about distances traveled and places
visited. At times it refers to influence, power, and
appropriate or inappropriate activities. On still other
occasions it relates to issues of personal confidence,
internal doubts, and spiritual struggles. In these ways,
the openness of the metaphor not only kept us focused
but allowed for the interplay of many perspectives.

Another meaning of the concept of space comes
directly from Elise Boulding's The Underside of History.
In this social theory she develops the concept of space
as directly referring not only to the actual physical
space but also to the learning which occurs as one lives
and works within particular environments. For example,
women in hunting and gathering societies know the ter-
rain in which they live and move. They learn to know
what kinds of berries and roots grow in what kinds of
places. They learn to feel and sense the environment so
that they can sustain the family diet if there is no
other food supply. This makes them watchful, conservative, and essential to the lives of the whole tribe.

The women in this study understand themselves to
live in a world where the potential for a New Creation
can be actualized. They learn from activities in home,
Meeting, and public world. They claim these learnings
are human learnings, available to all who would live in
relationship to the Light, Teacher, Spirit, and that of
God Within. They were led to being shaped and shapers.
This makes them faithful, authentic, daring, audacious
and, we believe, of considerable importance to the
ongoing struggle to make and keep life human.

Notes

[1]Mary Maples Dunn, "Women of Light" in Women of America, eds. Carol Ruth Beekin and Mary Beth Norton (Boston: Houghton Mifflin, 1979), p.

[2]Edwin Scott Gaustad, Historical Atlas of Religion in America, rev. ed. (New York: Harper and Row, 1976), p. 26, and Population Abstract of the United States, Vol. I, John L. Andriot, ed., (McLean, Va.: Andriot Associates, 1983).

THE INFLUENCE OF QUAKER WOMEN ON AMERICAN HISTORY

Biographical Studies

INTRODUCTION
DRAWING A PROFILE OF AMERICAN
FEMALE PUBLIC FRIENDS AS SHAPERS
OF HUMAN SPACE
Carol Stoneburner

ALTERNATIVE RELIGIOUS PERSPECTIVES AND PRACTICES

The pattern of interaction of women public friends with the larger society is grounded in the religious tenets and practices of Quakerism or the Religious Society of Friends.1 Quakerism burst forth out of the tumult of mid-seventeenth century England. A time of political, economic, social, and religious chaos and strife, it was the matrix of political and scientific revolution, the death of feudalism and birth of a new socioeconomic order, and a multitude of religious counter-cultural visions, programs, and experiments.

The most important movement to emerge out of this turmoil was Puritanism. While multifaceted it initially focused on the reform of worship and church government in the later years of Queen Elizabeth. Puritans wished to cast away all forms and practices that were not based on scripture, such as the office of bishop, liturgical prayers, and vestments. As time passed and the controversies within the Church of England became more volatile, Puritanism became not only more powerful but began to address connected issues in the larger society. Convinced that England had become an ungodly nation, Puritans, with their belief that scripture is the authority for individuals and societies as well as the conviction that the Holy Spirit can work in and transform sinful selves, saw themselves as having been called to reform individuals, church, and nation.

It was a time of overt hopefulness and expectation. In this chaotic but creative situation, a number of radical visionary groups appeared, most of them basically religious in their orientation, such as the Levellers and Fifth Monarchy Men. Various forms of millenialism were directly connected with these hopes. Much, if not everything, seemed possible with God being ready to bring about changed persons and a changed society. The world, with its various forms of idolatry, apostasy, and injustices, was going to be turned upside-down and set aright.

Quakerism: A Radical Puritan Reform

It is not surprising that with all of this turmoil many individuals felt cast loose from any type of deeply felt, reliable, and sense-making spiritual mooring, and consequently joined or explored a variety of Christian churches before finding one that satisfied them. Such a person was George Fox (1624-1691), the founder of The Religious Society of Friends. Having gone through a long search and a radical transformation himself, Fox preached, taught, and practiced a radical type of Christianity, rooted in "spiritual Puritanism," similar to, and perhaps directly connected with, left-wing Protestant groups on the Continent. He and all early Quakers believed that true religion was not just a segment of life but should shape all aspects of life, and that authentic worship needed no forms or rituals but was directed by the Spirit of God alone. One historian describes this degree of ecclesiastical radicalism graphically:

If the outline of iconoclasm may be regarded, only for diagrammatic purposes, as a declivity, with Roman Catholicism at the top of the hill and Quakerism at the bottom, then the Baptists are on the foothill. To limit the process of reductionism and stripping the Christian religion to what was believed to be its essential in England, it began with the lopping off of the Pope, the liturgy in Latin, images and five of the sacraments, thus forming the Church of England. The Presbyterians subtracted the role of bishops and established the parity of ministers, assisted by lay elders. The Independents, like the Presbyterians, exalted preaching and celebrated the sacraments of Baptism and Holy Communion, while decentralizing church government even further to the extent of local autonomy. The Baptists followed the Independents, but eliminated Paedobaptism in favour of believers' Baptism by submersion, and made church membership depend upon conversion and the gift of the Spirit. Finally, the Quakers completed the process of interiorisation by eliminating all the sacraments, claiming that they had the experience of sanctification without the ritual that had usually accompanied it, and doing away with a professional ministry.2

If mainline forms of Puritanism were counter-cultural, Quakerism as a left-wing form of Puritanism was more so.

Radical Quaker Language and Thought

The central and seminal theological belief of George Fox and his followers was that there was "that of God" within each person. The process of conversion, called "convincement" by them, was the personal experience of knowing God in one's inner being. They called the inner presence of God various names: "indwelling Christ," "Inner Light," "Teacher within," "Truth," and of particular interest to us, "the Seed." Such metaphors speak to the belief that accompanying and expanding the revelation of God known in Jesus Christ is the on-going revelation of God to any and all persons and the divinely given and awakened inner potential to respond to this divine presence.

An extensive spiritual process called (by seventeenth Century Quakers) the "Lamb's War" is described in considerable detail in the paper by Elise Boulding, "Mapping the Inner Journey of Quaker Women." Here it needs to be noted that there were two dimensions of the Lamb's War. The first was the inner struggle to be aware of and responsive to the inner Seed. The second was carrying out the new relationship with the presence of God through transformation of the larger society. By coming through the purgative "flaming sword" of the first part of the Lamb's War, Quakers were prepared to be participants in bringing forth the "New Creation" (George Fox's phrase for the transformation of the world).

The outward signs of this spiritual struggle were both negatively and positively expressed. Believing that the Church in England was practicing empty forms not grounded on personal religious experience, early Quakers occasionally interrupted the clergy and liturgy at these services, and refused: to be members of the Church of England, to pay tithes to the state for the support of the church, to take oaths of allegiance to the state, to pay special homage to persons because of their social rank, and to kill or to aid military endeavors.

The more positive outward signs were the gathering together in silent (unprogrammed) meetings for worship of God, and the willingness, even eagerness to be led by the Spirit of God to speak about one's personal experience of God in worship, to preach to non-Quakers about the sins of the old order and the possibility of a new creation, to suffer imprisonment and persecution, to articulate testimonies for moral and righteous living, and to adopt a life-style focused on spiritual growth.

The Society of Friends shunned many traditional ecclesiastical patterns because it saw itself as the true church. It developed a number of alternative practices, such as using: a lay ministry (open to men and women), Queries and Advices to replace doctrinal statements, Testimonies to replace creeds, Meetings for Business with separate structures for men and women, a redesigned marriage ceremony, spiritual journals as a form of discipline and as a way to instruct those new to the faith, recording members' births and deaths, and the Society's official actions, writing general epistles, and publishing tracts. The concept of the sacredness of all life in the New Creation replaced the particular sacraments of Communion and Baptism. Quakers built meeting houses, started schools for girls and boys, oversaw the apprenticeship of the young of both sexes, and provided care for Quakers imprisoned for their beliefs and for the family members of the imprisoned and those away on the traveling ministry.

While Quakers provided great support for their members, those who did not conform to a pattern of right-living--who married non-Quakers, paid church tithes, took oaths of allegiance, or fought in wars-- were disowned ("read out of Meeting").

Over time Quakers created a leadership class. They authorized traveling public ministries, designated spiritual elders and overseers, appointed clerks (chairpersons) to run meetings and "recorded" persons who were especially effective preachers; and developed a consensus form of decision-making for carrying out actions and disciplining members. In time, both men and women filled all of these roles.[3]

Gender and Spirituality In Early Quakerism: The Lamb's War

Contemporary social historians, both in period studies and in general histories of women in America, have accurately noted the effects on Quaker women of the alternative tenets and practices described above.[4] The religious justification for women speaking in public to interpret their faith; the leadership training possible within the separate women's Meetings for Business and in most parts of the Quaker leadership class; the formal education provided for girls; and the articulation of a Testimony (principle) of equality of persons have been seen as important innovations of Quakerism. Social historians have also described the profound effect Quaker women have had on their non-Quaker American sisters by acting as role models of alternative behaviors.

What has been less discussed is the spiritual empowerment Quaker women experienced through the process of convincement (variously called the Lamb's War in the seventeenth century, the struggle for purity in the Quietist Period of the eighteenth and early nineteenth centuries, and the wrestle with conscience in the nineteenth and twentieth centuries). Contemporary feminist theological study of women's spirituality does, however, remind us that examination of the spiritual process of women should be separated out and silhouetted against the religious experience of males. Otherwise, the male experience will be seen as normative and the particular insights of women may be lost.5

Quakerism has stressed the spiritual equality of men and women. This is a by-product of the belief that it is the Spirit of God which acts and speaks through persons, and which is not gender-bound. There are important places where the female and male experience of spirituality may be similar. These will be noted, but ways will also be suggested in which subtle variations of the acculturation of women and men have provided different experiences and thus different understandings—first as inner struggle to be responsive to the divine within and later as outward struggle to transform society.

Personal Transformation of The Lamb's War: Interplay of
Spirit and Nature

Both men and women fought against the Light which
penetrated the darkness of their sinful lives and consequently exposed a considerable amount of distressing
self-knowledge.   This caused a quaking of the human
spirit (one basis for the name "Quakerism") for men and
women.   Both sexes had to fight against the desire to
fill their lives with distractions so that they could
avoid despair.   Quaker spirituality involves, therefore,
the determination not to flee but to wait patiently and
quietly for the Light to flood one's life.   Waiting
patiently may have been a more usual process for females
because of their socialization. However accounts of both
sexes suggest that this was a central but exceedingly
difficult struggle for everyone.

To glimpse better what Quakers believed about the
presence of God within the self, it may be helpful to
designate this as experience of "the Other."   This
phraseology suggests the radical difference between the
human self and divine presence.   Quakers did not believe
each person had a little piece of divine substance in
their souls.   Instead they believed that each person had
the God-given potential to respond to the presence of
divine otherness within their very being.[6] While the
metaphor of the Light describes the exposing process of
spirituality, the metaphor of the Seed captures both the
sense of "otherness" and the need for receptivity.   The
Seed already is present.   The spiritual process is to
acknowledge its presence and nurture its growth and
development.   Such growth changes the believer.   Ideas
and feelings about the self are transformed.   Where once

there was isolation of the self, there now became a
relationship of self and Other. "Living in the Light"
is the normal Quaker phraseology for this and it
describes both the scrutinizing ("Light") and the
relational qualities ("Living in") of this spiritual
process.

While both men and women struggled against and came
to affirm the relational in their lives,[7] women had a
different vantage point because as women they had been
socialized to see the importance of living in relationship to various others and to use this to shape their
lives. One quintessential experience of the other for
many women was procreation (pregnancy, childbirth, and
childrearing). To become aware of, willing to affirm,
and creatively react to the natural seed of the other
growing within could be a profoundly altering experience. A woman thus learned to accommodate and respond to
the other. She was both helpless and responsible. She
was vulnerable unto death, yet gave new life through the
blood and milk of her body. Pondering this natural
mystery, her perspective as a person was altered. A
pregnant woman could not afford to live in isolation.
She had been shaped, but also became a shaper in creating a caring environment for the child. (Although we
are focusing on the human learnings of relationship
learned in maternity, women who were not mothers, as
well as men, would and did have comparable natural
experience, which brought about this human learning of
relational living.)[8]

Often the important human learnings which are
gained through maternity are assumed to be, and
designated as, instinctual or merely natural. It is not

usually acknowledged that a psycho/social transformation has occurred for women to be able to care effectively for the new life. Received tradition in our culture generally associates pregnancy and childbirth with passivity not action, with instinct not social learning.

How then did the procreative experience affect Quaker women? If the above line of reasoning is accurate, it is quite possible that each type of responding to the seed, in spiritual convincement and in procreation, illuminated the other. An important consequence of this was the conviction that there is not a necessary division between spirit and nature, the latter identified with negative qualities. Both male and female Quakers often used dualistic language, but they seem to have been groping for a way beyond the necessary identification of some aspects of reality with sin and darkness. It has been argued that the strong interest in science for many Quakers, both men and women (see papers on Maria Mitchell, Ann Preston, and Lucy Gaynor), was the result of the conviction that the natural world is not dead and inert but sacramental, that is, manifesting the presence of God. For the self that has been transformed in the spiritual struggle, all of creation can also be seen as transformed--self and the nature world are part of the New Creation, as Fox indicates in a famous passage:

> Now was I come up in spirit through the
> flaming sword into the paradize of God. All
> things were new and all the creation gave
> another smell unto me than before, beyond what
> words can utter. I know nothing but pureness
> and innocency and righteousness, being renewed

up into the image of God by Christ Jesus, so
that I say I was come up into the state of
Adam which he was in before he fell.9

All aspects of existence could be distorted by sin, but
similarly all aspects could be perfected. Without the
necessary dualism of spirit and nature, study of the
natural world and spiritual understanding influence each
other. For at least some Quaker women this interaction
between the spiritual and natural probably occurred in
the reception and nurturance of the biological and
spiritual seed.

Societal Transformations of the Lamb's War: Interplay
of Spirit and Nature

This interplay of spiritual and natural was not
only a part of the transformation of the self within but
led to the effort to transform society without, the
second phase of convincement or Lamb's War. For women
the caring for others--not only children, the infirm,
and the aged at home, but the poor, the imprisoned,
Indians, slaves, the victims of war, the disenfranchised
in the public realm--was fundamentally religious. Of
course women have traditionally performed some of these
tasks, but they were seen as primarily attached
(Luther's term was "nailed") to the home in a subser-
vient role to the husband as a result of the Fall
(Luther) or because God initially ordered creation in
this hierarchical manner (Calvin).10 In contrast,
Quaker women were seen as spiritually equal before the
Fall in the original creation and after they had experienced salvation in the New Jerusalem/ New Creation.
This opened the possibility for Quaker women to act in

the public sphere as well as in the home. At the same
time women's traditional familial roles were also not
downgraded. Even when a woman felt led by God to leave
her family to preach--or later to do reform work--there
was no sense that such a decision was an expression of
devaluing the significance she had discovered in her
maternal role.

Another area in which the interplay of nature and
spirit had a transformative effect upon social behavior
was in the Quaker attitude towards sexual conception.
Throughout most of its history, mainline Christianity,
especially through the broad influence of St.
Augustine's theology, held that Adam's sin was passed on
to a child in the act of conception which itself was a
result of the sin of lust. Sexuality after Adam was, in
this view, always distorted by sin. Living in the New
Creation, Friends, on the other hand, believed sex to be
free from the weight of sin. As Jerry Frost comments:
"If at marriage the parents either had attained or were
working toward perfection, sex for them contained no
taint and their children would be innocent."[11] This
understanding is echoed and extended in the nineteenth
century by Susan B. Anthony in a letter to Elizabeth
Cady Stanton in which Anthony was reporting on a debate
on "the sexes" and on "sex":

> To me it is not coarse or gross, it is simply
> the answering of the highest and holiest
> function of the physical organism, that is
> that of reproduction. To be a Mother, to be a
> Father is the last and highest wish of any
> human being, to re-produce himself or herself.
> The accomplish[ment] of this purpose is only

through the meeting of the sexes. And when we come into the presence of one of the opposite sex, who embodies what to us seems the true and the noble and the beautiful, our souls are stirred, and whether we realize it or not, it is a thrill of joy that such qualities are reproducible and that we may be the agents, the artists in such re-production. It is the knowledge that the two together may be instruments, that shall execute a work so God like.12

Another altered understanding of nature and spirit is Quaker women's response to not having the traditional Protestant sacraments of Baptism and the Lord's Supper. These were rejected by both male and female Quakers because of their iconoclastic attitude toward all external rites, and because God was not distant, but present in the soul. They also rejected them because in other religious groups the sacraments were dependent upon a specifically ordained--which meant male--priest-hood or ministry and denied the important Quaker conviction of the priesthood of all believers (including women). Giving birth, washing (both activities of Baptism), and feeding (activity of Communion), important traditional parts of women's lives and work, were made into holy acts performed by male clergy in other Christian churches. In Quakerism, women were not taught to receive submissively these sacraments from hands of male authority, but were taught to participate actively in the sacramental qualities of all life.

A final area in which women had special understand-ing is the challenge to male hegemony. Although seventeenth century male Quakers radically challenged the leadership of church and state in disturbing ways and were persecuted for them, it was their prerogative as males to do so. For Quaker women as females it was not. In their preaching, their interpretation of the gospel, their traveling missions, and their willingness to accept persecution if necessary, they attacked not just the civil and ecclesiastical status quo, they also challenged traditional social norms of appropriate female behavior. Within the interplay of nature and spirit in the New Creation this attack on gender definitions was not only social but religious. Hence part of their religious task was articulation of an alternate view of women's role.[13] Such articulations are referred to over and over again in the essays of this volume on women as public friends. There was a range of viewpoint and some disagreement among women public friends about the role of women. There was often tension as well with other Quaker women who downplayed or rejected their role of shaping society. But for female public friends the articulation and example of a alternative/different role for women was a religious task.

Within the Society of Friends the Wilkinson-Story schism (1673) was partly caused by the empowerment of women through the establishment of Women's Meetings for Business. George Fox wrote two epistles defining women's right to preach. And in 1666, Margaret Fell—later to become Fox's wife—wrote the tract "Women's Speaking Justified, Proved and Allowed of by the Scriptures, All Such as Speak by the Spirit and Power of the Lord Jesus" precisely to counter the many attacks on the claim that God can call women to preach. Hugh Barbour's essay on "Quaker Prophetesses and Mothers in Israel" demonstrates the way Quaker women persisted in carrying out these public ministries in spite of dissent within Quakerism and persecution in England and America.

These formulations expressing the importance of women as shapers of public space (thus articulating new roles for women) are one of the significant contributions Quaker women have given to the larger public. These religious formulations, rooted in integration of ordinary/natural and spiritual life, energized, such women in very powerful ways. This is true even in later periods when public friends spoke in secular language and categories. As participants in the New Jerusalem /New Creation, where dualism and hierarchy are overcome in the interplay of nature and spirit, Quaker women not only experienced inner change but became agents of world-transformation.

Profile of Quaker Women as Transformers/Shapers of Society: Public Friends

In order to outline a group profile of the female public friends included in this study, the life of Margaret Fell Fox is explored and her activities categorized. This list of categories forms a paradigmatic pattern of characteristic behaviors which were repeated again and again by the Quaker women who are the subject of this study, even though the historic period, the geographical location, and the theological framework of Quakerism itself, kept shifting. In other words, what stays relatively constant and becomes a tradition, learned and repeated by women of a number of generations, is not a set of particular beliefs or a theologically cogent viewpoint but a way or pattern of interacting with the world. At numerous historic points, the living example of one woman, shaping her life as a public friend, will be the inspiration and the model for women of the next generation. The particular phraseology expressing the religious motivation may not be the same from one generation to the next, but the same types of activities will be employed.

Paradigmatic Margaret Fell Fox

Margaret Fell Fox (1614-1702) was born of landed aristocracy in northwestern England. She was raised to fulfill the expectations of a gentlewoman who is "born to oversee a household."[14] When she married Judge Thomas Fell and moved into Swarthmore Hall, the manor house of Ulverston, she was seventeen years old.

They had a family of eight children, seven daughters and one son. Because Judge Fell was often away working in the courts of law and as member of the Long Parliament, and because it was expected of women of the manor, Margaret Fell was involved in administering the farms and tenants of the estate, buying and selling livestock and grain, overseeing the iron forge and lending money and supervising trade. She was also involved in carrying out religious duties fitting her role in Ulverston. These included seeing that there were daily prayers and Bible study and supporting the parish church and the permanent clergy. She was also used to entertaining visiting clergy (conformist and non-conformist) as well as persons on state business.

She saw that her seven daughters were tutored in reading and writing, and trained as managers. She urged them to be capable of being financially independent and to carry on their own business both at home and when traveling. All of the Fell women traveled alone when called upon, managed their own affairs and aspects of business, and were prepared to act with independence like their mother.

Margaret Fell, in fulfilling her responsibility to entertain traveling ministers, met George Fox and became convinced of the "Truth." Judge Fell had already shown considerable tolerance of non-conformist clergy. He was probably initially dismayed, nonetheless, at the almost complete conversion of the members of his household, family and servants, to Quakerism. But when he became acquainted with George Fox, and other early Friends, he soon opened his home for Quaker worship. Although he maintained his own responsibility for the local parish, and did not join The Society of Friends he often sat in his study with the door opened onto the room where Friends gathered in silence for worship.

Margaret Fell became an active Friend. She spoke (preached) in Meeting for Worship as the Spirit moved her. She entertained traveling Friends. Since Quakers were often persecuted, she wrote them in prison; sent funds to care for their needs; oversaw the care of their families; and protested to the authorities (church and state) about the persecutions. With George Fox, she promoted Women's Meetings for Business. She was counselor in person and by letter to Friends as they moved throughout the world. And she wrote public epistles and tracts which articulated the meaning of

Quakerism. These writings give evidence of a women well versed in Biblical and theological discourse.

Thomas and Margaret Fell had a long mutually supportive marriage. After his death the protection of his estate by the State was withdrawn and Margaret Fell was herself persecuted for her Quakerism. Before this period she had used her influence with the King and state leaders to soften the persecution of Friends. In doing this, she had documented the conditions in the prisons. In 1660 she published "Declaration and Information from Us and the People of God Called Quakers to the Present Generations, the King and both Houses of Parliament." She visited the King. At one point, she obtained the release of George Fox from prison. In 1669, eleven years after Judge Fell's death, Margaret Fell married George Fox.

At the instigation of her son, who had not become a Quaker, Margaret herself suffered three long imprisonments, and the distrainment of her livestock and funds. She was praemunired (lost the protection of the King). Still she wrote letters, protesting to the government, and encouraging friends to travel for the faith. She also developed contact with and wrote to and about the Jews in Holland.

It becomes clear why Margaret Fell is often called the "Nursing Mother of Quakerism." Swarthmore Hall was the organizational hub of the newly developing Society of Friends. There she administered the Kendal Funds, which were used to support traveling missionaries, and kept in touch with all of Quakerism's far-flung activities--such as William Penn's Holy Experiment in

Philadelphia.

Summarizing this woman's life, she spoke, articulating and interpreting the Christian faith herself; wrote theological arguments and published an alternative religious and social vision; formed a network with others in the Quaker movement, providing financial, material, and psychological support for them; organized activities of others in both the temporal and spiritual; traveled independently; developed contacts with Jews and others to share her alternative perspective, to honor theirs, and to work together when possible; confronted directly and sought to shape the thoughts and actions of government officials at every level; administered aid (social, medical, financial, and psychological) to Quakers far and near; educated and trained her own daughters and many other women for spiritual and social independence and equality of personhood; created a rich family life and helped build a home for her own family, the local community, and others who visited from afar; entered into and enjoyed two marriages--acting as an independent and yet mutual partner with her husbands, and formed a center for the developing Society of Friends.

Patterns of Behavior of Women Public Friends

Quakerism was fortunate to have a female leader of this stature and prestige. She was clearly more trained and more skilled than most of the early female converts to Quakerism. Yet a number of the same elements that were present in Margaret Fell's life can be found among leading Quaker women who came from much poorer backgrounds. For instance, Mary Fisher, a servant, untrained in many of the ways of the world, nonetheless, traveled and preached throughout much of England, even going into the university cities where opposition from the church and learned society was quite intense. She visited the Sultan of Turkey. And she was one of the first Quakers to visit and preach in the Puritan Commonwealth of Massachusetts where she was whipped and jailed under the Quaker Act. She later visited South Carolina, where her granddaughter became a noted Quaker preacher, and was buried in Charleston. Belief that they were instruments of the Spirit of God enabled such women as Margaret Fell and Mary Fisher (rich or poor) to act and shape the environment.

Later in America during the nineteenth century, Quakers were predominantly from the middle class and thus had access to training, education, and networks of power. For them the major force behind their active faith was also the sense of spiritual presence and obedience. Models such as Margaret Fox and Mary Fisher served as authorization for a full range of involve-ments. Even though they, as middle-class women, were most susceptible to the mores of the "cult of true womanhood" (the privatized domestic sphere), they knew about women who had acted and ministered in the public realm as well as in the smaller spheres of church and family. The dichotomy of public and private sphere could not compete with such liberating knowledge.

The roles of seventeenth century Quaker women pre-sented in Hugh Barbour's paper are preachers, writers, counselors, visitors, helpers of the poor and needy, organizers, prophetesses, and travelers. He states that

although they shared many of these same roles with
Puritan women (excluding preaching), there was both a
communal style (associated with Women's Meetings for
Business and Sufferings) and a religious intensity
which marked a different quality for Quaker women.

In the comparative study of Quaker and Non-Quaker
women in The Dictionary of Notable American Women, (in
the Appendix) a similar pattern emerges of Quaker
women's public roles as preachers, speakers, and
reformers. They were involved in education, and in the
administration and organization of religious, reform,
and secular groups. They were involved in the analysis
of social ills, whether slavery, the poor, prisons, the
city, mental institutions, "sweated labor," native
Americans, or the role of women in the larger society.
They initiated political action as a result of their
analysis, and they formulated new theories to articulate
their findings and suggested new solutions to social
problems. They were well represented among the earliest
women doctors, scientists, and naturalists and among
entrepreneurs. The majority were married, although
singleness did not carry a negative connotation for
Quakers. There was better than average family stability
within their families, and there was a strong pattern of
partnership between husband and wife. And there was
also a propensity for organization and for travel. The
latter meant an interest not only in local issues but in
national and world problems--and often in the connections between these areas. Traveling also meant not
only traveling oneself, but providing hospitality in
one's own home for other travelers. A picture of a vast
social/religious network of women and men (at least in

terms of their relatively small numbers) opens out in this profile of Quaker women.

In this profile we find a pattern of public, active, shaping behavior. It began to emerge as early as 1652 and it continues up to the present. During some periods, traveling and preaching predominated. In other, traveling for organization was the primary emphasis. Social analysis, the formulations of alternative social visions, and the employment of political and legislative means to shape the culture were more important in the last hundred years, but all of these facets are present to some degree earlier. The pattern itself continues to influence or function as a model for women inside and outside the Society of Friends.

THE QUAKER HOME AS PRIVATE AND PUBLIC SPACE

The reasons for and the pattern of Quaker women's public stance have been explored. The focus now shifts to the way these beliefs and activities have affected the institution of the family and the reshaping of the Quaker home. Quaker women did not denigrate the role of the family. Those who were married lived full domestic lives and had a better than average marital stability. Significant examples of husband and wife patterns of equality and cooperation are described in the essays in this study. And it will be seen that the care of children and kin-folk provided activity and meaning. So in many ways, Quaker women continued to function in the family in a manner that was compatible with the social norms of the time.

Blanche Hersh, in Slavery of Sex, suggests that her
nineteenth century sample of 51 female abolitionist
reformers (more than a quarter of whom were Quakers) did
not seriously question either the definition of the
family or the appropriateness of some special spheres
for men and women. But they advocated a third sphere, a
public sphere, shared equally by men and women.15 This
study of Public Friends shifts the discussion, however,
from the family and special spheres to the home, noting
significant changes in understanding the space of family
life itself. The home continued to be private familial
space but it also became public space. In fact, the
distinction blurred as a multitude of activities were
carried on in the same space. Consequently a multitude
of social learnings occurred within the home.

Swarthmore Hall, the home of Margaret and Thomas
Fell, and then of Margaret and George Fox, served as a
model. The homes of William and Gulielma (and later,
Hannah) Penn in England and Philadelphia, Isaac and Mary
Penington in England, and Robert and Christian Barclay
in Scotland were yet other early models. The homes of
artisans and later, middle class Quakers, in both
England and America contain the same comings and goings
of Public Friends, such as transactions of Society of
Friends's business, hospitality for visitors, secret
hiding places or respites for those in conflict with
authorities, and meetings to discuss, strategize, and
organize ways to alter the society.

What were the consequences of this altered perspective and different behavior associated with the home?
First, it meant that Quaker women were often able to
behave as traditional women and as public women in the

same space. Second, Quaker women learned the important
skills of caring for people and nurturing growth. These
were enormous assets to the Society of Friends and to
the larger world as well. Third, the home became something more than the base or place of a marriage. It
became the place where a single woman, like a married
woman, could invite the world in on her own terms. A
quotation from a nineteenth Century speech entitled
"Homes for Single Women" by Susan B. Anthony expresses
this attitude.

> The charm of all these women's homes, is,
> that their owners are `settled' in
> life;--that the men, young or old, who
> visit them, no more count their hostess'
> chances in the matrimonial market, than
> when guests in the homes of the most
> happily married women. Men go to these
> homes as they do to their gentlemen's
> clubs,--to talk of art, science,
> politics, religion and reform,--they go
> to meet their equals in the proud domain
> of the intellect,--laying aside, all of
> their conventional `small talk for
> ladies.'[17]

Fourth, the home and the family were places, along with
the Meeting and Quaker schools, where children were
taught about the world and were shown equality between
the sexes in ways more advanced than in the larger
society. They were places of leaning the alternative or
counter-cultural tradition. Fifth, homes were necessary
organizational spaces. In any new movement, or in any
developing social organization, there must be places for

meetings, for planning, for strategy sessions, for articulating alternatives and testing ideas. It is not a surprise that the first Woman's Rights Convention in 1848 was planned in the home of a Quaker woman, Jane Hunt of Waterloo, New York, near Seneca Falls. The physical and symbolic reminder of the transforming power of this meeting is found in the Smithsonian Museum in Washington, D.C.: a tea table. Certainly the tea table symbolized the cult of true womanhood. But here we have that symbol transformed by another perspective. The tea table became a symbol of power and change, not the symbol of passive luxury. In the essays in this volume, it will be seen that a number of homes are "organizational" hubs: Susan B. Anthony's home, shared with her sister, Mary, was the Headquarters of the American Suffrage Movement for many years; M. Carey Thomas' "Deanery" at Bryn Mawr College was a place where the women of the college interacted with men and women from the larger world; Alice Paul's home/work space, Villa Barthalona, in Geneva, Switzerland, was the base of operations for seeing to it that women's rights were incorporated into international laws and the place of refuge for women fleeing Nazi Germany; and countless homes safely hid escaping slaves or provided hospitality to abolitionists in their travels. It is impossible to count the homes that eighteenth century Charity Cook stayed at in her traveling ministry; in each home she performed a ministry to each member of the family as she accepted their hospitality. The "Quakerage" in China combines public and private lives. There would scarcely have been the spread of the Society of Friends or of the movements of abolition, woman's rights, temperance, or peace, if the homes of Quakers and other like-minded

persons had not been used as bases of operations for
these causes and the people traveling on behalf of them.

Sixth, the home was so connected to the Meeting and
the Meeting House within Quakerism that there was trans-
ference of meaning and even of activity between the two.
When there was no Meeting House, Meetings for Worship
and for Business were carried on within homes. Mary
Maples Dunn's work (in progress) studying the interrela-
tionship of spaces, functions, and designs for colonial
American Quaker homes and Meeting Houses draws attention
to the way that equality of space (for women and men)
was built into the very architecture of Quaker Meeting
Houses in America, with an equal side for women and for
men. This enriches and expands her earlier scholarship
on the impact of Women's Meetings for Business disowning
("reading out of Meeting") Quakers who had married non-
Quakers. The effect of this practice during the
"Quietist Period" in American Quakerism led to a serious
demographic loss in the numbers of Quakers in this
country. The "purity" of the meetings, however, was
sustained. Yet she reminds us, this was the very period
of "feminization of religion" within mainstream Protes-
tainism, the time when women became both the numerically
dominant population within the memberships of churches
and even more subordinate persons with regards to church
leadership. Within Quakerism the "reading out of
Meeting" meant that there remained within the small
Quaker sect a fairly evenly divided congregation of men
and women, and the power of women and men within the
Meetings remained more balanced.[18] This tendency to
support equality whether in architecture or membership
demographics did affect the idea and practices of the
home.

Perhaps when one is aware of the transformation of the home and family within Quakerism one gets a different vantage point on one of the most puzzling and seemingly contradictory kinds of work that is discussed in the final papers of this collection. First, one sees the work of Florence Kelley, advocate of very strong protective legislation for women and children in this country. She was acutely aware of the need to insure that the home, women, and children were not exploited during the most intense periods of industrialization and urbanization. Consequently she advocated legislation to protect the home. Second, in what many viewed as a counterproductive action which might be dangerous to the home, Alice Paul advocated the Equal Rights Amendment to the Constitution. Was she, as a single woman, simply insensitive to, or against, the home and family? For many years these two perspectives were at war with each other and the issue seemed to be the home and family versus individualism and human rights.

This struggle is clarified by Amelia Fry's essay on Alice Paul, which shows her concerned not just with the principle of equality of the sexes, but also with the role of nurturance women have traditionally learned within the home. Paul was convinced by anthropological studies that women were by nature more nurturant and thus that legal equality would not threaten domesticity and family life. She was not advocating, therefore, an individualism which was anti-home or anti-nurturant. Florence Kelley, on the other hand, was convinced by her father and others in economic and political life, that the larger industrial companies would not care for women, children, and the family without protective legislation. She thought men might eventually gain some control over their lives and work in industry through organizations and unions, but women must be protected by the state.

This dilemma seems to have been resolved in our decade in various ways. It has been richly addressed by the social theory advocated by Elise Boulding in The Underside of History where she reminds us that nurturance is learned by anyone, male or female, in the home, or in any other space, where the function is that of caring for less able persons (children, the ill, the aged). Thus the ability to nurture is not dependent upon gender, and the home does not have to be threatened by the principle of legal equality. Neither should the larger society be threatened by the principle of equality. But the accompanying concern must be the realization that caring for people, nurturance, is as important a human function as other work performed by men or women in the more public spaces of life. As Progressive Friends realized in the mid-nineteenth century, men needed to learn nurturance just as women needed to learn to speak, organize, and act in public.

Five Historical Examples of Quaker Homes as the Coinherence of Private and Public Space

Descriptions of five Quaker homes will conclude this re-interpretation. First consider the seventeenth century palatial estate of Viscountess Anne Conway, in Warwickshire, England. Ragley Hall was the place of discussion of such men as Cambridge Platonist Henry More, scientist William Harvey, and physician and scientist Francis Van Helmont. Serious philosophic-scientific and religious discussion were carried on with Anne Conway as a magnet figure and an active participant. When she turned to Quakerism late in her life, its leaders, George Fox, George Keith, William Penn, Isaac Penington, and Robert Barclay, corresponded and visited with her. Anne Conway seldom left her estate because of severe migraine headaches. She was attended by many of the famous physicians of that day and eventually Van Helmont became a resident physician. She, nonetheless interspersed her life of pain with the kind of dialogue and discourse described here. Her own writing was to become influential on Leibnitz's philosophy. There was a strong affinity between Quakers' views of the New Creation and her anti-dualistic philosophical understanding of the natural and spiritual world. There was also a strong bond between the quiet Quakers, many of whom she hired as servants in her home, or entertained as visiting Friends, who spoke to her about their own sufferings. It is in what she called the "sufferings" or "purifications," what Quakers called the Lamb's War, that she found companionship with the Quakers.[19]

The second reference is to Elizabeth Hooten, George Fox's earliest convert and an early traveling minister. She traveled to Puritan Massachusetts especially to build a house (with permission from the King of England) as a safe haven for Quakers. She was no better received, carrying this permission and grant from the King, than other Quakers. Under the Quaker Act she was not allowed to enter, stay in, or even get water from any house in the commonwealth. She was imprisoned, whipped thirty lashes and abandoned. Homes, where one could be welcome, were understood at the very beginning to be important to Hooten and other Quakers who knew first-hand about persecution and being homeless.[20]

The third reference is to Tanglewood, the home of Emily Howland, nineteenth century reformer and philanthropist, which she inherited from her father and mother. She lived in the 15-room house in rural Sherwood, New York, most of her adult life. A woman of considerable wealth, she worked for education of freed slaves and for the equality of women. Tanglewood was used as a place to entertain traveling reformers, and to house teachers for a school she established next door. Her niece, also a single woman, lived about six houses away (within a very small village) in another house of similar size. Rather than combine households, each maintained and used large homes in ways informed by the practices of earlier Quakers.[21]

The fourth reference is to Lucretia Mott's large dining room which seated more than twenty. There is an interesting account by Susan B. Anthony about dining at the Mott home. There was a large party at dinner (a regular occurrence) and the discussion ranged over reform and political affairs. As the meal came to a close, Lucretia Mott went into the kitchen and got a wooden bucket with water and soap. These she brought to the table. While the discussion continued at the table, Lucretia Mott washed the dishes and Susan, who was seated at her side, dried them as they continued to participate in the conversation. Such an image gives us insight into the intermeshing of private and public actions expressed in Quaker hospitality.[22]

The fifth example is Hull House, that pioneer settlement house in the midst of the squalor of twentieth century Chicago. Jane Addams, raised by a Quaker father; Edith and Grace Abbott, active as Friends throughout their lives; Florence Kelley, a Hicksite Quaker by birth and practice, came together with such other women as Ellen Starr and Sophonisba Breckinridge to create this space where all kinds of persons could meet. It was also a place where social reformers (men as well as women) could dwell in community at the heart of a blighted urban city. One catches glimpses of Jane Addams at home with the immigrant population which shared Hull House. At the same time, she shared this, her enlarged home, with colleagues involved in social analysis and working for social justice. They visited factories and tenements. They surveyed sanitary conditions and proposed ordinances and standards of public health. They participated in the development of social theory at the University of Chicago, and they joined forces with others in the Progressive movement to create legislation for a more humane environment. But a major part of their impetus to work for social change came from living in a settlement house which created a bridge between different social classes and ethnic groups, between private and public space.23

PUBLIC FRIENDS AND DIFFERENT MODES OF SHAPING HUMAN SPACE/SOCIETY

The impulse to transform and reshape culture has persisted within Quakerism since the seventeenth century. But the ways in which this impulse has manifested itself has been influenced by the multiple agendas of the larger society and the possible initiatives and responses of the Society of Friends.

In seventeenth century Colonial America, Quakerism took root and attempted to create and sustain a theocracy in Pennsylvania. It created enclaves in Rhode Island, Long Island (New York), New Jersey, Delaware, Maryland, and North and South Carolina. It struggled to maintain a presence in colonies such as Massachusetts and Virginia. This already suggests three different modes of interaction: (1) theocratic; (2) sectarian influence which is appreciated or at least tolerated by the larger culture; and (3) sectarian influence which is repulsed by the larger culture and yet functions as a significant alternative and critical perspective.

By the end of the seventeenth century, Quakerism had moved from trying to achieve control of the society, to turning inward to consolidate the diverse members of the Society of Friends and to create a sectarian righteousness which would inform, or at least shame, the larger culture. This is usually called the Quietist Period and it dates from roughly 1700 to 1827. Quakers came to perceive themselves as a "peculiar people" during this period. The paper on Charity Cook by Algie Newlin describes many of the ways that this stance was limiting but also some of the ways it was empowering for women Public Friends.

The social, political, and religious agenda for all of America changes as the nineteenth century opens. The Christian evangelicalism of the Second Great Awakening, Jacksonian democracy, European inspired Enlightenment thought, Transcendentalism, the shift from an agrarian society to a commercial economy fueled by industrialism--all combined to cause incredible social change.

Quakerism had to respond. The impulse to be active reformers surfaced. Simultaneously, the impulse to be even more sectarian, even tribalistic, grew. The impulse to evangelize the world was re-emphasized within parts of Quakerism and profoundly influenced by other Protestant denominations. This was often accompanied by the desire to "get along," to move away from the stance of "peculiarity" and appear more like other well-educated evangelical Protestants.

Quakerism experienced tremors and splits. In 1827-28, a significant schism occured and separate Yearly Meetings of Hicksite and Orthodox Quakers were soon established in main areas where there was a significant Quaker presence. Hicksite Friends, named for traveling minister Elias Hicks, were more concerned with the authority of the Inner Light and the power of the continuing revelation of God. They were also more likely to be rural rather than urban. Although Hicks himself was in strong opposition to Friends being engaged in social and political actions with non-Quakers, some more liberal Hicksite Quakers built on the principle that the leading of the Inner Light directs one to overcome social ills and injustices. These Hicksite Quakers (some of whom later became Progressive Friends) were willing to join with other Christians concerned about slavery, temperance, women's rights, etc., and work in and with more secular groups. This created tensions among the Hicksite Friends, as well as between them and Orthodox Quakers.

Orthodox Friends, influenced by evangelical Protestantism, were more focused on the divinity and the saving death of Jesus Christ and on the authority of the Bible. They were usually more urban, and although they still maintained a separatist quality in worship and in family and social gatherings, they were more likely to be engaged in economic and commercial enterprises with the larger American society. They represented comparative wealth and urbanity and were not always willing to share power with rural Quakers. Traveling English Quakers (no schism occured in England) attempted to mediate between these two groups but they were theologically now closer to the Orthodox Friends.

This schism was felt not just at the Yearly meeting level, but also in Quarterly and Monthly meetings. Even some families experienced the divisiveness. And the unity of Friends was further splintered in 1845 with Gurneyite Friends split off from Orthodox Friends and then divided again in 1877 into Gurneyite and Wilburite (Conservative) Friends. Each division claimed to be the more authentic Religious Society of Friends.

Questions of sectarian purity, of power within the Society of Friends, and of significantly different interpretations of the best mode or modes of interaction with the larger society are basic to these divisions. It is worth noting that a religious society with no national or international body for unity and discipline breeds diversity and tension. And the larger agenda of the culture clearly sets that stage for Quaker confusion. It should be noted for our purposes that the separate branches of Quakerism all continued to reflect

the whole spectrum of interactive modes between engagement and withdrawal from the larger society.

Urbanization, the growth of management and labor
conflicts in industry, two world wars, the decline of
colonial empires, and a growing internationalism are
features of the agenda in the twentieth century.
Progressivism, socialism, other secular movements for
change, a growing desire for world government and/or
international law are responses to these problems.
American Quakerism also developed two major responses,
the American Friends Service Committee (A.F.S.C.) in
1929 and the Friends Committee on National Legislation
(F.C.N.L.) in 1943. The leadership for both was drawn
primarily from conscientious objectors of the First and
Second World Wars. Thus, males predominated. Quakers
tended to focus their social actions through these
groups rather than through Monthly or Yearly Meeting
actions. There also continued to be a plurality of
ideas about how the Society of Friends should interact
with the larger society, and so the twentieth century
continued the multiplicity of the nineteenth. Women
seem, however, to have lost some voice within the
official organization of Quakerism (less representation
in A.F.S.C. and F.C.N.L.; the growth of a class of
pastors/clergy in programmed meetings; merger of Men's
and Women's Meetings for Business in all branches and at
all organizational levels; decrease of the selection of
women as clerks of Yearly Meetings, and the continuation
of the fact that only one woman has been president of a
Quaker college). It is not surprising that twentieth
century Quaker female Public Friends hovered at the edge
of the Society of Friends (moving in and out).

The dilemma faced by female Public Friends, of whichever branch and in whichever period, is apparent. There was no one approved way to maintain the stance of being true to spiritual insight, part of the Society of Friends, and engaged with the world. Only two generalizations seem legitimate. The more a branch of Quakers, or an individual within a branch, accommodates or adjust to the definition of mainstream Protestantism (either in beliefs or in practices), the less likely female Public Friends will develop and persist. Secondly, the tensions in the nation are reflected in the lives of female public Friends.

A Basis for Comparison: Six Non-Quaker Women and Six Modes of Interacting with Quaker Women for Socal Change

To better understand the complexities created when a group of women set out intentionally to change the larger society--while that society is itself in spasms of change, the identity of the group (Quakerism in this case) is being modified, and the definitions about the actions of women are evolving--we will explore briefly six non-Quaker women interacting with Quaker women drawn from the three hundred years of this study. Our exploration will demonstrate that there has been a multiplicity of ways in which Quaker women have related to and affected culture; that Quaker women have provided various kinds of leadership in the movement of American women into more public spaces; that this leadership is always in interaction with other non-Quaker women leaders; and that Quaker women are an important part of the unfolding history of women in America.

American women have redefined their roles as they moved from privatized to more public spaces. Females interpreted and analyzed their own faith or belief systems, spoke in public, demanded and obtained education, organized gender-based groups, became critics of the social climate, and acted as reformers by posing religious, social, legal, and political alternatives. While these have developed chronologically to some degree, they overlap with each other in significant ways. The overall movement, however, does seem to break like a sequence of waves. Outlining those waves, we shall distinguish six ways non-Quaker women have related to Quaker women, as: precursor and mentor (Anne Hutchinson), more radical religious and social initiator (Mother Ann Lee), more conservative adversary (Catherine Beecher), close personal collaborator (Elizabeth Cady Stanton), complementary strategist (Frances Willard), and simultaneous founder who later becomes interdependent (Lillian Wald).

Anne Hutchinson, Precursor and Mentor

Anne Hutchinson (1591-c.-1643)24 was already at odds with American Puritan orthodoxy in Massachusetts Bay Colony before the advent of Quakerism. She was married to a respected businessman, William Hutchinson, and was the mother of twelve children. She was influenced by John Cotton, a minister who emphasized the covenant of grace over against what he saw to be an undue emphasis upon the covenant of works. Anne Hutchinson held that the covenant of Grace implied an indwelling Spirit of God. Her particular interpretation of these beliefs, her leadership in discussion of the faith by men and women within her home, her strong influence on many women in her role as midwife, and her impact on several male leaders within the colony, left her vulnerable to attack as an antinomian heretic who wished to turn upside down the whole (patriarchal) structure of this Puritan errand into the wilderness. In September 1637, a synod of churches condemned her for her efforts. In November 1637, she was brought before the General Court and accused of "traducing the ministers and their ministry." She was banished from the colony the following spring and kept in custody during the intervening time. In March of 1638 she was excommunicated before her banishment. A close friend, Mary Dyer, supported her throughout these trials and publicly accompanied her out of the church after the excommunication.

Anne Hutchinson left Massachusetts Bay Colony for an island in Narragansett Bay. After her husband's death she and her children moved to Long Island where she and all but one of the family were massacred by Indians. Mary Dyer and her husband William Dyer were subsequently banished and excommunicated for being followers of Anne Hutchinson. They settled in Newport, R.I., until 1652 when they visited England. During the five-year period in England, Mary Dyer became a follower of George Fox and part of the Society of Friends. The doctrine of the Inner Light was similar to Anne Hutchinson's antinomian heresy. When the Dyers returned to New England in 1657, Mary was imprisoned for another kind of heresy--Quakerism. She was banished again, returned, and was sentenced to be hanged. The pleas of her husband saved her for another banishment.

Her third intentional return to Massachusetts Bay Colony assured her death by hanging on Boston Common in 1660.

Here one senses that the alternative religious perspective, in two similar but different articulations, threatened the hegemony of Puritan leaders by posing the dangerous possibility of individual experience and interpretation of faith. Neither Anne Hutchinson nor Mary Dyer advocated religious tolerance, per se. Rather, they claimed their personal right to interpret their own religious experience. In doing so, they made their stance an option for other men and women. Anne Hutchinson and Mary Dyer were judged both for their inappropriate female behavior and for their alternative belief in the inner spirit. The effect was death for both women. Yet each symbolized a redefinition of feminine spirituality and the need for religious tolera- tion for both men and women. Anne Hutchinson led the way, Mary followed.

Anne Lee, More Radical Religious and Social Initiator

Anne Lee (1736-1784)[25] was born in England. She was a serious-minded young woman who worked in the textile mills until her marriage to Abraham Standerin in 1762. In 1758 she had become acquainted with James and Jane Wardle, former Quakers who belong to an off-shoot of Quakerism called "Shakers." Lee experienced four painful childbirths and the death of four infants. This physical and mental anguish convinced her of the sinfulness of sexuality. She took this powerful personal conviction with her when she joined the Shakers. Ann was imprisoned for breaking the Sabbath and during that period had a "grand vision" of the Garden of Eden. Her decision to advocate celibacy grew out of this. In her vision, she also experienced the indwelling and intimate presence of Christ. This vision led her to see herself as having a divine mission to complete the work of Christ. Others, among the Shakers, perceived her as Mother Ann, the Second Coming of Christ.

In 1774, Ann, Mother of the New Creation, and her followers moved to America. By 1776 the first Shaker community was established in Niskeyuna, New York. By her death in 1784, plans for eleven other Shaker communities were underway.

Ann Lee, like the Quakers who influenced her, advocated an alternative society, a "new creation". Like the Society of Friends, Shakerism supported equality between the sexes, separate male and female structures of leadership, simple living, pacifism, a familial organization for living which was both separate from the larger culture but deeply hospitable to it, and belief in the personal experience of the divine. Unlike Quakers, the Shakers advocated celibacy (but did not extend this to other anti-nature stances), authorized ecstatic expression of religious experience, shared property in common, and established separate communities.

Shakerism developed in America during roughly the same time as the Quietist Period in Quakerism. Both advocated living the pure alternative life as a type of "witness" to the larger culture. Shakerism was more radical in its withdrawal. Partly for that reason,

Shakers were unable actively to shape the larger society. Rather, their alternative posture provided a living critique and example.

Another celibate, communal, and religious alternative of the period was the development of American orders of Roman Catholic monks and nuns. In particular, the nuns provided places for female leadership to evolve and an authorized vision of service to the larger community by single women. Both Catholic sisters and Shakers pose a more radical alternative vision for American society than Quakers. This more radical religious stance and practice provided social, psychological, and political space for the Quaker alternative vision. Because Quakers did not advocate celibacy (even though they extended the definition of the home and family), Quaker women were perceived as acceptable leaders for other non-Quaker women in a way that their celibate sisters were not. Here the radical alternative helps to legitimize some aspects of Quakerism and provide space for Quaker women's leadership.

Catherine Beecher, More Conservative Adversary

Catherine Beecher (1800-1878),[26] daughter of Presbyterian clergyman Lyman Beecher and sister to numerous brothers who were ministers and to three sisters, one being Harriet Beecher Stowe, became a strong advocate for the education of girls and women, the importance of the domestic sphere (where she offered practical household advice as well as ideological support of the Christian home) and education for the physical well-being of girls and women. She perceived this as a form of ministry, which stressed the major, although unheralded and unappreciated, role of women in the culture (particularly as teachers and as mothers). She was a major advocate of the moral superiority of women, which was seen as the result of the self-sacrifice women gained through maternity and in the submission of their wills to God and to father and husband. Using Jesus as a model of self-sacrifice, women gained special authority within the domestic sphere.

Beecher drew on the kind of power residing in notions of the female sphere which Nancy Cott describes in The Bonds of Womanhood. She extended this sense of separate-from-male but common-to-female experience and drew it full scale into her version of the cult of true womanhood.

Beecher's stress on the special spheres of women put her in direct opposition to Quakers Sarah and Angelina Grimké. First of all both of the Grimké sisters articulated their views in public and were denounced for this kind of gender-inappropriate behavior not only by the ministers of Massachusettes ("Pastoral Letter" by the Congregational Ministerial Association of Massachusettes in 1837) but also by Catherine Beecher in letters to the sisters. Angelina's "Appeal to the Christian Women of the south"27 and Sarah's Letters on the Equality of the Sexes and the Condition of Women were also examples of Quaker women suggesting the category of humankind as an alternative concept to the separation of male and female spheres. Catherine Beecher was strongly opposed to such conceptualiztion.

The tension over Beecher's understanding of separate spheres of men and women and the insistent alternative perspective for human rights and human engagement advocated by the Grimke' sisters demonstrate the two crucially different nineteenth century perspectives on women's place in society. Although Beecher clearly intended to extend women's influence, she could not support aggressive measures such as suffrage, or strategies of change, which might diminish the special role and sphere of women. Many Quaker women, like the Grimke' sisters, found her perspective (certainly the dominant one in the nineteenth century) unacceptable. Throughout her life Beecher was in overt opposition to any serious alteration of women's private role or the "nature" of the family.

The opposition of view alluded to here suggests that one role Beecher played was to interpret clearly and definitively the mainstream concept of the evolving sphere of women. This allowed some Quaker women, and others who advocated more active roles for women in ever-increasing areas of the society, to shape their alternative views against a powerful female voice. This dynamic probably assisted both parties and their separate ideologies. As Beecher dignified the bonding together of women in their special, limited sphere, the Grimke' sisters extended this bonding to not just middle class "true women" but working-class women and, most importantly, slave women. When slave women were incorporated into the female bond, the negative quality of human bondage was added to the definition of feminine experience. "Thine in the bondage of womanhood" was Sarah Grimke's epistolery closing. It was also her opposition to and call for movement away from Beecher's

endorsement of limited sphere and moral superiority.
Elizabeth Cady Stanton, Close Personal Collaborator

Elizabeth Cady Stanton (1815-1902)[28] is legendary
for her fifty-one year relationship to Quaker Susan B.
Anthony. Although there were differences in their
temperaments, abilities, some of their beliefs, and
sometimes their strategies, these two women worked
together for the cause of women's rights almost their
entire adult lives. Whether it was running petition
drives, organizing conventions, publishing The
Revolution, addressing legislators, sending letters,
working on speeches, fund-raising, lecture tours, or
attending to some of the familial duties of the Stanton
home, this female partnership symbolizes a close kind of
female camaraderie and cooperation. Yet it was not an
exclusive relationship. Each of these women had
numerous other close personal and working relationships
with other women. Nor was it utterly unique. The
history of American women is rich in female partner-
ships--Lucy Stone and Antoinette Brown Blackwell, M.C.
Thomas and Mary Garrett, sisters such as Sarah and
Angelina Grimke, Catherine Beecher and Harriet Beecher
Stowe, Emily and Elizabeth Blackwell, Lucretia Mott and
Martha Wright. Some of these relations excluded men.
Some surely were the primary emotional ties for the
women involved. Whatever the degree of closeness, such
relationships as that of Elizabeth Cady Stanton and
Susan B. Anthony sustained the women's rights movement.
Its closeness threatened some parts of the Society of
Friends but energized and freed these two women.

Frances Willard, Complementary Strategist

Frances Willard (1839-1898)[29] moved the Women's Christian Temperance Union (W.C.T.U.) from "a praying society dedicated to temperance" to a strong women's movement, solidly rooted in the Midwest, which prompted not only "temperance"--total abstinence and legal prohibition--but also a broad range of other causes. These causes were labor reform, "social purity" (concerned with prostitution and the legal age of consent) in marriage, health and hygiene, advice to young mothers, city welfare work, prison reform, work with young Negroes and a Department of Peace and Arbitration. It is said that Frances Willard thought of the WCTU as a school to interest women in life beyond the family circle, so that they might take a more active and useful part in society. Symbolized by an organizational badge, a white ribbon for the purity of the home and with a slogan "For God and Home and Native Land," the W.C.T.U. created the social climate for more religiously and politically conservative women to enter into the national political fray. Over two hundred years after Quaker women came to understand the religious basis for public action, Willard helped other Protestant women to take these steps and also urged them to enter the developing internationalism of the late 1880's.

It is readily accepted that in the latter days of the suffrage fight (after Frances Willard's death but before the decline of the W.C.T.U.), it took the three-pronged strategy of conservative action (W.C.T.U.), ardent activism (the combined American and National Suffrage Associations under the leadership of Carrie

Chapman Catt), and more militant feminism (Women's Party under the leadership of Alice Paul) to achieve the final ratification of the nineteenth amendment. There were Quakers in each of these camps (several Quaker women were national leaders and state officers of W.C.T.U.), and it took this kind of complementarity of emphasis and strategy to achieve that particular forward wave.

After the suffrage struggle was concluded the central group developed into the League of Women Voters which drew procedural process from the consensus model of some of its Quaker leaders and membership. The W.C.T.U. continued to play the role of involving women in social issues in what seemed to be moderate to conservative modes. The more radical Women's Party moved to extend the struggle for women's equality with the 1923 introduction of the Equal rights Amendment to the U.S. Constitution. Again complementary and different perspectives and strategies kept the forward thrust breaking in new waves. Quaker and non-Quaker women worked together in all three complementary facets.

Lillian Wald, Simultaneous, Separate Leadership Becoming Inter-dependent

Lillian Wald (1867-1940)[30] in 1891 entered nursing school. Two years later she enrolled in Women's Medical College, New York City, for further training in nursing. Soon afterwards she organized nurses for work in the tenement house area of the lower east side of Manhattan. That year she and Mary Brewster, friend and fellow nurse, moved into the area to live and work, and identify themselves with the neighborhood. By 1895 she was able to establish the Nurses' Settlement at 225 Henry Street. By 1913, Henry Street Visiting Nurses Service had 92 nurses and was making 200,000 annual visits in homes. Between 1893-94, Lillian Wald and others had expanded their work to the Henry Street Settlement House, with seven houses on Henry Street and two uptown branches. Between 1900-1910, she had helped establish the first public school nursing program, and the Department of Nursing at Teachers' College. By 1912 she was the first president of the National Organization for Public Health Nursing.

This work is parallel to, though unconnected with, two different developments in Quaker women's experience. The first is the role of Quakers (men and women) in the establishment of the Female Medical College (1859) in Philadelphia. Like the program for nurses at Henry Street, this endeavor trained women in the medical professions, as doctors as well as nurses; authorized women to move into new vocational/professional positions; formed strong networks of women who learned their practice in urban areas; and assisted in the development of the field of public health, a new profession for doctors and nurses and one ripe for women's interests.[31]

The second and, probably, the more obvious development was Lillian Wald's creation of a settlement house similiar to that founded by Jane Addams (raised as a Quaker) and her cohorts (several of whom were raised as Quakers and three of whom remained active Friends) at Chicago's 'Hull House' five years earlier. At Hull House, the multifaceted program did not have a strong a

medical base, but the newly educated middle-class women
came with very similar goals. As Jane Addams wrote:

> I gradually became convinced that it
> would be a good thing to rent a house in
> a part of the city where many primitive
> and actual needs are found, in which
> young women who have been given over too
> exclusively to study, might restore a
> balance of activity along traditional
> lines and learn of life from life itself;
> where they might try out some of the
> things they have been taught. . . .[32]

"Life itself" proved to be a powerful teacher. At Hull
House, Florence Kelley learned by investigating
sweatshops; Grace Abbott learned from working with the
immigrants; Alice Hamilton surveyed and inspected
dangerous trades; Julia Lathrop entered the work of
public welfare; Louise DeKoven Bowen observed the
juvenile courts; and Ellen Starr worked with a variety
of ethnic groups to preserve their cultural inheritance.
Jane Addams learned by doing, administrating and
writing. All of these women assisted in the creation of
new fields of academic study and the creation of new
professional fields open to women.

By 1900 these parallel settlement house adventures
were joining forces. Lillian Wald and Florence Kelley
worked for the creation, in 1904, of the National Child
Labor Committee (Kelley lived at Henry Street from 1899-
1924). In 1912, President Taft appointed Julia Lathrop
to head the Children's Bureau of the Department of Labor

at the suggestion of Lillian Wald. In 1919, after the U.S. Congress passed the first child labor act, Grace Abbott became head of Child Labor Division. By 1914, Lillian Wald, Jane Addams, and Florence Kelley were all engaged in the American Union Against Militarism. From then on, the women from these originally separate but parallel endeavors are intermingled personally and professionally in a vast network of men and women engaged in what we call the Progressive Movement. They created new fields, strengthened the relationship of academic research and education to life, worked with politicians for more humane legislation, and created many varied organizations to address people's problems in urban settings.

Often the same impulse--whether for education, health care, or against slavery, alcoholism, urban blight--brings forth local independent action simultaneously in different areas. Both Quaker and non-Quaker women have initiated these actions and then through interaction have shared the benefits of separate but parallel experiences. The whole became richer for the separate beginnings and for the mixing of women from a variety of religious backgrounds.

Two brief comments conclude this analysis of independent but parallel endeavors. The foreign mission fields also allowed other newly educated women to find and create professional opportunities. As James Cooley's paper on Quaker women missionaries in China demonstrates, such women found the same openness for service, personal financial independence, and the possibility for more professional creativity in the many separate but parallel foreign missionary outposts, as the women of the Progressive movement found in urban areas in the United States.

Second, although the missionaries had to be explicit about some religious motivation to qualify for these new opportunities, the American urban female professionals and reformers played down their religious motivation and turned to the secular language of Progressivism and/or Socialism. Yet this use of secular language and views did not obliterate, the religious motivation undergirding these women's lives. For both groups of women, the missionaries and the urban reformers, learned from each other's separate beginnings. Internationalism and peace issues moved to a central place in all of their experiences, their beliefs, and their leadership and became a significant religious/social agenda.

CONCLUSION

We have sketched a profile of public Quaker women acting over three hundred years. We have seen how they interact with the Spirit of God, their families, Meetings, like-minded women (and men), and the larger world. Trying to transform important dimensions of the whole culture by using some of the alternative models and visions of the Society of Friends, these women formed a living network across the decades. One generation of women taught and inspired the next generation until a tradition was formed, and then shaped the women involved and they in turn shaped, with varying degrees of success, the world in which they lived.

Notes

[1]The primary sources on seventeenth century Quakerism used are: Hugh Barbour, The Quakers in Puritan England (New Haven: Yale University Press, 1964); John Punshon, Portrait in Grey: A Short History of the Quakers (London: Quaker Home Service, 1984); and Elbert Russell, History of Quakerism (New York: Macmillan, 1942).

[2]Horton Davies, Worship and Theology in England: 1603-1690 (Princeton, University Press, 1975), pp. 495-96.

[3]John Punshon, op. cit., pp. 85 and 95. During the 17th century women were not included as overseers and as part of Yearly Meeting before single-sex Meetings were established. Later women were not part of Representative Meeting for a period in the 19th century.

[4]See: Clarkson, Thomas, A Portraiture of Quakerism, 3 vols. (New York: Samuel Stansbury, 1806) for early reference to Quaker women's public and private character. Some of the more contemporary sociologists and social historians who develop this theme are: Carol Ruth Berkin and Mary Beth Norton, eds., Women of America (Boston: Houghton Mifflin, 1979); Elise Boulding, The Underside of History (Boulder, Colorado: Westview Press, 1976); William Chafe, The American Women: Her Changing Social, Economic, and Political Roles, 1920-1970); (New York: Oxford University Press, 1972); Eleanor Flexner Century of Struggle (Cambridge: Mass., Harvard University Press, 1959--revised and published by Atheneum, 1972); Antonia Fraser: The Weaker Vessel (New York: Alfred A. Knopf, 1984); Miriam Gurko, The Ladies of Seneca Falls (New York: Macmillan, 1974); Blanche Glassman Hersh, The Slavery of Sex: Feminist-Abolitionists in America (Urbana: University of Illinois Press, 1978); Janet Wilson James, ed., Women in America Religion (Philadelphia: University of Pennsylvania Press, 1980); Linda K. Kerber and Jane DeHart Mathews, eds., Women's America: Refocusing the

Past (New York: Oxford University Press, 1982); Gerda
Lerner, The Female Experience: An American Documentary
(Indianapolis: Bobbs-Merrill, 1977); Judith Loeber,
Women Physicians: Careers, Status and Power (New York:
Tavistock, 1984); Rosemary Radford Reuther and Rosemary
Skinner Keller, eds., Women and Religion in America,
Vol. 1 and Vol. 2 (New York: Harper and Row, 1981 and
1983); Rosemary Reuther and Eleanor McLaughlin, Women
of Spirit (New York, Touchstone Books, 1979); Alice
Rossi, ed., The Feminist Papers: From Adams to
deBeauvoir (New York: Bantam, 1973); Page Smith,
Daughters of the Promised Land: Women in American
History (Boston: Little, Brown and Co., 1970); Anne
Firor Scott, Making the Invisible Woman Visible
(Urbana: University of Illinois Press, 1984).

5This section of Quaker women's spirituality is
informed by a number of feminist theologians: Carol P.
Christ, Diving Deep and Surfacing: Women Writers on
Spiritual Quest (Boston: Beacon, 1980); Elizabeth Clark
and Herbert Richardson, eds., Women and Religion: A
Feminist Sourcebook of Christian Thought (Boston:
Beacon Press); Mary Daly, Beyond God the Father:
Toward a Philosophy of Women's Liberation (Boston:
Beacon, 1973); Barbara Leslie Epstein, The Politics of
Domesticity: Women, Evangelism and Temperance in Nine-
teenth Century America (Middletown, Conn.: Wesleyan
University Press, 1981); Amanda Porterfield, Feminine
Spirituality in America from Sarah Edwards to Martha
Graham (Philadelphia: Temple University Press, 1980);
Kathryn Allen Rabuzzi, The Sacred and the Feminine:
Toward a Theology of Housework (New York: Seabury,
1982); Rosemary Radford Reuther, ed., Religion and
Sexism: Images of Women in the Jewish and Christian
Tradition (New York: Simon and Schuster, 1974); and
Reuther, Sexism and God-Talk: Toward a Feminist
Theology (Boston: Beacon, 1983).

6Influential in the discussion of women and relational
modes are Jesse Bernard, The Female World (New York:
The Free Press, 1984); Nancy Chodorow, The Reproduction
of Mothering: Psychoanalysis and the Sociology of
Gender (Berkeley: University of California Press,

1978); Carol Gilligan, <u>In a Different Voice:
Psychological Theory and Women's Development</u>
(Cambridge, Mass: Harvard, 1982). The necessity to
extend this relational mode beyond the female world
(and make a major aspect of the human agenda) is a
theme of Elise Boulding in <u>The Underside of History,</u>
<u>op. cit.</u>

[7]Seventeenth century Quaker men and women distrusted
familial relationships, including mother-child, because
they could function as distractions to the spiritual
struggle. They also, however, came to various degrees
of new understanding of these relationships as they
were more convinced of their role in the New Creation.

[8]Focus on female spirituality is beginning to pose some
new questions about male spirituality. In this paper,
the spiritual process creates a challenge to norms of
appropriate female behavior. One wonders whether the
same process of convincement (which can lead to an
integration of spiritual and natural) may not have led
some Quaker males to move more fully into activities
usually assigned to women. In particular, an exploration of the twentieth century Quaker males who declared
themselves conscientious objectors to war and subsequently became involved in major human service and
refugee work of the American Friends Service Committee
might find this the reverse image of Quaker women's
action in public spaces.

[9]George Fox, <u>The Journal of George Fox</u>, ed. John L.
Nickalls (London: Religious Society of Friends,
1975), p. 127.

[10]Rosemary Radford Reuther, <u>Sexism and God-Talk: Toward
a Feminist Theology</u> (Boston, Beacon, 1983), pp. 97 -98.

[11]J. William Frost, <u>The Quaker Family in Colonial
America</u> (New York: St. Martin's Press, 1973), p. 66.

[12]Elizabeth Cady Stanton and Susan B. Anthony,
<u>Correspondence, Writings, Speeches,</u> ed. Ellen Carol
DuBois (New York: Schocken, 1981), p. 67.

[13]This is in contrast to most Protestant understanding
of the function religion as endorsing and enforcing the
acceptance of the normative, submissive behavior of
women. Although Barbara Welter is discussing nineteenth
century religion, the same sentiments could be applied
for all three centuries of this study. "One reason
religion was valued was that it did not take a woman
away from her `proper sphere,' her home. Unlike partic-
ipation in other societies or movements, church work
would not make her less domestic or submissive, less a
True Woman." Dimity convictions: The American Woman in
the Nineteenth Century (Athens: Ohio University Press,
1976), p. 22.

[14]Information and phraseology from Hugh Barbour,
"Margaret Fell Speaking," Pendle Hill Pamphlet 206,
1976.

[15]Blanche Glassman Hersh, op. cit., p. 204.

[16]William C. Braithwaite, The Second Period of Quakerism, 2nd ed. (Cambridge: University Press, 1961), p.
446.

[17]Susan B. Anthony, "Homes for Single Women," Susan B.
Anthony papers, Library of Congress.

[18]Mary Maples Dunn, "Women of Light," Women of America,
Carol Ruth Berkin and Mary Beth Norton, eds. (Boston:
Houghton Mifflin, 1979).

[19]Marjorie Hope Nicolson, Conway Letters: The Corres-
pondence of Anne, Viscountess Conway, Henry More and
Their Friends, 1642-1684 (New Haven: Yale University
Press, 1930).

[20]Elbert Russell, op. cit., p. 106.

[21]"Emily Howland," in Dictionary of Notable American
Women, 1607-1950 and Judith Colucci Breault, The World
of Emily Howland: Odyssey of a Humanitarian (Millbrae,
California: Les Femmes, 1976).

[22] Ida H. Harper, The Life and Work of Susan B. Anthony (Indianapolis, Bowen-Merrill, 1898), Vol. 1, p. 122.

[23] "Jane Addams" in D.N.A.W.: 1607-1950.

[24] "Anne Hutchinson" in D.N.A.W.: 1607-1950 and Horatio Rogers, "Mary Dyer Did Hang As a Flag" in The Quaker Reader, ed. Jessamyn West (New York, Viking, 1962).

[25] "Mother Ann Lee: in D.N.A.W.: 1607-1950 and Catherine Beecher by Kathryn Kish Sklar (New Haven, Yale University Press, 1973).

[27] Angelina Grimke, "Appeal to the Christian Women of the South" and "Letters to Catherine Beecher" in Alice Rossi, The Feminist Papers (New York, Bantam, 1974), pp. 296-305 and 319-322.

[28] "Elizabeth Cady Stanton" in D.N.A.W.

[29] "Frances Willard" in D.N.A.W. and Lydia Jones Trowbridge, Frances Willard of Evanston (New York: Willett, Clark and Co., 1938), Anna A. Gordon, Thee Beautiful Life of "Frances Willard (Chicago: Woman and Temperance (Hartford, Conn: Park Publishing, 1883).

[30] "Lillian Wald" in D.N.A.W. and Beatrice Siegel, Lillian Wald of Henry Street, (New York: Macmillian Publishing Co., 1983).

[31] "Ann Preston" in D.N.A.W.

[32] "Jane Adams" in D.N.A.W.

QUAKER PROPHETESSES AND
MOTHERS IN ISRAEL
Hugh Barbour

To precede this array of women scholars should evoke modesty in any man who can aspire to that virtue. My role is simply to provide the matrix, the ground or seedbed of history, in which their plantings can be rooted. Elizabeth Grey Vining, in her Ward Lecture at Guilford College in 1955, 1 pointed out that a sign of the strength of Quakerism from its beginning was its treatment of women, not as a special group, nor even as equals, but simply as people. This vision also underlies the title of our symposium and Melvin Keiser's preliminary paper. Nevertheless, my role is to describe roles, as played by women in early Quakerism.

The vivid facts about these women have been known and assembled for up to two generations, notably by Mabel Brailsford, Emily Manners and Isabel Ross.2 Here we also may record the debt of Quaker history in general to Caroline Fox and Caroline Stephens in the last century, and in our own to Elizabeth Brockbank, Isabel Grubb, Amelia Gummere, Margaret Hirst and Lucy Hodgkin writing in English, to Auguste Jorns and Amelia Vogelklou Norlind in nordic Europe, to Janet Whitney's and Elizabeth Vining's biographies and Jessamyn West's and Elisabeth Hering's novels, to Elfrida Vipont Foulds in all these fields, and to archivists like Barbara Curtis, Treva Mathis, and Opal Thronburg. Has any religious movement been as well served by its women historians as Quakerism?

The roles of early Quaker women nevertheless need better analysis, all the more because they never received formal titles. These roles overlapped and ultimately merged as the spirit led. But as preachers, both within the silent Quaker Meetings, and on missions to bring a message out into the world, and also as writers of tracts, early Friends spoke of themselves as prophetesses, divinely inspired. Secondly, as counselors to each other and younger Friends in general, as visitors and helpers to the sick, the prisoners and to poor Friends, and as organizers of these activities through the network of Women's Meetings, Margaret Fell and others were called Mothers in Israel, (which may remind you of Robert Frost's invocation to the Lord God of Hostesses).3 These two sets of roles seem at first to divide into the sacred and the secular. Part of my concern will be to show this distinction as ours, not theirs. For them it was all under the Light. On the other hand, neither prophetic nor mothering roles at first implied any new status within the family, in the economic market or on the social ladder. Even the Quaker organization, the network of Women's Meetings which will make the third main section of this paper, stabilized new human relationships only gradually.

The place for women in the Puritan culture around Quakerism can easily be seen either as too dark or too glowing. An age of no nuns had no roles for women in the Church, even as deaconesses, nor any in the universities. The ridicule against the few Baptists preacheresses and Ann Hutchinson underlines the usual norms. Even in his own family, the father was expected to lead the prayers.4 A community with no nobility, like Massachusetts, had also no place for patronesses of

saints and writers, like a Lady Conway or Princess
Elisabeth of the Palatinate, whose role in old England
combined high rank and spiritual depth. Moreover, the
Puritans had little patience with either courtiers or
courtesans, and hence with women's usual roles in
Baroque politics, stage drama or the arts.   Is any
Puritan sermon against women as scathing as a Mozart
libretto by Da Pointi? Puritan Englishmen may indeed
have given women more respect, allowed them more
integrity, and shared more of life with them, than men
in most ages before or afterward.   The medieval
tradition of shared work on the farm or in the
workshop, had given women firm but limited status
alongside their men in guild or common field, but fuller
family partnership probably resulted when these
communities lost their hold on individuals.5 Spinning,
weaving and tilling in every household had not yet been
pushed down by machines. The "Dame school" and the
parsonage school were still crucial in each village,
teaching women to read, write and keep accounts, if not
much more.   Above all, religious experience found new
centrality in family worship. Puritan diaries and death
memorials show the same sharing of deep purposes between
men and women, who were companions in spirit even when
physically separated, as do early Quaker journals.6 A
large part of the Journal of John Banks, for instance,
is made up of letters to and from his wife. Banks was a
Cumberland farm boy of only local education and little
religious background before his convincement as a Friend
in 1653. He felt called to travel in ministry only 15
years later.

Dear wife, (he wrote on his first journey), In that love that lasteth and still endureth, remaineth and increaseth in my heart to thee, is it, wherein I read and feel thee; the farther I am separated from thee, the nearer thou art unto me, even in that which length of time nor distance of place shall never be able to wear out, or bring a decay upon, feel the reach of my love in thy heart...

Ann Banks' replies were in the same spirit:

My dear and well beloved husband, unto whom my love reacheth, though separated in body for a season, according to the good pleasure of the Lord, . . . I dearly salute thee, in a measure of that . . . Truth that in our Life, our unity and fellowship . . . Dear Husband, by this thou mayst understand that I and all our dear children, with the rest of the family are all well, and as truly willing and content to give thee up to do service for the Lord, being satisfied it is in answer to his requiring thou art separated from us.[7]

Francis Howgill's last letter to his daughter, Abigail, reflects the same spirit, as did Margaret Fell's one surviving letter to her non-Quaker husband (also instructing the judge about Quaker publishing):

Dear Heart, mind the Lord above all . . .
to keep thee pure and clear and single
before him, without self-end whatsoever.8

The prominence of Quaker women preachers, nevertheless, travelling usually in pairs, was noted by Puritans
everywhere. They were the first Friends at London,
Oxford and Cambridge. Twelve of the twenty-two Quaker
challengers from England to Massachusetts before 1660
were women, though only 14 of the 68 in the next forty
years.9 Figures from Philadelphia and Wales show this
one-fifth proportion as fairly stable thereafter.10
Quaker women traveled more than men to far and dramatic
places, and the women's journeys fell disproportionately
within the first eight years after the religious
awakening on Firbank Fell. Those who went to judge New
England had mostly already traveled widely to preach
within England. The journeys and jailings of Katherine
Evans and Sarah Cheevers in the eastern Mediterranean in
1659-60 became equally famous, but Beatrice Beckley,
Mary Prince and Elizabeth Cowart also reached Papist
Italy. The pioneer visit of Elizabeth Harris to
Maryland, the courage of Mary Clark and Mary Wetherhead
lost at sea, and of Sarah Gibbons' drowning in a canoe
as she returned to Rhode Island, may deserve the same
prestige we usually give to Mary Dyer and Elizabeth
Hooton. The heroism of Mary Fisher before the Sultan
need not be left isolated in story-land.

These many exotic journeys show the prominence of
prophetic leading in the roles of women in early
Quakerism. Individually inspired women later dominated
the Shakers, the Amana Inspirationists, and Christian
Science, just as Antoinette Bourignon was "Light of the

World" to her own Dutch sect in Fox's day. But Friends were pioneers in expecting such "openings" to be given to all their members, women and men alike.11 The key Quaker Bible texts about their own movement were Joel 2:28 and its echo at Pentecost, when God's Spirit is poured out on all flesh, so that both sons and daughters shall prophesy. Those verses stand on the title page of Margaret Fell's own tract, Women's Speaking, which was in 1666, perhaps the first book by a woman on this subject. Her whole argumentation was biblical. She gave priority to the first chapter of Genesis, where God blessed male and female equally, and the second, where Eve is Adam's help-meet, over Chapter 3 where paradise was lost. Margaret plays with Paul's phrases about Christ as the Seed of the Woman, and the Church as his bride. She omits the "Song of Deborah" the blood-thirsty, the first named as "Mother in Israel," but otherwise she presents the prophetesses' succession from Miriam through Hannah and Huldah to the New Testament Anna and Mary Magdalene, the first to see the Risen Christ. Since Puritans constantly quoted Paul's ban on women's speaking in Church, Margaret made clear, like Fox and Fisher before her, that Paul said nothing against the Holy Spirit speaking through women.

Another witness to the central role of prophetic leading for early Quaker women is their writings. Two hundred twenty tracts published before 1700 represent the quantity of women's religious experience: 82 of the 650 early Quaker authors were women, and incidentally 30 of the 144 writers of Swarthmoor letters. The old campaigners, Barbara Blaugdone and Elizabeth Hooton, wrote like modern gradeschoolers (the latter's letter to "Mayor Bullock" of Derby in 1651 being the only document

I know which Fox recopied to improve the spelling). But most of these Quaker women wrote a neat script and used an educated vocabulary. Yet for most of these women, writing was a special event. Twenty-two of the 30 northern women wrote only one surviving letter, and 48 of the 82 published but one tract. Of the total of women's publications, moreover, from which we exclude some joint petitions, 36 percent represent what I have called Proclamations, essentially nothing but a prophetic message in about eight pages. This is double the percentage of such tracts in early Quaker writings by men; again, the women had 16 percent or double the men's proportion which were exhortations to those in political power.[12] By contrast, theological and other debating tracts against Puritans and other Churchmen represent only 8 percent of the women's titles, as against 21 percent for the men's, and if the ratio is based on the number of pages or sheets covered, the disproportion becomes several times larger. Theological debates were wordy. Most of the women's prophetic writings appeared in the 1650's during the outpouring of the first great missions. The other main groups of writings by Quaker women, notably Epistles (38, or 17 percent), and Memorials to dead Friends (22, or 10 percent), belong to the 1680s and 1690s. Nine to twelve women wrote partially autobiographical accounts, a high figure for that period, but they were shorter and simpler than the men's journals. Except for Margaret Fell, the nine Quaker women who published five or more tracts were little known as preachers or leaders: (Sarah Blackberry, Hester Biddle, Ann Dockwra, Dorcas Dole, Abigail Fisher, Rebekah Travers, Dorothy White and Joan Whitrowe). None except Margaret Fell had their written works reprinted as a collection. Most of their tracts did not outlive the immediate situation which called forth the prophetic message.

The right of God's Spirit to transcend ordinary social mores had been invoked not only by Quakers but by women halfway to Ranterism, such as Anna Trapnel, Martha Simmonds, and Hanna Stranger. In the public mind, these women's lives discredited the claims of all others who felt prophetically led. Some even among Friends were restless spirits: - it is astonishing how many married and settled far from their childhood homes. (For instance, Ann Clayton in Rhode Island, Mary Fisher in South Carolina). Alien and distant places into which they had forced their way gradually or suddenly became new homes. In relation to the conventions of respectable society, "leadings of the Spirit" might represent the release of impulses which neither men or women normally let themselves express, or perhaps even feel. The Antinomian Mary Gadbury was deserted by her husband, and then encouraged her lover, William Franklin, in his claims to be Christ re-incarnate, being shattered when he later renounced them.13 But Quakers as sober as Robert Barclay felt the call "to go naked for a sign," like the prophet Isaiah.14 Before Freudian insights were available, the shock to the ego would simply prove to an early Quaker that any impulse to "do likewise," if not evidently evil, must come from God. Quaker women made fewer such signs than did men, and none did so regularly, like Solomon Eccles or William Simpson.15 The women's signs, like young Elizabeth Fletcher's going topless at Oxford, were early and arresting, but not typical.

A more typical ploughing up of the psychic depths is shown by a letter to George Fox from Suzanne Arnold, a Quakeress about whom Geoffrey Nuttall himself could find no other information, but who described a dream like those of Woolman or of Mary Penington:

Dear ffrend:

I am moved to declare unto thee how it hath bene with me since I saw thy face in the flesh . . . Upon the seaventh day, when I departed from the being come about fiue miles, I sait me downe to rest, & sitting upon the ground a while I (was as) if I had bene taken out of the body, being not sensible [words torn out and blotted make the next two lines illegible] In the night I dreamed that I was carried into a p[leasant] garden [again a line is lost]. & as I came from the garden there stood in the way many outward enemies [?] & I was maid to stand [word lost] when I came at them & they was very vissius, but after awhile I was maid to come bouldly through the midst of them, declaring and spreading forth my hands at them, and they was all put to silence; & then I was brought to my outward being, and when I came there: there was a taull child brought Unto me which were clothed in whit Raiment and where soever I went It went with me, & the next day after, being the fift day of the weeke, wee had a meting at my outward

being. As I was wating upon the Lord in
silence, it came: "the manhoud of Christ
is witnessed." Upon the third day of the
seke after, there was at the next house
to ours a company of proud men, some of
them they call gentlemen which did hiely
dishoner the Lord in drinking & vaine
pastime which I was much burthened with
all, but at the presant I had nothing
given from the Lord & so I was willing to
be silent; but in the neight they was set
in my vewe and how it was with them, so I
was wakened by the mighty power of the
Lord working in me & I was commanded to
write, & in obedience to the Lord I was
maid to rise out of the bed in the night
& writ unto them, & in obeying I had
s[weet] peace; and upon the seventh day
after, it came in great power: "heather-
to I have wrought and work thou;" and it
continued with me all the day, and on the
secand day of the weke, after, in the
morning, I was at our fire [?] & it came
unto me in great power: "I have chosen
thee into [blotted]." & so I Rest waiting
upon the Lord & desiring the [blotted] of
the Lord to pray for me, that I amy kepe
faithful & obedient unto the Lord iesus
Christ. Susanne Arnold16

The possibility remains that some blots on Susanna
Arnold's letter were no accident. Fox crossed out
phrases in other letters of intense affection to himself. Even Margaret Fell had signed with the whole

Swarthmoor household one such rhapsodic letter in 1652. The footnote seems to be in her handwriting:

> Thou knowes that wee have recived thee into our hearts, & shall live with thee eternally, & it is our life & joy to be with thee. And see my Dear heart, let not the power of darknesse separate thy bodily presence from us, which will be A greefe & trouble to us.17

Some early Quaker women, notably Dorcas Erbury, Mary Howgill and James Nayler's women disciples were so unrestrained they are usually dismissed as neurotic. Yet, it may be significant that though some younger women: - Elizabeth Leavens, Elizabeth Fletcher, and Elizabeth Williams, incautiously traveled preaching with only a male companion, the only sexual offense charged publically against any of the `valient sixty' was a man's, Christopher Atkinson's.

The issue of emotionalism goes deeper. Outbursts of joy and mutual affection easily overwhelmed newly convinced Friends because they had sat for agonizing weeks of bitter self-discovery under the searching Light . . . Their torments and their breaking through are impersonally described in journals such as Banks', Burnyeat's and Howgill's, and personally in letters like Richard Hubberthorne's. The spiritual pilgrimage, through intense self-judgment and purification, and the resulting impatience for the dawn, produced the symbols of the "the Lamb's War' within the heart. Later as the Camp of the Lord, those who had overcome within themselves carried the campaign to others. As in the Great Awakening or the Wesleyan movement, drastic changes in human habits and motives inevitably involved arousing intense human emotions. The process was recognized and intentional, however dangerous. On the whole, the women were as sober and wise in handling such emotions in themselves and each other, as were the men; perhaps indeed the women had more experience and maturity about this.

This carries over to our next concern, the work of early Quaker women as spiritual counselors. The role was less visible than that of the prophetic preacher, the call to minister less dramatic. Fox called the preachers to meet together before there were formal Elders or Overseers. But, in many cases, Friends recorded in their journals that at the beginning of their inner struggle "a Friend . . . being touched with a sense of my Condition, was made willing to read a Paper in the Meeting which was suitable to my Condition,"18 or spoke a few words of comfort. Often it is not made clear if the helper was man or woman, but usually men were expected to help men, and women to help women. This help was crucial in difficult cases; we have several letters in which women Friends were sent by men to Margaret Fell for guidance. In 1653, Naylor wrote to Margaret at Swarthmoor.

> As for Ellen Parr, I hear that she
> is come towards thee; inquire and send
> for her if she be not come to thee.
> Judge the death, but save the little
> thing which I have seen moving in her...
> Let her stay a while with thee, and show

her the way of love, which is much lost
in the heights.[19]

On another woman, perhaps a sister of the later
separatist John Wilkinson, Thomas Aldam was much more
severe; here Margaret's counseling merged with
discipline:

Dear sister M: FF:

In thee is the salt to savor the
unsavory spirits, which talk of truth,
but live in deceit . . . Here is a Friend
. . . which I have sent unto they house
from York (where Aldam was then in
prison), with Agnes Wilkinson, who hath
acted contrary to the Light in filthiness, and is case out with the Light,
with them who was partakers with her; as
a letter will let thee understand, which
Agnes is to deliver to thy own hand
sealed with my own seal: T.A. . . . . .
see the seal be not altered . . . My
brother G. FF. did write me to send Agnes
to her mother's house; she is cast out,
though she owns the condemnation kneeling
upon her knees at York . . . But, dear
heart, it is not yet right; for the seal
and the will speaks, from the sence of
the just in prison (within Agnes' heart);
and the will and the seal breaks out in
passion. And so the will gets ease, and
the judgment ceases, and the mind turns
from the sword. But a subtle appearance

in the condemnation it is to deceive the
simple, that she into unity may be
received . . . See that she be set and
kept to labor; that flesh may be brought
down, and the Life raised up to reign
over her will; which now doth her
filthiness condemn, . . . till the just
be delivered out of bonds . . . Take heed
of receiving her in amongst you hastily,
lest you take a burden.[20]

Cases of such counseling by Margaret Fell and other
Quaker women like Ann Downer and Mary Penington can be
read between the lines of Journals like Thomas Ellwood's
and letters like John Stubbs'. It was no empty gesture
that so many letters to Margaret Fell, like those to Fox
himself, conclude with a request to pray for the person
who wrote them.

Letters of spiritual counsel, like those later
written by Isaac Penington or Fox, or those between
Barclay and Princess Elizabeth, seem less common from
Quaker women,[21] but we can assume many were lost. It is
important to see this Spiritual counseling, however, as
part of the background out of which Fox felt a leading
of the Light to set up formally the Women's Meetings of
Friends, along with the women's more visible roles as in
caring for the sick, the prisoners and the orphaned.

The story of the organizational role of Isabel
Buttery, Ruth Brown and Ann Downer in setting up the
first Quaker Meetings in London has often been told.
Women also seem to have worked with Stoddard and the
Drings in overseeing Quaker publications through the

London printers. Several modern books (Braithwaite, Brailsford and Lloyd) have also reprinted in full John Crouch's account, telling how "some ancient women Friends did meet together . . . to inspect the circumstances and conditions of such who were imprisoned on Truth's account, and to provide things needful to supply their wants."22 Out of these which George Fox established, the weekly meetings of the "Box Meeting," the Women's "Two Weeks Meetings," both apparently about 1660, and a decade later the joint men's and women's Six Weeks Meeting, and the Meeting for sufferings came. The practical results of the women's care for prisoners can be seen in Ellwood's accounts of the crowded Quaker groups in Newgate and Bridewell in 1662, to whom women brought not only food and bedding, but tools to work at their trade.23 The sight of wives and lovers bringing to prisoners their meals and jailers' fees were common enough, as late as Elizabeth Fry's day; it was a sordid experience, but the only severe danger was infection. Suffering and imprisonment were understood as part of the Lamb's War. The Quaker women cared more religiously as well as more widely and efficiently for all Friends in a prison, and Quaker women prisoners benefited equally. But the heroines are Ann Downer, who walked 200 miles to Cronwall when Fox was in Doomsdale Dungeon; Ann Naylor, who came the next year from Yorkshire to nurse her errant husband in the Tower of London; and Margaret Fell, who came the length of England more than once to try to persuade the London authorities to liberate Fox.

Some of the other services done by early Quaker women were also not unique to Friends, being substitutes for welfare services intended under the Elizabethan

"Poor Law" or for what was still provided by the Church of England parishes. These included care for orphans and for those too old to support themselves. Teen-agers needed to be formally apprenticed in a craftsman's home and shop, to learn a trade. Farmers who had lost their barns and cattle by fire or sheriff's fines were given emergency help. Quakers become famous, not only for how well they helped their own poor, but also for and to non-Quakers. Yet here, again, the main difference between Quaker women and at least the charitable country gentlewoman was probably the more intensely religious and Meeting-centered spirit in which Friends felt called to their helping.

This element of ministry was gracefully but strongly expressed in Margaret Fell's letters about "the Kendal Fund," to support traveling Quaker preachers, particularly those in prison, and even more their families, between 1654 and 1658. To those who should give, she wrote:

> You may know the mystery of the
> fellowship, and be in that Mystery, in
> Unity with the Brethren; that so you may
> come to be one with them in their
> Sufferings, in their Tryals, Travels,
> Troubles, Buffetings, Whippings,
> Stockings, Prisonings.24

When the Conventicle Act persecutions of the 1660's threw most Quaker prisoners back upon local Meetings' resources, this first national venture faded, but when Fox set up the men's and women's committees in London they gradually became the new centers for aid. In 1671,

Fox proposed the nationwide system of W̲o̲m̲e̲n̲'̲s̲ M̲o̲n̲t̲h̲l̲y̲
M̲e̲e̲t̲i̲n̲g̲s̲, parallel with the essentially men's monthly
business meetings set up in 1668. Margaret Fell, whose
Women's Meetings at Swarthmoor and Lancaster had been
among the first established, wrote also a national
Epistle in Support. The functions of these formal
Women's Monthly Meetings remained mostly the same: the
poor, orphans, widows and prisoners.   The new element
which caused ardent polarization among Friends, and was
a spark for the Wilkinson-Story split, was the requirement that the Women's Meetings approve prospective
marriages.

Marriage again combined a traditional English issue
with a prophetic Quaker Testimony against parish clergy.
In addition, the Friends felt an intense religious
responsibility for individuals. Even apart from the
Civil Registration of marriages, under Cromwell's
Commonwealth in 1653, which had ended the monoply of
Parish clergy in recording marriages, the North-of-
England custom of "handfast marriages" before lay
witnesses had regularized common-law status. But Fox
was concerned to legalize Quaker marriages, children and
inheritances as early as 1653 and especially after new
marriage laws in 1656 and at the Restoration.[25] Along
with the consent of parents and weighty Friends, the
engaged couples were expected to show their "clearness"
from conflicting obligations before the Women's meeting.
Against the demand, and against the independent,
separate and almost equal status of Women's Meetings in
general, it was often the weightiest male Friends in
little local Meetings who protested. Their protest
upset George Fox, perhaps partly because it accused him
of seeking undue authority as a sort of Quaker pope,

whereas there is some evidence that he wanted to devolve authority from weighty individuals upon the Quaker community as an organized whole.26 The setting up of Meetings, and of Women's Meetings in particular, could claim religious validity, just in proportion as the Sense of the Meeting could claim the same divine leading and authority that had been felt by prophetic individuals. As late as 1680, in one of the first of Fox's sermons to be taken down in shorthand, he was still stressing authority as shared between men and women: in the day of Creation,

> God placed men in a blessed
> habitation . . . and set him in
> domination over all the works of his
> hands . . . God said to them "have
> domination," he did not say to them, "Do
> thou have dominion without thy wife," but
> he said to them "have domination," . . .
> Man was blessed and so was woman, and all
> things were blessed unto them.

Then Fox went on through the cycle of texts Margaret Fell had used: Deborah now also, and Hulda, and Magdalene at the Tomb, and Christ the Seed of the Woman.27

    Thus, through Fox's sense of a divine calling to set up the Women's Meetings, and through their shared leadings as they met for business, the prophetic role transformed the other aspects of Quaker women's work and relationships, and lifted them beyond either biblical legalism or social convention, without making women's rights as such a key issue. The challenge to the old pattern was not that it curbed women but that it curbed the Spirit of God.

An Epistle from the Lancaster Quarterly Women's Meeting went out to "Women's Meetings everywhere" between 1675 and 1680. Isabel Ross found a copy in Nottingham, and more recently Milton Speizman and Jane Kronick of Bryn Mawr found another in Philadelphia, and published it in the first issue of Signs. Copied by hand, like most such Epistles, it must have been widely read. It was evidently written by Sarah Fell, then Clerk of Lancaster Meeting, who had also taken over from her mother the management and account-books of the Swarthmoor Hall household. Once again, the argument began biblically, with Christ as Seed of the Woman, and all women as thereby adopted as the Seed of Abraham, "So here is the blessed Image of the living God, restored again, in which he made them male and female in the beginning . . . so that you may be helps meet, in the Restoration, and Resurrection of the body of Christ, which is his Church." Along with Miriam and Hanna, Sarah Fell was willing to notice the worldly women whom the Hebrew prophets condemned, and the women of Canaan and Samaria whom Jesus enlightened; and so Sarah moves on to the women who announced the Resurrection. Then the Epistle turned to the duties of Women's Meetings, which include overseeing the conduct of individuals, and presenting papers for condemning conduct that became "a publick offense," notably "if there be any that goes out to Marry, with the priests, or joineth in Marriage with the world." By this time, engaged couples were asked "to bring their marriages twice to the Women's Meetings and twice to the Men's." The Women's Meetings were also to oversee joint testimony statements against tithes, affirming each woman's own clearness from paying any; the women were to care for "the poore, and widdowes, . . . the sick and weak and Infirme or Aged," and to record all their decisions in a book, keeping account of all payments. Sarah concluded, as her mother had begun her tract a decade before, with the reminder that if women be in some sense a "weaker sex," it is the kind of weakness by which God's strength is made perfect, as his wisdom is made perfect in what seems human foolishness. Neither Saint Paul nor Carl Jung said it so well. Perhaps we can see the openness of Mary at the Annunication as the seedbed of Quakerism.

Notes

[1]Elizabeth Gray Vining, Women in the Society of Friends, given Nov. 11, 1955, Guilford College, N.C.

[2]Mabel Richmond Brailsford, Quaker Women, 1650-1690 (London, Duckworth, 1915); Emily Manners, Elizabeth Hooten, First Quaker Woman Preacher (London, Headley, 1914); Isabel ross, Margaret Fell, Mother of Quakerism (London, Longmans Green, 1949).

[3]Robert Frost, A Masque of Reason (N.Y., Hold, 1945).

[4]Cf. Carl Bridenbaugh, Vexed and Troubled Englishmen, 1590-1642 (Oxford University Press, 1967), p. 32.

[5]Christopher Hill, Pelican Economic History, Vol. II, Reformation to Industrial Revolution, (1969), p. 83. Bridenbaugh, op. cit., pp. 169-170, denies that women had guild rights. On Baroque Women, see Pat Rogers The Augustan Vision (London, Methuen, 1974), Ch. 9.

[6]See Owen Watkins, The Puritan Experience, Studies in Spiritual Autobiography (N.Y., Schocken, 1952); also William Haller, The Rise of Puritanism (N.Y., Harper, 1938).

[7]John Banks, Journal (1712), pp. 22-57.

[8]Abraham MS#1, correcting Ross, op. cit., p. 119, from microfilm. Howgill's letter new prefaces the 1696 edition of his works.

[9]Combining Rufus Jones, Quakers in the American Colonies (2nd ed., N.Y., Norton, 1966) with George A. Selleck Quakers in Boston (Cambridge, 1978) and "First Publishers of Truth in New England, 1656-1775" by G.J. Willawer, Jr., in Quaker History, 65, #1 (Spring, 1976), pp. 35-44.

[10]Elizabeth Vining reckons 12 women out of the 66 "First Publishers of Truth," and 32 of the 112 overseas visitors to Philadelphia Friends before 1773. The Lloyds of Dolobran in Wales recorded 36 women out of the 174 traveling ministers visiting there around 1700. (Arnold Lloyd, Quaker Social History, 1669-1738 (London, Longmans Green, 1950), p. 126.

[11]See J.G. Riewald: Reynier Janson of Philadelphia (Groninger, Wolters-Noorlhoff, 1970), Ch. 4.

[12]See Appendix by David Runyan for Hugh Barbour & Arthur Roberts, editors, Early Quaker Writings (Grand Rapids, Erdsman, 1973), based mainly on the titles in Joseph Smith's Catalogue of Friends Books (London, 1867, 1893).

[13]Her story was first explored by Allen Hole of Earlham. On similar cases, see G.F.S. Ellens, "The Ranters Ranting," in Church History, 40 (1971), pp. 91-107.

[14]Is. 20, where the prophet warned Hebrews they would be led naked into exile if they rebelled against Assyria.

[15]See Kenneth Carroll: "Early Quakers and `Going Naked as a Sign,'" in Quaker History 67, #2 (Autumn, 1978), pp. 69-87.

[16]Swarthmore Manuscript 4:37, punctuation modernized.

[17]SMS 3:24-6, cf. Ross, p. 37. This footnote includes Margaret's regret that Fox "shaked the dust of thy feet at him who would not receive thee, nor is worthy of thee, which shall be A testimony against him forever." Was this Henry Fell or the Judge himself? Fox added later a note that "he . . . was not long after convinced."

[18]John Banks, Journal, p. 5. Lloyd (p. 2) dates Quaker overseers from a Balby Meeting of 1656; Elders met regularly with Ministers from about 1698 (Lloyd, p. 128).

[19]SMS 3:326   July [1653] from Sedbergh.

[20]SMS 4:89, October 30, 1654, Thomas Aldam from York Castle.

[21]Isabel Ross preserves one from Margaret Fell to Anthony Pearson (p. 58 from SMS 3:100) and one from her to Caton & Stubbs as they returned to Holland (p. 70).

[22]Posthuma Christiana, (1712), section III.

[23]History of the Life of Thomas Ellwood (1714), pp. 188-9, etc.

[24]Margaret Fell, A Brief collection (1710), p. 97, from Miller MS #65. See Ross, p. 63 and Spence MSS III:18, SMS 1:210-12, 236-40, etc. on the Kendal Fund.

[25]See Lloyd, op. cit. pp. 49ff.; Hugh Barbour, The Quakers in Puritan England (Yale, 1964), pp. 177-9; Richard Vann, The Social Development of English Quakerism, (Cambridge, Harvard University Press, 1969, p. 103) on Quaker marriages.

[26]See Emilia Vogelklou, The Atonement of George Fox (Wallingford, Pendle Hill, 1969). Barclay's & Penn's arguments at this time nevertheless supported Fox's special authority.

[27]Fox, "Sermon at Wheeler Street," 1st of 4th month, 1680, see Barbour & Roberts, pp. 502ff.

MAPPING THE INNER JOURNEY
OF QUAKER WOMEN
Elise Boulding

Introduction: Twenty-Five Women

For this study of the inner journey of Quaker
women, I have chosen a group of women representing the
first five generations of English Quakers.   These
English women have served as role models to American
Quaker women by virtue of the fact that they were chosen
for inclusion in the fourteen-volume Friends Library
published by Philadelphia Yearly Meeting (Arch Street)
between 1837 and 1850.   By adding Margaret Fell, born in
1614, and Elizabeth Fry, who died in 1845 (neither of
whom are in the Friends Library), the study encompasses
the early period of activism, the movement to quietism,
and the beginnings of the rebirth of activism in the
Society of Friends.   The twenty-five women we are
considering all either kept journals or wrote many
letters, were active in the ministry within the Society,
and were considered saints by their meetings.   The
significance of their inclusion in the Friends Library
is that they were considered both inspirational and
doctrinally sound by the orthodox branch of Friends in
Pennsylvania.   They could be said to represent one
important stream of women's religious experience in the
first century and a half of Quakerism.

Their lives were very different from our own.   They
lived under more stress, whether from persecutions or
the constant presence of death and coffins and burials,

as children, spouses, relatives and friends died around them. They had to struggle with their identify as women called to public spiritual leadership in a world unfriendly to Quaker practice, and in local Meetings where a number of Friends, male and female, were lukewarm to the idea of women's leadership. They carried heavy household responsibilities, often worked side by side with their husbands in field or shop, nursed the sick in a far-flung kin network, attended and ministered at First-day and Midweek Meetings, Monthly, Quarterly and Yearly Meetings, and at numerous sittings for accomplishing the work of the local Friends' body. They visited the sick, helped the poor, taught the children of the poor, oversaw the local workhouses and visited the prisons and madhouses, in their own community. On top of all this they were called to travel in the ministry, sometimes on trips that took them away from home for two or more years at a time. They could do all this because they had a deep and powerful prayer life, but they also engaged in unremitting spiritual struggles as to the rightness of what they were doing. They thought of themselves as channels of God's will, not shapers of space. In fact, their prayer life was creating new inner space, and the conditions for a spiritual and social regeneration of the society around them were created by the overflow from that inner space.

Here are a few facts about these twenty-five women. Only ten of them had children. These ten nearly all had large families, however--seven to ten children. Nine remained childless in marriage, four marrying in or near their forties, after they were already well known as ministers. Six remained single all their lives. Yet all had heavy household and nursing duties as members of extended families. Some were of comfortable means like Margaret Fell and Elizabeth Fry, others were very poor like Elizabeth Collins who was sent out to be a houseworker at the age of five years when her father died. Apprenticed to a trade at sixteen, married at eighteen, widowed at twenty-two with two children, Elizabeth became a recorded minister of the Society at twenty-four. Other young women emigrated to America against their parents' will in their late teens, worked their way out of indentured service under great hardship, and became ministers in the new land. Whether rich, poor, or of moderate means, they all worked hard and prayed long. The average age of death for these women was sixty-eight, which means they lived considerably longer than their non-Quaker sisters of that era. Two lived to be ninety, ten lived into their eighties or nineties, five to their sixties, and five died at fifty or under. (For three no age at death is given).

Spiritual Formation and Spiritual Discipline

In other religious traditions, and most particularly in the Catholic traditions, there is a vast literature and some well-developed practices concerning the process of spiritual formation and the disciplining and reshaping of the "natural person" into the child of God. The priesthood and the religious orders offer experience and religious guidance for the infant soul on its journey toward God. In the Society of Friends there are only queries, not specific practices, and all guidance comes from the inward teacher. Yet the same high aspirations for spiritual growth are found among these women as among the Catholic saints. The writings of St. Teresa of Avila could be slipped in among the journal passages quoted here, and would not seem the least bit alien.

Because there was no external authority to guide, discipline and exhort them, these women disciplined themselves. In the gentler mode, they saw themselves as spiritual children, needing to be nurtured and protected as "natural" children do, in a kind of probationary childhood, until ready for harder things. (12:290) Sarah Grubb writes of the need to accept the pace of spiritual growth:

> I often wish that I could learn to be still when I have nothing to do, and instead of straining my eyes in the dark, and watching the breaking of day, to dwell quietly in the ward all night, believing in the light, and obediently working therein. The outward day breaks gradually upon us, and experience teaches us the certain indication of its approach, a dawning of light which we are not apt to disbelieve, nor doubt that the meridian of it will come in due time. As in the outward, we cannot hasten that time, no more can we with respect to divine illuminations. Does it not therefore remain to be our business, to wait for the light when a little of it appears, to believe in it, and that the fulness of the day will come, though we

do not now see it; remembering that
`blessed are they that have not seen, and
yet have believed.' This is what I
apprehend to be right to do, and what I
wish to attain. 912:314)

Then there was the long period, even for those who
grew up in the Society of Friends, of trying to adopt
the higher code of conduct that the religious call
demanded. Often in the early days it took the form of
struggling to use the fateful words thee and thou, which
marked a person as clearly having chosen to be a
publisher of truth. Elizabeth Stirredge recalls this
period in her own life:

For my part, I had a concern upon my
spirit, because I shifted many times from
that word. I would have said any word,
rather than thee or thou, that would have
answered the matter I was concerned in,
but still I was condemned, guilt
following me. I was not clear in the
sight of God; my way was hedged up with
thorns; I could go on no further, until I
had yielded obedience unto the little
things. Then I walked along, as I frequently used to do, when things came as a
weight upon me, where I might be private
from all except my soul's concern. Oh!
that desolate place where I used to
retire along, how many times hath my soul
met with my beloved there, who hath
sweetly comforted me, when my soul hath
been sick of love; and full of doubts,

for fear He had forsaken me. But blessed
be his name who liveth forever, he still
appeared in a needful time. (2:194)

Self will was seen as enemy, and had to be sternly
faced.

Sarah Grubb, in somber flash of insight:

I see abundant occasion to watch the
spring in myself from whence my rejoicing and
depressions come. Self is a subtle enemy,
insinuating itself into the company of the
purest intentions and approved services,
claiming a share of their peace . . . (12:312)

Mary Capper puts it:

In my private cogitations, found
self still alive, and that its branches
shoot in all directions, and still want
the pruning knife. (912;300)

Elizabeth Fry writes at age twenty, when she still
loved worldly things:

How much my natural heart does love
to sing: but if I give way to the
ecstacy singing sometimes produces in my
mind, it carries me far beyond the
center; it increases all the world
passions, and works on enthusiasm.
(Fry, 74)

True religion seems a subject of
that great importance; that we must not
play with it, either mentally or in word;
. . . I am not a friend to too many
religious thoughts; for thoughts are apt
to wander, and border on imagination.
Religion is a deep inward working of the
feelings and of the heart; we must not
look too much for the bright light on the
surface of things, but we must humbly and
quietly try to seek deep; attending to
the day of small things, trying to be
faithful in the little . . .

(Fry, 92)

These women are practising what Catholics would
call "religious discernment." They are subjecting their
thoughts, feelings, impulses, to criticism in the light
of the divine knowledge available to them. Because they
know they are to be channels for communicating God's
word to others, they judge themselves by the hardest
standards they know. Such

poor weak instruments ... required not
only the forming of the potter's hand,
but higher degrees of drying, and greater
heat in the furnace to prepare them, than
almost any other vessel; nay, if I may be
allowed the comparison, they are like
dishes that have to pass through the oven
for every service, and which, after they
are emptied, and the company has enjoyed
them, need more washing and care than any

other utensils at the table; and great
danger there is that, by indiscretion of
some sort or other, they will get cracked
or broken. I look with dread, I am bowed
down and dismayed at the sight of the
precarious standing of such, but
especially my own. (12:289)

Alternations of the stern and tender view of one's
spiritual growth are very marked in the writings of
these women. First, Jane Hoskens writes of being
carried like a lamb in the Father's arms, while he
patiently nurtures her newborn spirit, and she feels a
"fresh and large visitation of heavenly love," yet
suddenly the birth of the new creature in Christ Jesus
becomes a tearing experience:

Now I was mightily reached unto, and
stripped of all self-righteousness, and
my state was opened to me in such a
manner, that I was quite confounded, and
concluded that though I could talk of
religion, being made a child of God, a
member of his church, and an inheritor of
his holy kingdom, there was as much need
as ever to cry, Lord, have mercy on me a
poor sinner! not yet having witnessed
the law of the spirit of life in Christ
Jesus, to set me free from the law of sin
and death. Outward ceremonies availed
nothing, the new birth was wanting, and
must be witnessed, in order to prepare me
for the work whereunto the Lord had
called me, and was about to engage me in.

(12:462)

Jane kept reaching the point where she thought that now her rebirth was completed:

> . . . that I had nothing to do but
> sit contented under the enjoyment of
> Divine favour, rejoicing that I had left
> all and followed Christ . . . till one
> time being in a meeting, and sitting very
> contented under my own vine and fig-tree,
> a call arose in my mind; I have chosen
> thee a vessel from thy youth to serve me,
> and to preach the Gospel of salvation to
> many people; and if thou wilt be
> faithful, I will be with thee unto the
> end of time. (12:463)

Jane is shocked, because she doesn't even "believe" in women preaching!

All the women struggle mightily against being called to the ministry. There are usually three crises. The first is in accepting an inward call to serious holiness. The second is accepting a call to speak in Meeting. Some women struggled so hard against the inner call to speak that they became seriously ill, and the struggle could go on for several years. Spouses, children, relatives, an entire Meeting could become involved in these struggles. Alice Hayes became seriously crippled and had to be cared for by her husband before she finally broke the bonds. Margaret Lucas longed and dreaded to go to Meeting--longed for Divine sustenance, dreaded the call to speak. Finally she manages. Overcoming "slavish fear" she gets ready to kneel in vocal prayer:

> While I viewed the place, my soul
> secretly breathed thus before the Lord,
> `Here is the place of my execution; . . .
> This is the block whereon I must yield up
> the pride of nature, for a testimony of
> my obedience; remember me, O Lord! and
> the conflicts that I undergo to serve
> thee. Accept, O Lord! the sacrifice.'
> I then kneeled down; and when I arose,
> this came into my mind; `the life that I
> must now live, must be by faith in Jesus
> Christ." (Lucas, 13:201)

Yet there is still one more titanic struggle ahead, when the call comes to travel in the ministry outside one's local Meeting. Elizabeth Webb had a call to go to America. She become so ill while resisting it that when she finally gave in she had to be carried to shipboard on a litter.*

There are no objective reasons for these struggles. They are not simply neurotic symptoms of an unbalanced emotional life. First, there is the problem of redefining one's role as a woman to fit the exacting demands of public ministry, a problem that will be discussed in the next section. Second, there is the training for the life of the spirit and for the ministry which every woman must undergo who responds to the call.

*This may not be precisely correct. The journal account is ambiguous, and she may have meant simply that she finally decided to go even if she had to be carried aboard on a litter.

Lastly, there is the prospect of grueling hard work in travelling from meeting to meeting diagnosing spiritual ills and guiding individuals and meetings to the resources they need. Not the least of the grueling aspects of the travel was the physical danger and hardship involved: at sea, the dangers of shipwreck and being stopped by pirates and man o'wars: on land, the dangers of impassible roads and of brigands and thieves.

Quaker ministers are trained by God alone, and the training requires extraordinary inward attentiveness. Catherine Phillips, one of the tenderest and most loving of women ministers, has written about the divine training as she experienced it:

> The All-wise employer of true gospel ministers knows how to direct his servants, both as to the matter, and the manner wherein he intends it should be communicated to the people. I have admired his wisdom and condescension therein, when without forethought my speech has been accommodated to the capacities of those to whom it was directed. To such as be illiterate and ignorant, I have spoken in very low terms; and to those of more understanding in such as answered its level; while to the learned, and those of superior natural talents, I might say with the prophet, `The Lord God hath given me the tongue of the learned;' although I had it not by education. I have not wanted

eloquence of speech, or strength of argument, wherein to convey and enforce the doctrines given me to preach; of which I could say, as my Lord and Master did, my doctrines are not mine, but his who sent me, and his love, life, and power, have accompanied them, to the stopping of the mouths of gainsayers, and convincing of the understandings of many, of the rectitude and efficacy of `the Truth as it is in Christ Jesus." . . . all we can do is but little, and that little communicated by his strength, this is ultimately the language of our spirits; Not unto us, O Lord! not unto us, but unto thy ever worthy name, or power, be glory forever! Amen. (11:274-6)

Margaret Fell writes to Friends whose ministry has carried them to prison:

I do see the secret work of God going on in people's minds. Look not at the hard rocks, nor look at briars, nor at the thorns, nor at the mountains, nor the coldness, for . . . the true seeds-men must not regard the weather, the winds that blow; they sow the seed before the winter. There is a winter and there is a summer; there is a time to sow the seed, there is a time to reap. So the Lord keep you wholly in his power to himself, for there is never no fainting

but to that mind which goes from the pure
within, that . . . hath a joy in the
Earth. (Barbour: 11)

Even with the confidence that God has taken their
training in hand, there is the heavy burden of being
called to discharge the pastoral duty day after day, in
ever-new settings, among strangers, with few clues as to
what has been going on in a particular locality, what
individual agonies a Meeting harbors. Martha Routh
writes of this burden of ministry on a particular
occasion:

> When rising on my feet I felt it to
> be in fear and trembling; for while
> sitting under the renewal of baptism, I
> had to believe, that the state of the
> meeting was very complicated. But it is
> only for thee to read, Oh! fellow-
> traveller, thou who art able to do it, in
> a similar line, what it is to be so
> engaged, and how great the care and
> watchfulness which is necessary, even
> when under the holy annointing. The
> states of the people are opened like
> flowers in a garden, some appearing
> beautiful to the eye, and affording a
> pleasant saviour; others of a contrary
> appearance, yielding an offensive smell;
> others having little or no scent. To
> know how the culturing hand should be
> turned upon these, in order to help, is
> indeed a weighty matter; and nothing
> short of that adorable wisdom, which

alone is profitable to direct, can
accomplish it according to the divine
will. (12:456)

Sarah Stephenson was one of those who participated
in creating a new type of ministry for the Society of
Friends, a ministry to families in their homes. Before
her innovations, ministry was confined to public
meetings. She developed a way of "sitting" with
families in their living rooms so that spiritual
teaching could become individualized down to the needs
of the youngest family member. For thirty-one years
Sarah travelled up and down England visiting families,
and in the last sickness-ridden months of her life, as
long as she could travel at all she kept up a schedule
of three family visits a day. Few people, men or women,
could sustain such a pace and remain spiritually alive.

All of the women report ups and downs over the
years of their ministry. None achieves peace of mind
for once and all. They write of spells of "poverty of
spirit" and of dry seasons, of times when they fear
going to meeting for fear of "falling prey to the
devourer." A "dipped state of mind" is frequently
referred to. Sarah Grubb, one of the most widely
travelled, writes that:

> My travel hath long been through a
> waste howling wilderness where, (though
> surrounded with innumerable blessings)
> my mind hath been led mostly to feel
> itself like a pelican, and to wish for an
> outward situation similarly obscure, that
> I might ever be hid from the eyes of men,

of whom I often feel a fear that baffles
description.

Nine years after the first quote, still travelling,
she writes:

> I mourn over myself, not knowing why
> it is so with me. As to opening my mouth
> in our meetings, it seems as far from me
> as if I had never known such a concern.
> A painful gloomy exercise, or a wandering
> imagination, is what I have principally
> to travail through; and yet, having been
> acquainted with a situation of mind much
> more destitute than this, I dare not but
> consider the invisible support my soul is
> blessed with, as an object of reverent
> gratitude. (12:344)

The most fearful women are in a sense the most
courageous. Elizabeth Fry was full of fears from
childhood on, and fought them right up to her deathbed.
She writes resignedly of ups and downs; "yesterday's
manna is not for today." At age thirty-five she records
in her journal:

> . . . in the night I had a deep
> plunge, making me exceedingly low and
> nervous. The enemy appeared to come in
> like a flood: I sought after quietness
> and patience, and in due time felt a
> standard to be lifted up against him, for
> which mercy, may I not say, `Bless the
> Lord, oh, my soul, and all that is within

me, bless his holy name.' (Fry, 228)
    At age forty, at the height of her international
public activity:

        I Seldom remember being less able to
        come at Divine Consolation . . . am I
        separated in heart from my Lord? Have my
        public engagements diverted me from the
        life of self-denial, of daily taking up
        my cross? If this be the case, I cannot
        heal myself, I cannot help myself, I
        cannot bring myself back--and therefore,
        O Lord! Thou who graciously carest for
        thy children . . . be pleased to heal my
        backslidings, to help me, and as far as I
        have wandered from Thee, to bring me
        back. (Fry, 344, 5; age 40)

    Yet never is discouragement absolute. All these
women know that God will "bring them back." Their
spiritual discipline enables them to carry on in the
face of the buffeting of the spirit. They often use the
image of the Rock on which they rest, the Everlasting
Arms which hold them up, to signify that on which they
rely with such complete faith. Already at age twenty-
eight, Elizabeth Fry forsaw how her life would be, as
she struggled to balance family and Meeting and public
concerns and to keep her own religious identity intact:

        I have been married 8 years
        yesterday. Various trials of faith and
        patience have been permitted me; my
        course has been very different to what I
        expected, and instead of being, as I had

hoped, a useful instrument in the church militant, here I am a care-worn wife and mother, outwardly nearly devoted to the things of this life. Though at times this difference in my destination has been trying to me, yet, I believe those trials (which have certainly been pinching) that I have had to go through have been very useful, and brought me to a feeling sense of what I am; and at the same time taught me where power is, and in what we are to glory. (p. 133)

She will not give up: "the wall of preservation appears almost broken down, yet my heart says, I will not fear but that I shall at last praise him, whom I desire to be the health of my countenance and my God." (p. 150)

Being a Woman

In a study of great Spanish nuns, Sister Electa Arenal (1979; in press) comments that these women combine utter humility and determined self-assertion. These are exactly the qualities that characterize the women Friends we are considering. Confident to the point of arrogance, full of joyful self-assurance, when riding a wave of the spirit, they cower in a howling wilderness when they hit the troughs between the waves. Jane Pearson, one of those who struggled the longest before giving in to the call to ministry, and travelled the most widely afterwards, confessed that her mind was either filled with heavy clouds or heavenly radiance and peace. They dared not count on any support but divine aid, for the men in their meetings were not always supportive (John Story told the women to go home and wash their dishes), and neither were the women. The ministry sisterhood is a powerful one, but many women clung to more traditional roles and would not partici- pate in the women's meetings, or carry their share of meeting work.

The ministry sisterhood therefore had to carry on their own inner struggle as well as to struggle with unsupportive fellow-friends, with the larger world, and with the God who laid the ministry on them. Elizabeth Stirredge shouted back to God when she felt the call: "If women are supposed to be so unworthy, then don't use me!" Sarah Grubb learned to overcome her fear of going in to give messages to the men's meetings. In general, the women apparently tried to reason with the men and raise the consciousness of the women. Women ministers often called women's meetings and tried to establish women's meetings for business where they did not exist. Martha Routh writes especially of how her mind "was dipped in sympathy" for women Friends in America (less well organized than in England), and she tried to strengthen their sisterhood. Teaching girls, working with women in prisons and finding employment for poverty-stricken women were all expressions of sister- hood, although carried out in ways that we would find very maternalistic today. Women ministers supported each other by travelling together, writing to each other, visiting each other. They also developed close relationships with supportive men Friends. Alice Hayes writes of Francis Stemper that "he was a man of tender spirit, though not advanced in years, even as a nursing father." (2:76) The image suggests a creative transcendance of the traditional male role in one who was a good friend to women.

Judging from their journals, all these women had keen intellects, although they were continually at work subduing "the reasoner." They saw through the products of Oxford and Cambridge and felt real contempt for the mental and spiritual capacities of the professors. They were as apt to enjoy taking on a hostile man in public debate as not, although they paid a price later in spiritual penance for letting "the reasoner" get out of hand.

Catherine Phillips was perhaps one of the most vocal of the women in public debate on the position of women. Deborah Bell put down in a long letter to a woman friend what many women expounded in public; the biblical precedents for the active participation of women in the public life of the religious community. (It is much along the lines of Margaret Fell's "Women's speaking Justified." (Barbour).

Since women as prophets, visionaries, teachers and church leaders are not hard to find in either the Old or New Testament, the task of women Friends was not hard when they were arguing scripturally. However, the most telling argument against the women would be cultural rather than scriptural. Everyone "knew" where women's place was: in subjection. Deborah tells men that women are indeed in subjection--to God, not men!

> For we are far from usurping
> authority over the men, but remain in

true subjection, depending upon the Lord
our strength, and waiting for the
authority of his holy power, which calls
to this great work, and carries it on,
both in sons and daughters, to the praise
of his great name. (5:15)

The Inner Life

If God's indwelling and continual presence were not
the most real fact of existence for these women, they
could never have overcome all the obstacles to answering
the call of God in their lives. Their Journals all
indicate that they lived a life of continual inward
prayer. Several mention, including Elizabeth Fry, that
from the time of their first serious call to holiness,
often in their teens, they have never failed to awaken
into prayer each morning of their lives. The over-
whelming love they feel for God breaks through the often
tedious accounts of their travels in the ministry and in
public service. "Do with me as thou wilt, only let me
be thine!" Elizabeth Fry writes. One day, five of her
children are in bed with whooping cough: "but all
appears light, nay more than light, such sweetness has
covered my mind, little short . . . of joy and peace."
(187) Another day, "Yesterday, I experienced liveliness
of spirit without any apparent cause; nothing but free
mercy and grace . . . It is an unspeakable source of
gratitude to feel alive spiritually . . ." (197)

Sarah Stephenson, in an interval between long
journeys, writes:

Melksham, 16th of Sixth month, 1797

This morning, when alone, my soul was sweetly, unutterable so, overshadowed with the love and precious presence of the Beloved of my soul; who was pleased to break in upon it with the effusion of adorable kindness; under which I was enabled to supplicate the King of kings, through the medium of the pure spirit of his Son, the Lamb immaculate, for preservation and ability to such a poor despicable worm, to do whatsoever he might be pleased to employ me in; and humbly to crave preservation through this vale of tears; and at the close of time, that my poor spirit, through his adorable mercy, might be granted admittance, where forever I might worship Him, with the Lord Jesus. Amen. This, after a time of deep baptism . . .

1st of Eighth month, 1797.

This morning, sweetly opened into the Divine mystery of the coming of the adorable Son of the Highest, with the salutation of the angel to the mother of our dear Lord, attended with the precious feeling of his pure redeeming love to mankind, in order to purify, so as to make meet for union and communion with Him while here, and everlastingly to dwell with Him in a glorious eternity. (4:200)

Strict as these women are with themselves, they experience God's love freely, and they also experience outpourings of human love. Catharine Phillips writes, "I look upon love to be the governing passion of the soul." Elizabeth Webb writes:

> I am a witness for the Lord, that
> the shedding abroad of his love over the
> inhabitants of this nation, hath been
> like showers of rain in the spring time.
> I well remember that I told a Friend in
> London, I felt the divine extendings of
> the love of God so to flow to the
> people, as I walked in the streets of the
> city, that I could have freely published
> the salvation of God, which is near, and
> his righteousness, which is ready to be
> revealed, in the public places of con-
> course: the Friend said he hoped it
> would not be required of me. This I
> mentioned to convince thee that universal
> love prevails in the hearts of some who
> are unknown to the world, and hardly
> known to their own brethren; and this is
> not to be wondered at. (13:164,5)

Some of these bursts of inward song come in solitude, others come in the midst of journeys. Elizabeth Stirredge was imprisoned with three other Friends for meeting in public. It was a cold winter's night, the stone prison walls were icy, the earthen floor damp through the handful of straw meant to serve as a bed. Lying down to rest, with one thin blanket for cover, Elizabeth prays:

Oh! thou Physician of value, who
can strengthen both soul and body, be
with us this night, and all the nights
and days that we have to live in this
world. Then the Lord was pleased to open
my heart unto him, and to fill it with
his mercy and comfortable presence, inso-
much that I could have sung aloud of the
goodness of the Lord, and of his mercies
and blessings bestowed upon us. But
looking over my fellow prisoners, and
seeing them so sound asleep, I forebore
to open my mouth. In the morning there
came many people to the prison door, to
see how many of us were dead with our
hard fare; some of them were sure, as
they said that I was dead, for I looked
as if I would not live until the morning.
Finding us all alive and well, they
confessed and said, `Surely we were the
people of God, if there were any."
(2:205)

The lyric quality of Elizabeth Stirredge's
religious experience comes out a number of times in her
journal. Another example, also from a period of
travelling and active persecution:

`Lord, what shall I do to be saved?
I would do anything for assurance of
everlasting life; and if the Lord will be
pleased to accept me upon any terms, I
matter not what becomes of this body. If
I could find a cave that I might get

into, where I might mourn out the remainder of my days in sorrow, and see man no more,' I thought I could have been contented. But it pleased the Lord to open the eyes of my understanding, and to lead me by a way that I knew not, and to begin the first day's work in my heart, which was, `the spirit of the Lord moving upon the waters, and dividing the light from the darkness.' When the separation was made, I could see my way in the light, which was the 'light unto David's feet, and a lanthorn to his paths;' and it will order every one's goings aright, if they take heed unto it.

. . . my earnest cries were to the Lord, `to lead me by the right way, and to create in me a new heart, and renew a right spirit within me. Let me be unto thee, O Lord, what I am, and not unto man . . .

Oh! my soul can do no less than magnify the living God, who is worthy of praise, honour and renown, thanksgiving and obedience for evermore. And why so? Because he hath condescended to the lowest estate of his handmaid, and bowed his ear to my prayers, and had a regard unto my cries, and hath answered my request, and given me my heart's desire, which was to be led in the right way. (2:189)

On the whole these Quaker women are reticent about their inward spiritual exercises, however. They refer to them obliquely more than directly. When they do record them, it is often with expressed reluctance, as if what transpires between themselves and their God, those heights of joy, grandeur and mystery that are reached in communion with their divine source, will be thought inappropraite for a woman if made public. Patience Brayton breaks her own reticence to write:

> How often would my nature have flinched; but the hands of God would draw near, and cause me to tremble, so that I was enabled to say, thy will O Lord shall be my will and my guide, if thou wilt give me strength to perform thy work to thine honour, if I have only bread to eat, water to drink, and raiment to put on, so that I return in peace to my family and friends, whom I love in the Lord. He knoweth that my spirit is humbled in desires that I may bring no stain upon the blessed Truth. It is thou, O Lord! that has made the Truth near to me as my life; thou art a husband indeed, and a gracious Father, to support in all trials thy poor depending children, who are under thy preparing hand, that they may say in their hearts, in sincerity and truth, thy will be done.

And then she goes on to reveal her hesitations about writing:

How often does the dread of the
Father of mercies influence my mind, to
write in much trembling of my secret
exercises. I am at times afraid to write
and afraid to omit it, but I find my mind
easy in writing what I have inserted.
(10:450)

Sarah Grubb, in a letter to a friend, writes of
major new spiritual directions for herself in language
so allusive that one can only assume that her friend is
also accustomed to the language and understands whereof
she speaks:

Sixth month 1781. . . I have, after
contending my ground by inches, ventured
to set off towards a place which I have
often looked at with a kind of dread and
dismay; from an apprehension that it
strongly resembles that great city
Babylon, in which it is hard to be
preserved from tasting of the cup, either
in a greater or less degree; and where,
if there even be preservation from this,
deep suffering must be the consequence; a
state not likely for flesh and blood
readily to enter into. I can truly say
it is in great fear and abasement of
mind, that I advance towards it;
earnestly desiring to be kept to that
power which discovered the hidden things
of darkness, and shows us the different
sources of self-love.

Eleventh month 1781. . . We are
sometimes at a loss to account for our
own actions, because they proceed from
causes unsearchable to us, and which we
are led insensibly to comply with for our
own good, that that part in us which is
appointed for death, and which, by means
of the flaming sword, is totally
separated from the tree of life, may
receive no food or vigour to support it.
Since I saw thee, many and complicated
have been the concerns and feelings of my
mind; new causes and new anxieties have
occurred, from which I have seen great
need to procure a secret dwelling in a
quiet habitation, and to crave daily
assistance to abide therein, that my own
root might not be more impoverished, but
that by an inward attention to the voice
of the true Shepherd, a more intimate
acquaintance with him might be cultivated, and a greater subjection of spirit
experienced. (12:273)

Voices and Visions

If there is general reticence about the dealings of
God with the soul, there is nevertheless a willingness
to speak of the inward voice under certain conditions,
which it is giving the Friend in question a specific
mandate. So we often find women Friends writing of
words "intelligibly spoken" to their inward ear,
particularly during their early struggles to accept the

religious call, and the call to speak in meeting. Elizabeth Collins, the young woman mentioned earlier who went to work at the age of five, writes of "language intelligibly spoken to my inward ear: if thou art not more faithful, thy gift shall be taken from thee." (11:452)

Ann Crowley writes, "I intelligibly heard the still voice of my Master" in a call to the ministry. (7:465) Mary Dudley had been fighting against speaking in meeting. Sitting in meeting in extreme distress one morning,

> I had not sat long before a serenity long withheld covered my mind, and I thought I intelligibly heard a language uttered, which exactly suited my own state; but it so hung about me, as at my first appearance, though not anything like the same clear command to express it, that being lifted above all reasonings, before I was aware I stood on my feet with it, and oh! the rest I again felt, the precious holy quiet! (14:276)

Mary Alexander also held back for fear of being mistaken, when she felt the urge to speak, and was "under very great exercise":

> This was my situation one night in the beginning of the year 1789, when, after having lain a considerable time in close exercise of spirit, a light shined round my bed, and I heard a voice intel-

ligibly say: `Thou art appointed to
preach the Gospel." Immediately the
light disappeared, and I was left in an
awful, thankful frame of mind. (13:53)

Nothing less than the "intelligibly spoken word"
could help these women overcome their inhibitions
against daring to serve publicly as God's instrument.

Visions are also sometimes shared, as being an
extraordinary dispensation that should not be hidden,
although we can be sure the greater part of women's
visions from this period were never spoken of by the
visioners. Jane Pearson, who dies at eighty-one after a
long active life of travelling in the ministry
punctuated by much illness, had visions at the age of
seventy-one and seventy-seven which she recorded in her
journal. Presumably, she had other various visions when
she was younger, which she was either too busy or too
shy to record:

In the latter end of 1805, or the
beginning of 1806, I had a sickness, in
which I was confined for some time; and
one night as I lay in bed, between the
hours of nine and ten o'clock, being in a
solid, weighty frame of spirit, breathing
towards the fountain of all good, I
beheld with my spiritual eye, as clearly
as ever my outward eye beheld any
object, that the Ancient of Days
descended; his dread majesty enveloped as
in a cloud; and being emboldened through
his unmerited condescension, I begged for

a place in his glorious kingdom, when
unclothed of my mortal robes. I write in
awful fear. I thought it was granted,
and that I was allowed to proceed, if I
had any thing further. I then craved for
my only daughter the same favour. I
thought that too was granted.

I then lifted up my eyes and heart,
and mentally poured forth my soul,
saying: `Oh! Lord, the wickedness of man
is great;" my mind being expanded, and
bending in good will towards all; and the
answer I received was: `My mercy is
greater;' and the vision closed. But
oh! the contented calm it left. (4:462)

Prayer life is now absorbing more and more of her
waning energies, and shortly after the vision she writes
of prayer almost in the terms of the hesychasts, in the
Russian Orthodox tradition of linking prayer with
breathing:

A solemn time it was to me; for I
was much engaged in mental breathings;
the spirit helping my infirmities
inwardly to pray. A large portion of
heavenly bread was handed to me, without
much wrestling. (4:462)

And at age seventy-seven:

Oh! the pure silence that I felt, as
if Immanuel stretched forth his wings and

covered us: and that sublime and exalted
vision of the prophet was brought clearly
to the view of my mind, when he `beheld
the Lord sitting upon his throne, high
and lifted up, and his train filled the
temple. Above it stood the seraphim,
each had six wings; with twain they
covered their face, with twain they
covered their feet, and with twain they
did fly: and one said, Holy, holy, holy,
Lord God Almighty; the whole earth is
full of thy glory. And the posts of the
door moved at the voice of Him that
spoke, and the house was filled with
smoke.'

I inquired whether I was to divulge it or not.
(4:465) The answer was no, she did not need to speak
of it in meeting. Her energies were probably not equal
to it. But she did write of it.

Elizabeth Ashbridge, the intrepid teenager who
emigrated to America on her own against her parents'
will, was so abused by the master to whom she was
indentured that she was tempted to end her life.

Soon after this, I had a dream; and
though some ridicule dreams, this seemed
very significant to me, and therefore I
shall mention it. I thought I heard a
knocking at the door, by which, when I
had opened it, there stood a grave woman,
holding in her right hand a lamp burning,
who, with a solid countenance, fixed her

eye upon me and said, `I am sent to tell
thee, that if thou wilt return to the
Lord thy God, who created thee, he will
have mercy on thee, and thy lamp shall
not be put out in obscurity.' Her lamp
then flamed, in an extraordinary manner;
she left me, and I awoke. (4:185)

Not all visions come under such dramatic stress,
but they are usually recorded in connection with a time
of "dippedness of mind." Sarah Stephenson wanted to

. . . die like the beasts of the
field. But whilst under this distress,
sitting still one evening, the Lord was
pleased to cause a perfect calm to cover
my mind, and brought before me his
wonderful preservations and deliverances,
one after another, from my childhood to
the present time, as clearly as if
written in large characters: at the be-
holding of which my soul was humbled, and
faith in the mercy, goodness, and forgiveness of God, began to spring up in my
soul, and mercifully caused the clouds of
despair to disperse. (4:185)

In their efforts to be pure channel and fit
instrument, all these women distrust their own
imaginations. It is therefore of significance to
realize that most of them probably had highly developed
imaginations in spite of their own self-discipline. In
the Catholic tradition the religious imagination is
considered to be an important aid to spiritual growth,

when properly directed. There are also many warnings in Catholic writings of how, undirected, the religious imagination can cause a person to be deceived as to their own spiritual state. It is awesome to realize the extent to which these Quaker women, guided only by their inward teacher, were able to arrive at a powerful use of the imaginations they so carefully disciplined.

The visions show this to the fullest extent, but we see the imaging over and over again in the language of the journals as the women express what is happening to them. Images of nature's radiance and rebirth (Elizabeth Fry wrote, "I love to look through nature to see God."); of storm clouds; clouds of glory: of the Rock, the Everlasting Arms; of being dipped, of being stripped, of being, with all of nature, shaken to the point of sundering; of the Lord taking the wheels off one's chariot. All of these images recur again and again, along with one joyful image of being bathed in light. The women would not use their imagery to picture the stations of the cross, Catholic fashion, but they used it to acknowledge how God is present in every aspect of being, every mood, every feature of nature and humanity. Because they image the imageless God every-where, they cannot be lost, they cannot fall outside the realm of divine love and care. The storms and the radiance are both from God.

These women are spiritual athletes in the best tradition of the communion of saints from the beginning of the Christian era. They practise ascesis with the most rugged of the desert fathers. They do not read much, as far as one can tell from the journals, but when they do it is spiritual reading and in the manner of lectia divina, the ancient practise of monks, reading each word as a prayer. They practise unceasing prayer inwardly. They have an abundant overflowing love for God and all creation, and a profound humility about themselves as instruments. The Quaker tradition is by no means as sparse in spiritual guidance as it has been made to appear, and the spiritual guidance we can receive from the writings of Quaker women is a heritage long overdue to be rediscovered.

Family Life

    The concept of gender-bound reading has recently been introduced to the study of women writers. (Nancy K. Miller in Arenal.) You read in another's writings what you know of life because of your own experience as a woman or man. In examining the family experience of these Quaker women, that concept should be borne in mind. Other women can read into these journals a realm of experience of which men could not be aware. The actual references to family life are so reserved and sparse, with one or two notable exceptions, that it is easy to conclude that these women were indifferent to their husbands and children. They were continually struggling with their "natural affections," just as they were struggling with their imaginations, and with their intellectual capacities--the Reasoner in them. These struggles took place because they were more, not less, endowed with these faculties than other people. They imagined more, thought more, loved more than most of their contemporaries. However, even empathic reading of women's writings by women cannot overcome the gaps in understanding created by sheer absence of reference to

certain types of basic human experience that belongs in
the realm of family life. We must draw on Elizabeth Fry
for our only information on how these women faced childbirth, for example. She is the only one who even
mentions, although very indirectly, the experience of
being in labor. Having a low pain threshold since
childhood, each of her nine deliveries was a prolonged
nightmare. I learned to recognize, in reading her
journal, a certain somber tone that would creep into her
entries in the months preceding each new childbirth, and
came to know just when to expect such terse lines as
these: "Time runs on space. I desire my imagination
may not dwell on that which is before it. Every outward
thing appears nearly, if not quite, ready; as for the
inner preparation, I cannot prepare myself." (This a
couple of weeks before delivery.) Three weeks after the
birth: "A willing mind to suffer was hard to get at. I
longed to have the cup removed from me." (Fry, 142) One
line only, on the day before the birth of her ninth
child, when she was thirty-four: "Help, dearest Lord,
or I perish." The rest she kept to herself, and so did
all the other women who had nine, ten, or more babies.
Childbirth was "natural" but for many it was not without
fear and pain. None of these women died in childbirth,
but they had sisters who did.

                        Children

    The metaphor of the divine parent, the everlasting
arms, is central to the spiritual life of these women.
Why are they so free to express their love for God, and
so sparing in their expression of love for their own
children? For us the parent-child relationship and the

experience of human birthing is easily and naturally related to our experience of the divine parent and spiritual rebirth. The word "naturally" is, I believe, the key to the difference. Quaker women ministers partook of a religious culture in which the religious call was a call to follow Christ the inward presence and Christ the outward example. This meant literally a commitment to the re-making of the human individual on the pattern of the divine. The religious call has always meant this, the saints of every age taking it far more literally than others. What was different in the religious culture of the centuries previous to our own was that there was a strong sense of the sinfulness of the "natural" being of women and men. Human nature was not in itself good. It had to be reborn as divine nature through the cultivation of the Seed. The "oppression of the seed" is a term the women used frequently in their journals. They see the divine seed as being oppressed everywhere among the world's people, among Friends, and in themselves. Their work is to liberate the Seed, and to do this they have to be ruthless with the "natural parts" of their own being and of others. Concepts of the rooting out of self and self will, such as we saw illustrated from journal passages when spiritual formation was under discussion, extend to rooting out both natural affections and natural reason. Only God's love and God's reason had room in the reborn person. Since rebirth was not a once-for-all process, but a lifelong struggle against ever-renewed oppression of the Seed from human causes, one could never be sure when one's love was really a natural affection or was, as it should be, from the divine source.

This uncertainty was precisely what these Quaker
women struggled with, some more successfully than
others. Since they all had their share of human imper-
fections, and a highly developed individuality which
was--today we can say it as they could not--threatened
by the customary demands of motherhood, they were not
all equally fond of their children at all times.

Jane Pearson was one of the women who struggled
hardest with her motherhood. She was one of the most
widely travelled of the ministers, also the most prone
to sickness all her life. She herself recognized this
as related to the intensity of her struggle. (All the
women were in fact very discerning about their illnesses
and saw them as symptons of the struggle between their
natural and higher selves.) Even as a grandmother, she
was still struggling against affectionate feelings for
her grandchildren, and writes on one occasion when
setting out on new travels of how hard it is to go, but
that she dares not "let the affectionate part take
hold."

Elizabeth Stirredge was one of those who managed to
integrate her natural and higher feelings for her
children, but not without considerable struggle. One of
the first generation of Friends, she and her husband
were shopkeepers and had their goods repeatedly dis-
trained in the routine prosecution of Friends by the
authorities. Her calls led her to testify before King
Charles II about the persecution, to travel in the
ministry, and more than once the calls led her to
prison. She fought hard against the call to testify
before the king. Her children were young, and she could
not believe she was called to leave them:

Thus did I reason and strive against it, till my sorrow was so great, that I knew not whether ever the Lord would accept of me again. Then I cried unto the Lord again and again, `Lord, if thou has found me worthy, make my way plain before me, and I will follow thee; for thou knowest that I would not willingly offend thee.' But knowing myself to be of a weak capacity, I did not think the Lord would make choice of such a contemptible instrument as I, to leave my habitation and tender children, who were young, to go to King Charles, an hundred miles off, and with such a plain testimony as the Lord did require of me; which made me go bowed down many months under the exercise of it; and oftentimes strove against it. I could get no rest, but in giving up to obey the Lord in all things that he required of me; and though it seemed hard and strange to me, yet the Lord made hard things easy, according to his promise to me, when I was going from my children, and knew not but my life might be required for my testimony, it was so plain; and when I looked upon my children, my heart yearned towards them. These words ran through me, 'If thou canst believe, thou shalt see all things accomplished, and thou shalt return in peace, and thy reward shall be with thee.'

So the Lord blessed my going forth,
his presence was with me in my journey;
preserved my family well, and my coming
home was with joy and peace in my bosom:
everlasting praises, glory and honour be
given unto Him that sits on the throne,
and to the Lamb for evermore. (2:192)

At the age of fifty-seven, after one of the most
eventful lives of any of these Quaker saints, she sits
down to write her journal for her children and
grandchildren. The journal tells us, both directly and
indirectly, that she and her husband trained their
children to be partners in the outward struggle and
companions on the inward journey. Training the children
is a theme often on the minds of women:

The way you know; you have been
trained in it; and the concern of my
spirit is, that you may keep in it, and
be concerned for your children, as your
father and I have been for you. Train
them up in the way of truth, and keep
them out of the beggarly rudiments of
this world, that they may grow up in
plainness; and keep to the plain
language, both you and they; which is
become a very indifferent thing amongst
many of the professors of truth. But in
the beginning we went through great
exercise for that very word, thee and
thou to one person. (2:194)

The close of her journal is a beautiful prayer for her own children and God's flock everywhere, a powerful testimony to her own achievement in integrating human and divine love:

Bless my children, by preserving them in thy fear, cause them to remember thy mercies, from day to day; what thou hast done for them, and their father and mother, in their great affliction, when destruction and ruin were determined against us, and when we were almost past hope; howhast thou appeared, and confounded our enemies before our eyes! Lord, let these things never be forgotten by me, nor them, whilst we have a day to live upon the earth: but, sanctify all thy blessings and mercies bestowed upon us, and give us a thankful heart, and humble mind, and more and more unite us unto thee, and cause us to walk worthy of the same . . .

Therefore, strengthen my faith, hope and confidence, that I may steadfastly believe that thou wilt preserve my children, when I am gone to my resting place. Lord, keep my family and thy people, let not one of them be lost, or become a prey to the wicked one. If thou shouldest yet add more days to my life, let me not cease to pray for them and their offspring, that I may do my endeavour for their entrance into thy

blessed kingdom, so I shall go to my
grave in peace. And now, I do wholly
resign them into thy hands, knowing thou
art able to keep them through faith, and
to preserve them all their days, and to
do more for them than I am able to ask of
thee. Whatever exercise they meet with,
strengthen them, and bear up their
spirits, that they may not be overcome
with the temptations of the wicked one:
for, thy power hath been sufficient to
redeem my soul. Lord, once more do I
commit the keeping of my spirit to thee,
with my children, and all thy flock and
family upon the face of the earth, with
whom my soul is at peace and unity. I
feel the renewings of thy love at this
time, which is the greatest comfort that
can be enjoyed; therefore does my heart,
and all that is within me, return unto
thee all praises, glory and honour, with
hearty thanksgiving, and pure obedience
for evermore. (2:210)

Elizabeth Fry, who as we have already seen could
write more freely of her natural being than others,
gives us a glimpse of how the spiritual journey is
shared with children in daily life. Family meeting for
worship was part of the daily domestic rhythm, and the
children witnessed the upward soarings of the parental
spirit as well as the "dippedness of mind." One day
after family meeting she writes:

> I had to pour a little of my soul,
> there appeared to flow a current of life
> and love, as if we were owned by the Most
> High;   I felt my own like a song of
> praise . . . I certainly was much raised
> spiritually . . . (Fry, 208)

Elizabeth worries a great deal about the effect on her children of her public ministry, and consults with her brothers about this. Brother Joseph John Gurney reassures her that while the situation "is not what one would have chosen," it can do the children no harm to be exposed to concerns for the state of the world. Her children were as lively as she herself had been as a child, and she despaired of her inability to discipline them, but she loved them deeply. As adults, they were friends and companions to her. The death of Elizabeth's five-year-old daughter, Betsy, gives one glimpse into a sadness that none of the mothers among these ministers escaped--the death of a child. Her journey entry shows her struggling with feelings of rebelliousness against committing the once vivacious little spirit to burial:

> Dearest Lord, be pleased to arise a
> little in thy own power, for the help of
> thy poor unworthy servant and handmaid;
> and if consistent with thy holy will, to
> dispel some of her distressing feelings,
> and make her willing to part with and
> commit to the earth her beloved child's
> body. (Fry, 237)

Mary Dudley had to struggle harder than most to

integrate her parental and spiritual feelings, possibly because she had to struggle hard against her own parents as a young girl in leaving the family church to become a Friend. It had been necessary to overcome natural affection--considered as synonomous with obedience to parental wishes--to answer the divine call. She goes through the same conflict when her own children are born, since she has already been called to the ministry:

> Having a disposition naturally prone to affectionate attachment, I now began, in the addition of children, to feel my heart in danger of so centering in these gifts, as to fall short of occupying in the manner designed, with the gift received; and though at seasons I was brought in the secret of my heart to make an entire surrender to the work I saw that I was called to, yet when any little opening presented, how did I shrink from the demanded sacrifice, and crave to be excused in this thing; so that an enlargement was not witnessed for some years, though I several times took journeys, and experienced holy help to be extended. (14:287)

Time and time again the call to the ministry wins out over the calls of motherhood, but not easily:

> On returning to our lodgings found W.N., just come from a Clonmel; he informed that the young woman who had the chief care of my children had taken the

measles, and was removed out of the house. I sensibly felt this intelligence, and the struggle was not small to endeavor after and attain a degree of quietude, sufficient to discover the right path.

I went distressed to bed I think honestly resigned, either to go forward or return home, as truth opened. I got but little sleep in the night, and Knockballymaher (the meeting for which she was bound) seemed uppermost in the morning, so I rose early, and roused my companions--we set out, and after a rough ride for nearly two hours, got to meeting soon after Friends were assembled.

Through the continuance of that mercy which never faileth, all thoughts of home seemed dispersed, and I was helped to get a little to my own exercise--my lot through most of this journey--that of being dipt into sympathy with the imprisoned seed. (14:289)

The hardest call comes on the heels of the birth of her seventh child. Her journal editor writes that the youngest was

only ten weeks old, and her health was very delicate, so that the sacrifice was indeed great, but the merciful extension of proportionate assistance is thus acknowledged by herself:

> . . . `In the course of the embassy, many
> and sore were my provings, and of a
> closely trying nature my conflicts, but
> the arm of all sustaining help was near,
> and I feel thankful that this cup hath
> been drunk; for though mingled with deep
> and exercising sufferings, it has, I
> trust, tended to the further reduction of
> the creaturely will and choosing, and
> brought measureably into willingness to
> submit to the humiliating leadings of the
> holy hand.' (14:291)

One could argue that such behavior represents a rejection of parenthood and children, but the continuing contact, letters and expressions of mutual concern that continue until the death of each of these mothers argues against such simplistic explanations. Ruth Follows, an ardent logger of miles in the ministry and one whose journal reflects little but miles covered and number of meetings sat in, appears to prefer writing to her children over being with them. The note of self-pity in her letters about the hardship of being separated from her family does not always ring true, though again one cannot judge easily. Serious attempts at spiritual guidance intertwine with plaintiveness in her letters to her sons:

> To Her Son Samuel
> Donnington, Eighth month 27th, 1799

1777777272727272727272727272727272727272727772727272727272772727272727272727272727272727272 2727272727272727272727272772727272727272727272727272772

. . . Go on patiently--Is it not good for thee to feel thy own burthen? Consider how much greater difficulty thousands are not in, who have large families, and very little to support them with. I should be glad if I could say any thing that would be of service to thee, but thou well knowest that the best help is in thyself. O look there--ask of Him who 'giveth liberally and upbraideth not.' Neglect not thy chiefest duty of laying up for thyself treasure in heaven, and there is no doubt with me, that thou could then have a comfortable share of earthly blessings.

It is worth while now and then, to look a few years back at the situation the seemingly undone brother was in--in whom there was little hope of such a change as we now see; nor would he ever have so far conquered without a good and strong resolution. O that my dear children may all overcome the wicked one, that so I may salute you as young men, who are strong, having the word of God abiding in you.

To Her Son
Donnington, Tenth month 29th, 1779

We were glad to receive thine, and to find that a sense of good and a desire after it still attend thy mind; and perhaps thy poor body being afflicted

might be a means of arresting thy
attention, making thee sensible of the
uncertainty of this life, and raising
desires in thee to be prepared for a
better. Oh! the many struggles and
conflicts, with deep baptisms, that all
those who have desires are to be devoted
to God's service, and wholly redeemed
from every over anxious pursuit after the
things of this life. I, thy poor mother,
who for many years have been exercised in
the work of religion, am still sorely
beset, and often in great fear least I
should become a prey to the enemy.
(4:49)

Patience Brayton kept to her ministry even while
children (and husband) were dying at home, having begun
a lively service at the age of twenty-one. Most of her
travels were between the ages of thirty-eight and fifty-
four; the year of the death of her husband and two
children were apparently too much for her 'natural
affections." She remained home from age fifty-four
until she died at sixty-one.

Her letter to her daughter, Hannah, the year before
the family deaths shows how hard she was struggling.
That she wishes to be more and more given to the Lord's
requiring "whether I see thee more or not" sounds hard
and must be put in the context of her later behavior of
actually giving up travelling.

To Her Daughter
Namptwich, Old England, 25th of Second

Month, 1785

Dear Child, Hannah Brayton,

I have had thee in my mind for many days, with fresh remembrance what a dutiful child thou has been in the outward concerns of life. O my dear, I trust there is a blessing for thee in store, and I hope thou wilt labour for that blessing that fadeth not away; that the dew of heaven may rest upon thee in all thy undertakings; and if the Lord becomes thy director, thou wilt be directed aright, both in divine and outward things. I long to be more and more given up to the Lord's requirings, whether I ever see thee more or not; although thou feelest nearer to me than I can relate with pen, the favours of heaven I feel so near at times, surmount all other considerations; when that abates I long to see thee again, but I hope more and more to learn patience, in all my steppings along in this life, for I see the want of it more now than ever, in order to keep me low and humble: if I am exalted at any of these favours, then I shall be in great danger--I am ready to tremble, seeing the work so great. Oh, my child, though nature brings thee into my mind with nearness, yet believing there is one rich rewarder to them that hold out to the end; . . .

I remain thy affectionate mother,

Patience Brayton (10:459,60)

We see in the struggles of these women with their parenting role the foreshadowing of the struggles of today's women. The overarching concept of a divine love which could transform and encompass the natural affections was ever present as both a goad to the struggle and a solution to it. We shall see in the concluding section how the resolutions of these struggles came about in the last years of the aging saints.

Husbands

The Quaker testimony on equality in all human relationships takes on particular importance when applied to husband-wife relationships. It has consistently been one of the strengths of the Society of Friends, that when women and men marry, they take each other "with divine assistance," each promising to be to the other a loving and faithful spouse. Obedience is to God only, not to the husband. The patriarchal concept of wifely obedience that distorts the marriage covenant in the mainstream Christian tradition has no place in the Quaker marriage, as it had no place in the Anabaptist tradition out of which Quakerism came.

Partnership in obedience to God, however, was not necessarily easily arrived at in an era which had firm expectations concerning the submission of women. At least one of the women was physically abused by her husband when she turned Quaker after their marriage. This was Elizabeth Ashbridge, the intrepid adventurer who arrived in America in her teens as an indentured servant. True to the expectations of both the secular and the Quaker society, she endured uncomplainingly and won him over in the end. Alice Hayes, one of the first generation Quaker women ministers, used to be punished by her farmer husband for going to meeting. He relented some years later. When both husband and wife were Quaker, however, there was strong Meeting support for a woman minister once she had been recognized and recorded. Husbands who were unethusiastic about their wives' ministry generally therefore kept quiet about it. Those men who were outspoken against women in the ministry, like John Story, evidently had stay-at-home wives.

The affection of Quaker husbands and wives for one another was frequently commented on by non-Quaker writers. Clarkson's statement in Portraiture of Quakerism, (1806)

. . . that connubial bliss was the chief recreation of Friends, has often been quoted. Nevertheless, when the call to the ministry came, women had the same struggle between their natural affections and the divine calling in regard to their husbands that they had with their children. Sarah Grubb, whose public ministry began at age twenty-four, was much concerned about the danger of "settling down in outward enjoyments" when she married two years later. In fact, she took off on a major religious visitation to Scotland with a woman Friend just two weeks after her marriage, and was rarely at home as much as a month at a time afterwards. She had no children, unsurprisingly, and died the youngest of all these ministers, at the age of thirty-five. Here are her thoughts on marriage and the spiritual life, toward the end of her life, in a letter to a friend:

Twelfth month 1789. ---I have seen, in my short life, so much fallacy in human wisdom respecting matrimonial connections, and so much blessings showered upon an attention to simple uncorrupted openings, which have not at first appeared most plausible that I seem to have no faith left in any direction but that which the devoted heart finds to make for peace. In concerns of this sort, it is often very difficult for such to judge, because prepossession and inclination are apt to influence our best feelings. Natural affection bears some resemblance to sacred impulse; and therefore, methinks that this seed, though ever so right, must die in the ground before it be quickened and sanctified. In short, there are few openings, for our own and the general good, which have not to pass through this temporary death, few gifts but what are designed to be buried in baptism; and I wish thee, if ever thou possess a female companion, to obtain her as a fruit of the new creation; that so thou mayest reap those spiritual advantages which those enjoy, who, through the effectual working of the grace of God, drink together into one spirit, whether in suffering or in rejoicing; for without this experience,

Zion's travellers must find such connections to be secretly burthensome and
insipid. (12:346)

Her perceptive recognition that "natural affection
bears some resemblance to sacred impulse" goes both to
the heart of the conflict as these women experienced it,
and points to its resolution. Her trip to Scotland on
the heels of her marriage was not undertaken lightly.
In a letter to a friend at this time:

> . . . The sentiment thou drops respecting
> Scotland, is so exactly similar to my
> own, that it was like a little strength
> handed in the time of need; and I greatly
> wish, if the thing proved to be right, to
> be enabled to make a sacrifice of every
> selfish inclination, that my offerings
> and prayers in this one step, may be pure
> and acceptable to Him who sees in secret.
> But I often feelingly remember a saying
> of M. Peisley's (another much travelled
> woman Friend - ed.) that she was `torn as
> between heaven and earth,' and it many
> times is a matter of doubt, in which I
> shall centre. I have as much nature as
> most, and as great an aptness to cover
> myself with it, and live upon it; and
> though to be thus drawn from such a
> source, is cause of thankfulness, yet it
> seems like the pangs of death, and I
> sometimes query, whether my natural body
> will not fall under the operation. Was
> it not for experiencing now and then my

strength a little renewed, and my mind
clothed with the quietness of the
habitation which the arrows of the
archers cannot penetrate, I must fall to
the opposition of the enemy in myself.
(12:276)

Elizabeth Webb is the Friend who fell ill in
struggling against her call to go to America. Her
husband bore the full brunt of the struggle, and belongs
to the ranks of the unsung husbands of saints:

I then told my husband that I had a
concern to go to America; and asked him
if he could give me up. He said he hoped
it would not be required of me; but I
told him it was; and that I should not
go without his free consent, which seemed
a little hard to him at first. A little
while after, I was taken with a violent
fever, which brought me so weak, that all
who saw me thought I should not recover.
But I thought my day's work was not done,
and my chief concern in my sickness was
about going to America. Some were
troubled that I had made it public,
because they thought I should die, and
people would speak reproachfully of me;
and said, if I did recover, the ship
would be ready to sail before I should be
fit to go, &c. But I thought if they
would only carry me and lay me down in
the ship, I should be well: for the Lord
was very gracious to my soul in the time

of my sickness, and gave me a promise
that his presence should go with me. And
then my husband was made very willing to
give me up; he said, if it were for seven
years, rather than to have me taken from
him for ever. (13:172)

Catharine Phillips had no such struggle. Her
journal is almost a love song to her husband. She
married late in life, and they had only thirteen years
together. There is no shadow of conflict between the
divine and human love.

The time of natural affection betwixt us
was strong, arising from a similarity of
sentiments, which was strengthened by an
infinitely higher connection.

In another passage she emphasized the complementarity of
her ministry and their partnership:

An affectionately tender husband--ah, me!
how shall I delineate this part of his
character! Bound to me by the endearing
ties of love and friendship, heightened
by religious sympathy, his respect as
well as affection, was apparent to our
friends and acquaintances. His abilities
to assist me in my religious engagements
were conspicuous; for although he had no
share in the ministerial labour, he was
ready to promote it. (11:281)

She remarks elsewhere that their tie was "superior to nature, though nature had a share in it."

Anne Camm was even more lyrical about the divine human nature of the spousal tie. After the death of her first husband she writes:

> And by the quickening of his power, we were made one in a spiritual and heavenly relation--our hearts being knit together in the unspeakable love of God, which was our joy and delight, and made our days together exceedingly comfort-able--our temporal enjoyments being sanctified by it and made a blessing to us. How hard it was, and how great a loss to part with so dear and tender a husband, is far beyond what I can express. My tongue or pen is not able to set forth my sorrow. (1:476)

Anne Camm had twice the good fortune to marry a fellow minister, and they worked and travelled both separately and together. If we wonder how such a husband-wife team appears from the point of view of the husband, here is the record of John Bell about the life he shared with his deceased wife, Deborah:

> She was a loving and affectionate wife, and the gift of God to me, and as such I always prized her, a help-meet indeed both in prosperity and adversity, a steady and cheerful companion in all the afflictions and trials which attended

us, and a true and faithful yoke-fellow
in all our services in the church; for
being ever one in spirit, we became one
in faith and practice, in discerning and
judgment, and our concern and labour was
the same; which nearly united us, and a
life of comfort and satisfaction we
lived, our souls in the nearest union
delighting in each other; and the love
and presence of God, wherewith we were
often favoured in our private retire-
ments, sweetened every bitter cup, and
made our passage easy and pleasant.
(5:5)

It happens that Phillips, Camm and Bell all had
childless marriages. Undoubtedly it was easier to
develop this tender dual-nature relationship with a
spouse when there were no children present. For all the
appearances of equality for women which the practice of
recognizing women ministers implies, in fact the primary
feeling of responsibility for children fell more heavily
on the mother than the father. The stress created by
that asymmetry may well inhibit the dual-nature bonding
between parents which the childless couples apparently
experienced without effort. Each woman sought her own
unique balancing of the "natural" and the "spiritual" in
marriage. None failed completely to achieve some kind
of balance, but some found it more easily than others.

Friends

Friendships between women, and sometimes between married couples, could assume the same profoundly tender divine-human character as spousal relationships. Many of the journal records are really letters to friends, lovingly preserved by the other party and embodied in the memoirs of the deceased. Here is Quaker equality in one of its purest forms, as friends give spiritual guidance to one another, lend the spiritual ear to one another, and give wholehearted, undemanding support to one another. Letters to friends can be lyrical as those to spouses:

> Eight month, 1789. --Thou art, dear friend, an epistle written in my heart, where I sometimes read thee and thy mournful, humble steppings, with joy; consistent with the divine command to rejoice in his new creation, of which, in infinite mercy, thou art happily a part. (12:341)

The Last of Life, and the First

Intimations of an unseen presence, and a sense of the tension between at-oneness with and separateness from the surround, come very early to children. The apparent sensitivity to spiritual reality can be heightened by an early and frequent experience of death--death of adults, death of other children. All the women of our group have vivid recollections from early childhood of a sense of divine presence. They also have vivid memories of their fear of estrangement and separation from God and from their families, of being called too soon by the Angel of Death. Sin was a familiar concept at an early age, and they felt for the sin of disobedience long before they developed the inner disciplines of obedience. Salvation and damnation are themes they were made aware of as soon as they could talk, and they wondered anxiously when other children died whether these were saved or damned. As children, these women also exhibited unusual liveliness of spirit and capacity for sheer enjoyment of living. This liveliness of spirit and continually being reminded of death combined to set the stage for the titanic spiritual struggle each went through as a teenager and on into the early twenties, when they felt that the inward Christ was calling them to holiness. The tension was the stronger because they felt that what was required of them was possible, even if so many of their inclinations went the other way. Moments of great spiritual peace and joy alternated with despair, and they felt that the choice between salvation and damnation was really theirs. Once the battle was won and the call to the ministry answered, the fear of damnation disappeared, but the struggle for more perfect obedience went on.

I have emphasized in the discussion on spiritual formation how up and down the struggle to be a perfect instrument of God's will was, and how it continued over the years. The continual doing of God's will did not save the saint from anguish and despondency. What was done could never be enough. It is the lot of the saint always to demand far more of the self than ordinary people, so from one point of view these women were struggling at ever higher levels of goodness, toward more goodness, throughout life. Yet the "dippedness of mind" that attacked them also had a childlike quality. Can it be that the saint has a very prolonged spiritual childhood?

The spiritual childhood appears to come to an end, finally, in the last years. The everlasting arms hold the aging saint more steadily. There is a great sense of being near home, of mission accomplished, of greater tolerance of the human condition. There is also a wonderful sense of new spiritual growth, of new learnings, new experiences of God's love. Friends generally were very aware of this surge of spiritual wisdom and strength in their elder saints, and were careful to record their utterances when the saints were too feeble to write for themselves any longer. Family and friends were always gathered about in the final days, and one sometimes gets the impression that the bedrooms of the dying were almost crowded. If the dying took a long time about their business--sometimes this went on for months--the crowds came, went and came again. Deathbed utterances were particularly prized as glimpses of the glory ahead for all the rest, still at earlier stages in the spiritual journey.

All this emphasis on spiritual illumination from the dying is the more extraordinary when one realizes that most of them are suffering severe physical pain in their final months, and particularly in their final days and hours. They know what is expected of them by others. More important, they know what they expect of themselves. Sometimes they fear they may not be up to the final trial of pain on the path to glory, and pray for endurance. Mary Dudley was reported to have spoken in this manner:

> Afterwards, when under considerable suffering of body, she prayed for patience, and added `Oh! if I should become impatient with the divine will, what reproach it would occasion. I feel poor and empty, and when lying awake am not able to fix my thoughts upon what I desire and prefer but little things present, and this tries me. David speaks of having songs in the night, but I sometimes say, these meaning intrusive thoughts, are not the Lord's songs.' (14:365)
>
> Several times when taking leave of her family for the night, she solemnly uttered this short petition, `Gracious Lord, prepare us for what is to come.' And when suffering from pain, and the feeling of general irritation, she frequently petitioned, `Lord, enable us to trust that thou wilt never lay more on me than thou wilt give strength and patience to endure,' adding, `Pray that I may have patience.' (14:366)

The initial shift from a life of great physical activity to a life limited by physical incapacity can be a trying one. We can follow the progression in Jane Pearson from the first exclamation, "I dread being at ease in Zion!", to the more contented "the older and more infirm I grow the more I am enlarged in mind." At seventy-five, reading her old journals, she "feels a renewing of ancient power." She continues to prepare spiritually for her great transition:

> Previous to this precious season, I had had very great openings into divine things, pertaining to another life; things so sacred as not to be meddled with; which brought me to think I should soon be gathered; and in looking at the ministry I had been gifted with, although I felt no condemnation, my gift seemed as if it might be taken from me, yet not in displeasure; I had such siftings in meetings, and was so emptied, as from vessel to vessel. 94:464)

At age seventy-eight, the transition is still in process:

> Although I am exceedingly shaken, and my hand very unsteady, yet if it is right for me to leave to posterity, the memorable condescension of the Almighty to me, a poor worm, I shall be able to make it legible. Upon the 13th of the twelfth month, 1813, sitting in the evening by my fire-side, with company about me engaged in conversing, I felt a strong attraction heavenward, which I was glad to feel: and a gracious God seemed pleased to bow his heavens and come down, directing me to dismiss every doubt respecting my own exit; for that he would

take me in his mercy and support me
through what might befall me; and my
charge was, never more to doubt of my
eternal rest. Also respecting my
grandson, I was charged to doubt no more;
for that repentance had been granted even
to him at a late hour. The spirit of
intercession was poured forth upon me
with much energy, as seemed to rend the
very heavens, --O my soul! never forget
that season, nor ever cease to extol a
merciful God, in pardoning transgressors:
in this instance, mercy has covered the
judgment seat to a hair's breadth.
(4:466)

At age seventy-nine, we find the last journal entry in
her own hand:

Ninth month 19th, 1814. --This
morning I again had the most strengthen-
ing, consoling evidence of Divine favour,
that my poor frame could bear; letting me
know that as my strength decreased, his
watchful care over me increased; and
although he had seen meet nearly to
deprive me of my outward hearing, he had
increased the inward so surprisingly,
that I often seem to fall down before him
in astonishment; my mind being so
expanded and enlarged, that as naturals
abate, spirituals increase; and my dear
Redeemer allows me at seasons, to repose
as upon his bosom. (4:467)

Sometimes in the long months of physical pain before the final days a kind of spiritual torpor sets in, a numbness of mind, and then this clears as the end nears. Again, Mary Dudley may be taken as typical of many, as she rouses to pray with family:

> `Wash all in the laver of regeneration, and grant the renewings of the Holy Ghost, that Thou gracious Father mayest be praised in time, and with the dear Son of Thy love, everlastingly receive glory and honour, thanksgiving and renown. Amen and Amen.'
>
> Her voice was remarkably strengthened for this exertion, and she afterwards observed, `What a mercy to be favoured with a little fresh feeling; without the fresh feeling what is all expression, what is any thing?' (14:363)

Later, as her sufferings increased, she was able to separate her physical suffering from her spiritual state, the necessary precondition for the final glorious passage.

> Being tried with restlessness, and the desire for frequent change of position, she sweetly remarked, `It is only the body, it does not get within; all there is peaceful, quiet trust'. (14:367)

Other friends experience a gradual withdrawing of
the attention from outward things and indicate their
wish not to be distracted from the pull toward the final
passage. This was the case with Sarah Stephenson:

> The 22nd, a Friend proposing to read
> a letter from one she knew and loved; she
> asked whether it was interesting. A part
> of it was read; but as she appeared
> indifferent, the Friend left off, lest it
> should fatigue her. On this, she said,
> `I seem to be got past these things;' and
> added after a pause, `by saying so, I
> mean I do not wish to have my attention
> drawn out." (4:211)

Sarah's final passing was accomplished with much
inner serenity along with the outward suffering:

> Her strength was much decayed; and
> on the 26th of the fourth month, which
> was second-day, her breathing was become
> difficult and painful, and she felt great
> oppression of body. `This,' said she,
> `is wearing work,' but nevertheless she
> lay very still, as she had been enabled
> to do during the whole of her illness;
> and several times desired not to be
> disturbed. After a hard fit of coughing,
> with a discharge of phlegm, which left
> her much spent, she said, `It will be
> right, let it be which way it may; and
> that is better than all the world. it
> seems as if it must be nearly over now; I

have so little strength left.' A little
after, she seemed to be uttering praises,
saying, `How good, how good!' and
appeared like one engaged in sweet
supplication. A Friend asking her how
she did, after a pause she replied, `I
cannot say much: but my King reigns.'
Afterwards, at three different times,
being very weak and her voice low, she
was understood to say, `death-bed;--I am
passing away;--Lord, take me.'

Asking what o'clock it was, and
being told about one, she said, `Time
passes slowly.' Feeling increased
difficulty of breathing, pain in her
stomach and great oppression at her
chest, she said, `Give patience,' with
which, that she was largely endued, those
around her could witness. Again, she
asked the time of the day, and said, `I
love quietness, don't let me be
disturbed.' Soon after, finding herself
sinking fast, she seemed desirous of
taking her last leave of those around
her, and saluting them with dying lips,
said, `Farewell, farewell.' (4:212)

Much beloved Anne Camm knew she was ready:

Observing some of them to weep, she
said, `Be not concerned for me; all is
well--I have only death to encounter, and
the sting of it is wholly taken away--the
grave has no victory, and my soul is

ascending above all sorrow and pain. Let me go freely to my heavenly mansion--disturb me not in my passage.'

She then desired the Friends present to go to meeting, adding, `Let me not hinder the Lord's business, but let it be chief in your minds, and faithfully done by you all, that at the end you may receive your reward. Mine is sure--I have not been negligent, and my day's work is done.'

Apprehending that the hand of death was upon her, and finding her pain increased, she earnestly besought the Lord to help her through the last conflict; saying `O my God--O my God, thou hast not forsaken me--blessed be thy name, forever. O my blessed Lord and Saviour, who suffered for me and for all mankind, great pains in they holy body upon the cross, remember me, they poor handmaid, in this my great bodily affliction. My trust is in thee--my hope is in thee only, my dear Lord. O come, come, dear Lord Jesus, come quickly and receive my soul. To thee I yield it up-- help me now, in my bitter pangs.'

Her husband now kneeled down by her and prayed that the Lord would make her passage easy, and their prayers were graciously heard and answered. She had no more severe pain, but gently drew her breath shorter and shorter. She observed, that it was good to leave all to the Lord; and calling upon those present, said, `O pray--pray--pray' --and so fell asleep in Jesus, in a good old age, being in her seventy-ninth year. (1:479)

When Elizabeth Fry, who had fought the fear of death all her life, lay dying, her relatives gathered around to go down to the Valley of the Shadow with her, ready to support her struggle to the very gates of death. They knew there could be an anguished moment-- not everyone dies tranquilly. But Elizabeth in the end fought her battle alone, lying unmoving and silent through a long night and then whispering in the morning to her maid Mary: `Oh, Mary, Mary, it is a strife but I am safe."

The journey is accomplished. God has touched each of these women in their very early years, and returns as a beloved companion to guide them through the gates of death. In all the decades in between there has been an alternation of struggle and tranquility, of stormy clouds and radiant light. On their own inward journey they have reshaped the world around them, and transformed themselves. They always knew where the main direction lay, and they always knew they would make it to port. To the last woman, they would give God the glory. I do not believe it would be wrong, however, for today's Quaker sisterhood to give them the glory, too.

Women included in this study

1614-1702	Margaret Fell
1627-1705	Anne Camm
1634-1706	Elizabeth Stirredge
1657-1726	Alice Hayes
1689-1738	Deboreh Bell
1712	(Journal written) by Elizabeth Webb
1693-1760	Jane Hoskins
1701-1769	Margaret Lucas
1704-1775	Sarah Morris
1713-1755	Elizabeth Ashbridge
1717-1757	Mary Neale
1718-1809	Ruth Follows
1726-1794	Catharine Phillips
1733-1794	Patience Brayton
1735-1816	Jane Pearson
1738-1802	Sarah Stephenson
1743-1817	Martha Routh
1750-1820	Mary Dudley
1755-1831	Elizabeth Collins

1755-1845	Mary Capper
1756-1791	Sara Grubb
1758-1840	Mary Hagger
1760-1810	Mary Alexander
1773-1826	Ann Crowley
1780-1845	Elizabeth Fry

Bibliography

Arenal, Electa
    1979   "The Comment is Catalyst for Autonomy" in
            Anthology on women in Hispanic Literature,
            ed. Beth Miller, Berkeley: University of
            California Press (in Press).

Barbour, Hugh
    1976   Margaret Fell Speaking. Wallingford, PA:
            Pendle Hill PUblications.

Clarkson, Thomas
    1806   A Portraiture of Quakerism, 3 Vols. New
            York: Samuel Stansburg.

Evans, William and Thomas Evans, eds.
    1837   Friends Library: Comprising Journals,
    1850   Doctrinal Treatises and other writings of
            members of the Religious Society of Friends,
            14 volumes, Philadelphia: Joseph Rakestraw,
            Printer.

Fry, Elizabeth
    1974   Memoir of the Life of Elizabeth Fry.
            Montclair, N.J.: Patterson Smith

Miller, Nancy K.
    1979   "Women's Autobiography in France: for a
            dialectics of indentification," unpublished
            paper cited by Arenal in Anthology on Women
            in Hispanic Literature, ed. Beth Miller,
            Berkeley: University of California Press
            (in Press).

CHARITY COOK
Algie I. Newlin

Charity Cook was a prominent Quaker Minister of the eighteenth and early nineteenth centuries. She lived through the last years of an age in which all Quakers were bound together by spiritual ties and lines of communication into one Society of Friends. In her lifetime it was possible for the same Quaker interpretation of the Christian faith to be given at Bush River, Cane Creek, Philadelphia, Newport, Kendal, London, Belfast, or Pyrmont, Germany. Charity carried the Quaker message to Friends in all of these places. Five years after her death this era ended when the Hicksite Separation began the tragic process of splitting the Society into antagonistic bodies which would have little or no communication between them.

Her life gives a clear illustration of the role and importance of the itinerant female minister in the spread of Quakerism and in its survival. It has been said of her kind that ". . . their ministry was the lifeblood of the Society." The flow of that lifeblood was not just from the strong Quaker centers to the outlying provinces, as Rufus Jones puts it, but it was also flowing from meetings in the back-country to those who were better known.

Charity's life was caught up and swept along by the two most significant migrations in American Quaker history. One, which caught her family when Charity was four years old, scattered approximately sixty local meetings through the Southern Piedmont from Pennsylvania to Georgia. The second, which moved Charity from the South in her sixtieth year, spread Quaker meetings across the Middle West.

As a far-ranging woman minister, Charity Cook gives a clear revelation of the equality of women with men in the ministry of the Society. One of her contemporaries asserted that no distinction is made as to the powers of usefulness between men and women."[1] Charity never used the terms: "women's liberation," or "woman power," or "feminist movement." They were not in her vocabulary. She did not need them. She did not need a constitutional amendment to enable her to vie with men in the strenuous role the travelling minister. In that day the public ministry was probably the only avenue open to Quaker women for distinctive service to society in general, and Charity Cook made use of it to the limit of her ability. She seems to have taken her liberation for granted; considered it a gift of God, her birthright in the society of Friends. It seems obvious that she felt no restraint because she was a woman or because she was the mother of eleven children. She appears to have evaded no hardship which a male itinerant minister might have had to face. She rode horseback for thousands of miles, much of it through winter months, to visit most, if not all the Friends' Meetings between Georgia and Massachusetts.

Her husband, Isaac Cook, was no drone in their fifty-eight-year partnership. He was an elder and an active leader in the work of their monthly meeting. He seems to have considered himself a divinely appointed, home-keeping partner of Charity, the travelling minister. By caring for the home, the children and the farm in Charity's absence, he must have felt that he was fulfilling his part of the partnership and enabling Charity to accomplish her divinely appointed mission. He made it possible for her to be away from home and from their children on many occasions, some of them for several months at a time, and once for several years. For nearly thirty years Isaac met his responsibilities in the partnership as faithfully as Charity did hers.

Charity Cook was a product of the frontier backcountry of the South. For the first forty years of her life she was never away from it. She was born on the 13th of 12 Month, 1745, in a relatively new Quaker settlement on Monocacy Creek a few miles south of Frederick, Maryland. Her grandfather, James Wright, had been one of the founders of the settlement two decades earlier.

When Charity was four years old, her parents, John and Rachel Wells Wright, loaded pack-horses with their seven children along with essential tools, utensils, and supplies to make the hazardous journey to a frontier 300 miles away to start a new Quaker settlement. Their destination was the Cane Creek Valley in the southern part of what is now Alamance Country in North Carolina. At that time the nearest Monthly Meeting to this new settlement was Carver's Creek, about forty miles north of Wilmington. Their certificates of membership in the Society of Friends were sent to that meeting.

It seems quite certain that John Wright had gone to this frontier spot during the previous spring and summer. Following the pattern of frontier emigrants, he and men from other families who were planning to emigrate had gone out together, selected tracts of land, established some sort of claim on them, built log cabins and planted limited crops. When their objectives were achieved, these men returned home and made preparation for emigration with their families, probably the following spring. Enroute to the frontier, group or caravan travel offered as much security as was possible in that day. It would have been foolhardy for one man, or even one family, to attempt the journey alone when several of their relatives and neighbors were intending to emigrate to the same frontier. Accidents, illness or injuries might prove fatal to the lone traveller or lone family, but a group travelling together might provide assistance to each other in critical situations.

In the spring of 1749, the Wright family moved out of Monocacy, on the road to the southwest.[2] Other families must have joined them at Hopewell, near the present city of Winchester, Virginia. The first part of the journey was over the unimproved but much travelled road to the Southern Piedmont. The last half, south of Staunton, was over Indian trading paths which would not accommodate wagons.

On the long, precarious journey this family must have made a picture worth recording, if there had been anyone to do it. John Wright was thirty-two years old, Rachel twenty-eight, and their seven children ranged in age from ten years to three or four months.[3] One can imagine that John walked. Rachel and the older children might have taken turns walking and riding, while Charity and the two younger children rocked along in their reserved seats on the horses, the baby's basket being tied securely to one of the saddles.

Beginning a new life on a frontier with a family of seven small children seems at best a gamble. A one-room cabin with a half-loft was close quarters for a family of that size. The stock of corn and other meager crops which John Wright had stored in the cabin the year before provided a limited food supply. They must have had to rely on wild game for meat, and from the creek they may have taken fish, mussels, eels, and frogs. Only the barest necessities in tools, utensils, clothing and household furnishings could have been brought on the pack horses. Most family necessities had to be improvised and made by hand. Though some of the settlers may have been unable to read or write, it is a mistake to think of them as unlearned. They were highly trained in numerous skills which enabled them to survive on the frontier.

Research has uncovered nothing about the first meetings for worship held by the earliest settlers on Cane Creek, but there is reason to believe that they were held regularly. Enough is known about the beginning of some of the other Quaker settlements to indicate that settlers began regular meetings for worship soon after their arrival. There is a tradition that early New Garden Friends held meetings for worship in the woods, using logs for benches until houses could be built. Cane Creek Friends had been in the habit of regular attendance of meetings for worship before they emigrated to the south. If that had not been true, their Monthly Meetings would have not granted them certificates of membership to be taken to North Carolina.

Two women among the first settlers were deeply concerned with the religious discipline and spiritual stamina of the group. They were Rachel Wells Wright, a minister, and Abigail Overman Pike, who would soon be recorded as one. With these two women in the emigrating party it is easy to assume that meetings for worship were held along the way and at Cane Creek from the time of arrival. Less than two years after they reached Cane Creek, the leadership ability of these two women was revealed in their appointment by Cane Creek Friends to go to Eastern Quarterly Meeting in Pasquotank County nearly 300 miles away to request the establishment of a Monthly Meeting for these backcountry settlers. It was nearly 600 miles round-trip, and these two women rode horseback every mile of the way.

Charity Cook did not learn to read or write until after her marriage to Isaac Cook. It seems unlikely that there were any schools at Cane Creek while the Wright family was living in that community. Charity seems to have had a keen mind which she must have used in a learning process fit to life in the backcountry. In the last half of her life she became one of the most able and widely travelled ministers in the society of Friends. It now seems probable that in the course of her development on Cane Creek she came under influences which fixed in her mind concepts and aspirations which helped to guide her through a remarkable career as a minister. A major part of this influence may have come from five ministers who exerted great influence among Quakers during this period. All of the five were women.

The first and most influential of these was likely to have been Charity's mother, Rachel Wells Wright. By the time Charity was thirteen years old, there were thirteen children in the Wright family.[4] Although two of them were married before Charity's thirteenth birthday, there were still eleven children in the crowded cabin of this family. Charity saw her mother in full command of this beehive in addition to seeing her work outside the house at the barn and in the fields. In addition to these responsibilities her mother played an important role in Cane Creek Meeting. With the help of her husband, Rachel was able to visit Friends in the Cape Fear Valley where disorders were threatening the existence of two meetings. She was also able to go for long visits among Friends in Virginia and northeastern North Carolina.

There was also Charity's aunt, Hannah Wright Ballinger, a sister of Charity's father and an able minister and active member of New Garden Meeting, thirty-five miles away. Aunt Hannah had nine children, but nearly half of them were adults before Charity was thirteen years old. There can be little doubt about frequent visits between the Ballinger and Wright families in their respective homes.

The third minister who was well known to Charity was Abigail Pike, a near neighbor. Either she or Hannah Ballinger accompanied Rachel Wright on each of her visits among Friends in Eastern North Carolina or Virginia. Abigail had nine children also, enough to bring the total for these women to thirty-one, a number sufficient for a local Quaker Meeting. It is quite obvious that these three women were adept at arranging for their husbands to take charge of their respective households in addition to responsibility for their farms during the absence of their wives on long journeys in the gospel ministry. This pattern of life in these three families could hardly have escaped the attention of Charity and the other children.

During her Cane Creek years Charity Wright's education for the ministry went beyond the lessons found in the life of her mother and the other two women-ministers. When she was nine years old, two relatively young, unmarried women came from the British Isles and stopped at Cane Creek for about one week just after New Year's Day in 1754. Both were Quaker ministers. Catharine Payton, from England, was twenty-six years old, and Mary Piesley, from Ireland, was thirty-six. They were the first ministers from overseas to visit the Cane Creek settlement. Their journey on horseback would take them to nearly all the Quaker meetings between Charleston, South Carolina, and Dover, New Hampshire; and what they had to tell would attract the attention of Charity or any other child. The stories of their mission and journey, their adventures on stormy seas and frontier trails, and their description of England and Ireland and the Quakers in those two countries likely held the attention of young and old.5

During their week at Cane Creek, Catherine Payton and Mary Piesley certainly must have been in the Wright home. It is possible that they made it their headquarters. When they began their journey to Dunn's Creek and Carver's Creek in the Cape Fear Valley, Charity's father was one of the two men chosen by the Monthly Meeting to accompany them on their 150-mile journey. These two young women ministers likely gave a new and broader dimension to Charity's preparation for the ministry.

Charity's childhood at Cane Creek was not to be finished without a traumatic experience which might have alienated any girl of less stamina from the Society of Friends or blocked the remarkable career which the future held for her. Just prior to her fifteenth birthday, as nearly as can be determined, someone in the Women's Meeting accused her of having an affair with a man in the Cane Creek Meeting. She persisted in denying the charge but to no avail. After a few months, the unbending Women's Meeting disowned her on April 4, 1761. On that same day the Men's Meeting disowned the man in the case for "telling scandalous tales about several of the young women in the meeting,6 which fact may raise some question about the action of the Women's Meeting. By adjusting the date of her birth under the Gregorian Calendar to the new calendar, it may be found that she was only fourteen when disowned, instead of a few months past her fifteenth birthday. In either case, according to the present research she was the youngest member of Cane Creek ever to be disowned by that Meeting.

Charity appealed her case to Quarterly Meeting. The formidable committee of weighty men Friends from New Garden Monthly Meeting, appointed by the Quarterly Meeting, tempered the decision only slightly by recommending that she be retained in membership if she would admit her guilt and make an acceptable apology.7 This she would not do. It was a bold move. The Monthly Meeting, following the directive of the Quarterly Meeting, announced the testimonial against her on December 5, 1761, probably more than a year after the complaint against her was made in Cane Creek Preparative Meeting.

This case was caught up in the most complicated schismatic crisis in the history of Cane Creek Monthly Meeting. For some unknown reason the Meeting avoided any reference to the crisis in its minutes. It seems probable that Charity's mother, Rachel Wright, sharply criticized the way the Monthly Meeting dealt with her daughter. Rachel, a minister of long standing, knew that criticism of actions of the Monthly Meeting was considered to be a serious offense. She gave an apology for her action which was accepted by the Monthly Meeting as satisfactory, but when she asked the Meeting for a certificate for herself and her children to transfer their membership to Wateree Monthly Meeting in Camden, South Carolina, within whose limits they had already moved, some members of the Meeting objected on the grounds that Rachel Wright had not been sincere in her apology to the Meeting. This gave discontented members of Cane Creek Monthly Meeting the opportunity to challenge the control of the Monthly Meeting by what they considered a small body of "select" or "weighty Friends."

When approximately six months passed with the Monthly Meeting still unable to act upon Rachel Wright's request, she appealed to the Quarterly Meeting to prod the Monthly Meeting to act upon it. This immediately resulted in a confrontation between the Quarterly Meeting and the dissatisfied members of Cane Creek Monthly Meeting. When after dealing with the dissident members for six months the Quarterly Meeting attempted to discipline them, they appealed the case to the Yearly Meeting. It was the decision of that body that Rachel Wright deserved a certificate but that the Quarterly Meeting had exceeded its authority in granting it, and that the Quarterly Meeting should not have attempted to discipline the dissident members of Cane Creek.

The Quarterly Meeting and the Yearly Meeting wrestled with this case for nearly one and one-half years. By patience, persistence and the erosion of time, the crisis finally came to an end. The report of the Yearly Meeting was followed by a lull in the disorder at Cane Creek. During the next five years most of the dissatisfied members had either migrated to Georgia and South Carolina or had been disowned for various reasons. On March 7, 1767, more than five years after Rachel Wright had asked for a certificate to transfer, Cane Creek Meeting of Women Friends granted one for her and her children to Wateree Monthly Meeting.

On December 3, 1768, one year and nine months after the Women's Monthly Meeting had met it responsibility to Rachel Wright, "Charity Cook sent a paper of condemnation to this Meeting for her former misconduct which was received as satisfaction." One month later on January 7, 1769, the following appears in the Cane Creek Minutes: "The Friends appointed to prepare a certificate for Charity Cook have prepared one which was approved and signed." At that time Charity had been married to Isaac Cook for approximately seven years and was the mother of three children. It is presumed that by this action Cane Creek Monthly Meeting sent Charity Wright Cook's right of membership to Wateree Monthly Meeting, to which Bush River Friends would belong for another two years before they were given the privilege of holding a Monthly Meeting.[8] Since all the records of the Wateree Monthly Meeting are lost, Charity Cook's "paper of condemnation" is not available. Nothing is known   about its character or content, and no additional explanation or information about the note of apology is likely to be found.   By this exchange, it seems safe to assume that Charity's conscience was now free, if it had ever been otherwise.   The door was open again for free communication between her and Cane Creek Monthly Meeting.

Charity Cook's first decade at Bush River was a period of eventful years in her preparation for a career as a travelling minister.   At the beginning of the decade she had married Isaac Cook.   Information about their wedding may be in the lost records of Wateree Monthly Meeting.   No account of it has been found.   If they were married under the oversight of Wateree Monthly Meeting, she had been accepted into the membership by her own request.   If it had been a civil ceremony, Isaac's membership in the society of Friends would have been in jeopardy for his "marrying contrary to discipline."   So it can only be taken for granted that they were married.   The date of the wedding is not known, but their first child was born December 23, 1763.[9]   Such knowledge prompts the assumption that they were married in the first quarter of that year.

Charity had known Isaac Cook during her last three years at Cane Creek.   The encounter which she had with Cane Creek Monthly Meeting was as well known to him as to anyone.   The birth of their first child launched them into child rearing, and by the end of the decade there were five little Cooks in the cradle or underfoot.   In this decade, another of Charity's achievements was learning to read and write; quite likely with the help of her young husband.   Within four years after Cane

Creek restored her membership, her gift in the ministry was recognized by Bush River Monthly Meeting,[10] which suggests that she had been active in the spiritual life of that Meeting for several years. When she was recorded as a minister, she was only twenty-seven years old. In the early history of the Society of Friends, many young men and women became ministers, but in the 1770's this was rather uncommon. The two other Friends who were recorded at the same time as Charity were approximately twice her age: one was fifty and the other fifty-four.

Testimony against war was one of the concerns stressed by Charity in her ministry. She spoke to London Yearly Meeting on this subject during one of the early years of the Napoleonic War. In addition to her knowledge of the Quaker attitude toward war, her testimony must have been sharpened by her experience in war-times in America and Europe. She moved to Bush River during the time in which the Cherokee Indians were on the warpath in that area, late in the years of the French and Indian War. A few years later bands of robbers, ruffians and other lawless people roved the backcountry of South Carolina in which Bush River was located. The Regulators in South Carolina organized vigilante forces to protect innocent people in the area. For a time Charity Cook was close to the area of military operations. These disorders were followed within a few years by the outbreak of the Revolutionary War. Bush River was the scene of some of the worst aspects of that war. Here Whigs and Tories engaged each other in what appeared to be a war of extermination.

Quakers incurred the ill will of both sides by refusing to join or aid either. Near the end of the war, Joseph Cook, the sixteen-or seventeen-year-old son of Charity and Isaac Cook,". . . was taken prisoner by a band of pirates" (probably one of the bands of armed robbers which roved the backcountry of the Carolinas during much of the war period). When these men became convinced that Joseph would not join them, they told him they would have to shoot him. While they were discussing plans for his execution, Mary Herbert, a girl about Joseph's age, appeared. She told them that Joseph belonged to her and that they would have to let him go. When they refused, Mary grabbed Joseph in her arms and started off with him. The captain of the band, evidently amused and convinced that the girl would not be able to carry Joseph very far, shouted: "When you put him down we will start shooting." Mary Herbert must have mustered her full physical strength, for she carried him out of range of the guns of the armed band and ". . . in all probability saved his life."[11] Two years later Mary established a legal claim to Joseph by marrying him. In this way she took her place in Charity Cook's long line of strong-willed women.

On her numerous religious journeys in America, Charity Cook rode horseback for thousands of miles from meeting to meeting and home to home in every Yearly Meeting in America. For this remarkable achievement she might be called a "Quaker Circuit rider." Her major concern in visiting a local meeting was to visit every family in the meeting. She said it was an "arduous task,' but no evidence has been found to indicate that she ever shirked it. In one meeting, it took her two weeks to visit sixty families.[12] The journals of travelling ministers show that many of them gave of their time and energy to this type of ministry. When, during the course of the present research, the striking assertion was found that the ministry of the travelling Quaker ministers was the "lifeblood of the Society," it was thought to refer to the life of Charity Cook and some of the other widely-travelled ministers. The author is now convinced that this "lifeblood" was flowing mainly through the ministry of family visits. It appears to have been a most effective way of touching the lives of Friends of all ages.

During the first five years after being recorded, Charity seems to have restricted her ministry to her own wide-spread Monthly Meeting. Then a minute of Bush River Monthly Meeting for the 30th 11th Month, 1776, shows that she was breaking through local bounds to begin her career at large in the Society of Friends. The minute reads:

> Our friends Mary Pearson and Charity Cook informs (sic) this meeting that they have a desire to visit the monthly meeting of Friends, in Georgia, with particular families thereto belonging, with which this meeting concurs and appoints William O'Neal and Henry Milhous to accompany them.

The entire Minute is quoted because it gives the pattern for the travelling ministry of women ministers: two women travelling together, family visits, special reason for going and two men appointed by the Monthly Meeting to accompany and assist them with problems of transportation and other matters along the journey. Upon their return from Georgia, the two men reported to Bush River Monthly Meeting that the visit was satisfactory to them and to the Georgia Friends. Nothing was said about hardships along the way. Their visit among Georgia Friends was in December, a few months after the Declaration of Independence. Later in the war, Abel Thomas, a Quaker minister, followed a nearly identical route to that taken by the two women a few years earlier. In his Journal he reports:

> We were told that it was as much as our lives were worth to go over the (Savannah) River: that the Indians and white people were joined together in their bloody designs.

> We rode the River in great danger, the waters being so rapid and the bottom so rocky.

While he barely escaped being murdered, no evidence has been found that Charity Cook was threatened. She must have found the Savannah River just as dangerous, however.[13]

As seen from one perspective, Charity's religious journey to Georgia (her first venture in the travelling ministry outside her own community) was made when the family was poorly prepared for it. She was leaving her husband with seven children. The oldest was thirteen and the youngest was just three months old. The thirteen-year-old son was hardly old enough for much responsibility around the farm. The two oldest daughters were ten and eight--too young to care for the baby and other younger children. The journey to Georgia was a test of Charity's effectiveness in the travelling ministry as well as a test to Isaac's ability to meet the household and farm responsibilities in Charity's absence. Charity made this first trip at the age of thirty-one; her last was made forty-five years later in her seventy-sixth year.

When the second religious journey was made in 1782 to meetings in North Carolina and Virginia, two of Charity's daughters were sixteen and fourteen years of age. The ninth child was a sixteen-month-old boy. The two older daughters were able to carry much of the responsibility for the care of him and of the other young children. On this occasion, as with the later journeys made by Charity, Isaac was left with the management of the household and the farm, but his children were old enough to give him much of the assistance needed in daily tasks.

During the first decade of her itinerant ministry, all of Charity's four journeys were made in the South in company with Mary Steddom Pearson. Mary was twenty-four years older than Charity. This association was probably a valuable experience in Charity's ever expanding religious and spiritual development. Her concern for the religious vitality of Friends' Meetings was one of the compelling forces which kept her on her rounds to meetings in need of spiritual nurture. Itinerant ministers have left the impression that Friends in Charleston were never strongly attached to the Truth, and the Revolutionary War threatened the Georgia Friends with dissention. Charity was led to visit among Friends in one of these meetings on two occasions and three times among the Friends in the other.

In 1787 after five forays for Truth in the South in which she had gone into most if not all the meetings and homes of Friends in Virginia, North Carolina, South Carolina and Georgia, Charity Cook's concern led her to break out of the South and visit Yearly Meetings in the North. A certificate for this journey was granted by her Monthly Meeting on March 27, 1787. This mission was one of longer duration than some of the earlier ones, but through experience and growth the members of the family who remained at home were better able to fill the gap left by Charity's absence. She could trust God and Isaac to meet any need or emergency. On her way north she stopped to attend the sessions of the North Carolina Yearly Meeting held at New Garden. There she became acquainted with Sarah Harrison, who would become one of her companions ten years later in a memorable journey through some of the war-torn German states. It must have been a thrill for her to be in Quaker meetings in Philadelphia and in the northeast where she could meet some of the leading Friends of that day. She was in Philadelphia while the National Constitutional convention was in session. It certainly must have attracted her attention.

On the 28th day of 5th Month, 1796, Bush River Monthly Meeting recorded this significant Minute:

> Our esteemed Friend Charity Cook
> laid before this meeting a weighty con-
> cern that attended her mind for several
> years to pay a religious visit to our
> Friends in Europe as truth may open the

way with which this meeting unites.

One strange aspect of the beginning of this dream mission which had "attended her mind for several years" is that she spent nearly sixteen months, accompanied by her sister, Susannah Wright Hollingsworth who was also a minister, visiting many of the Quaker meetings in Virginia, Maryland, the western and eastern parts of Pennsylvania, New York and all of New England except New Hampshire before taking the boat to Liverpool. Why, one asks, did she undertake this long succession of visits over a wide range of American Quakerdom? It certainly prolonged her absence from home and family. Did her intuition tell her that this experience would be valuable in her preparation for interpreting American Quakerism to Friends in England, Ireland and Germany? It must have been just such a valuable experience. She met and established ties with many of the leading Friends of America, and some who were visitors from England. Martha Routh was one of them, and from her Journal we get much of our information about Charity's experience in New York, New England and on the boat to England.

On "Tenth Month, 17, 1797," the Severn, a small sailing boat with Captain Goodrich in command, left New York harbor for Liverpool with Charity Cook and two other women ministers of the Quaker faith, Martha Routh and Mary Swett, on board. Among the passengers were other Quakers, among them Elizabeth Wood and William Wigham. For one month and five days the Severn made its way through storms which were about as rough and continuous as the Atlantic could muster. Of the Quaker group, Charity was the best sailor. As if the rough sea were not enough, the Quaker passengers were tormented by a bunch of raucous men who peppered them with ridicule and broke up some of their meetings for worship. Charity was the only one who could silence them. This she did by the power of her vocal ministry.

The voyage was made during the early stage of the Napoleonic Wars, while Britain and France were in a desperate struggle for the control of the Atlantic Ocean. The Severn was stopped and boarded by men from the war vessels of both France and Britain and by men from a French privateer. The women knew that their ship might be taken to some distant port or even destroyed at sea. The armed ruffians from the French privateer were especially obnoxious and menacing. They ransacked everything on board in search of valuables which they could confiscate. Evidently the Quakers had nothing they wanted, but when an especially severe storm burst open the door and filled Martha Routh's cabin, forcing her and Charity Cook to stand on the bed and on a table, she said she would rather have two such storms every day than meet one French privateer.[14]

When finally the exhausting voyage was completed and they landed at Liverpool, Charity did not take time for rest, nor did she hasten to London to meet Friends there. Instead, she visited all the Friends in the area of Liverpool and then moved her base to Kendall.[15] To her that area must have been holy ground. It was Fox country. Here Quakerism had been painfully born. In this area were Swarthmore Hall, several historic Meeting Houses and even some of the "dirty stinking prisons" where numerous Quakers had suffered and where some of them had died. What a thrill the scenes of this sacred history must have given this self-taught Quaker woman from the backcountry of the Carolinas.

Charity Cook was in England for nearly three years. By inference from her earlier behavior, we may rest assured that she visited most, if not all, of the meetings and homes of English Friends. Elizabeth Fry indicates that Charity's several visits in her home became rather monotonous. It excites one to realize that a woman of her background could be able to minister satisfactorily to English Quakers, among whom were the intellectually elite of the social Friends. It is known from various sources that she was able to do this, but ample evidence comes from the fact that English Meetings endorsed her certificate for travel with commendations which the ever frank English Friends would not have done if they had had any doubt about it.

On July 21, 1798 three women ministers, Charity Cook, Sarah Harrison and Mary Swett, left London for Hamburg and the war-torn continent of Europe. They knew that there was war on the North Sea and on the continent of Europe as well as on the Atlantic Ocean.

Their voyage across the North Sea was a spectacle in Quaker history. The ship on which they had passage was in a British convoy to protect them from the French navy or from privateers. Charity was accustomed to meeting dangers, but one wonders if she did not become excited during this episode in her journey standing on the deck of her ship with British warships on either side bristling with the heavy guns and plowing the North Sea toward Hamburg and three months of surprising adventures in a troubled land.[16] Their attempts to hold meetings and meet people in Hamburg were not encouraging. Their Quaker "task force" then headed inland. If we had a picture of this invading party, it might have shown a carriage heavily loaded with three American women, an English driver, a German interpreter, baggage and more than 700 books and pamphlets--their "ammunition." A few days' journey to the south brought them to four German meetings, all in Pyrmont Monthly Meeting. They visited each meeting and most of the houses of Quaker families.

At Minden, a fortified town, they had a dramatic experience. When their vehicle reached the gate of the town at night, the occupants of the carriage were questioned rigidly by the soldiers on guard. Then, the man in whose home the German Friends had been holding their meetings was ordered not to allow any meetings while this strange company was in town. The next day was First Day, however, and the regular time for meeting for worship. So, meet they did, and the German Friend was promptly arrested. Then the military commander ordered these feminine intruders to hold no more meetings in Minden. The order came only a few hours before time for Preparative Meeting and, of course, these activist women thought it right that they should attend. Near the time for the meeting to close, officers with a band of soldiers interrupted, drove the assembled group out of the house and nailed the door closed.

The commotion attracted a large crowd to the front of the house. The mob and the excitement were spiritual adrenalin to the Bush River evangelical Quaker. As Sarah Harrison described the scene:

And Charity feeling herself warmed
with gospel love, began to call the
people to repentance, through Lewish
Seebolm as interpreter.

But Truth, it should be added, was not given much
time to flow through Charity's lips.   Sarah Harrison
continuted;

. . . the officers came like roaring
lions, commanded silence, taking Lewis by
the shoulders drew him away,so Charity
was under the necessity of holding her
peace.17

At last Charity had met her match.   The rough men
on the Severn had not been able to silence her, but this
German military officer did.

At Pyrmont, a resort center, it was Charity who
spoke to the meeting which was attended by the so-called
"great folk of Germany" vacationing there. From Pyrmont
the heavily loaded carriage moved toward Frankfurt on
the Main River.   At Friedberg, about twenty miles north
of Frankfurt, they encountered difficulties which
changed their direction but did not silence them.   They
drove into the town, found an inn, took rooms for each
of the five, rented a hall and put out invitations to a
public meeting.   When about 100 of the townspeople
assembled, the governor of the town accompanied by a
band of soldiers interruped the meeting and demanded to
know by whose authority the meeting had been called.
When he was told that ". . .it was under an apprehension
of religious duty . . .," the governor was neither

amused nor impressed. He ordered the group arrested.

They were taken to their inn, their trunks were opened and searched, their rooms were locked, and the five were forced to spend the next five days and nights together in the common room of that hostelry, guarded by two soldiers who were discreet enough to look the other way while the women dressed. A guard was kept outside the door, and a group of soldiers patrolled the street in front of the building.[19] When had a band of Quaker women demanded such a heavy guard?!

The governor, the magistrates and the other officers of Friedberg took batches of their books and pamphlets home with them for careful reading. Among the books were Barclay's Apology and Penn's No Cross No Crown. They were searching frantically for evidence which would help to prove that these three women were spies trying to enter France in their version of a Trojan Horse. Charity and her co-conspirators must have been so elated that they were grinning like Cheshire cats. What better way could have been found to get Quaker propaganda read by such prominent people?

At length they were acquitted of the charge of spying, but they were told that they must turn back to the north and that, if they attempted to go on to Frankfurt or into France, they would certainly be treated as spies. When they entered their carriage to depart they were stopped and handed a bill demanding payment for the expenses of their trial and military custody. The women almost exploded. They told the governor that payment would imply an admission of guilt which they "could not admit," and if it had any bearing

on their freedom of religion they would go to prison
before they would "violate their conscience by complying
with payment."

When the governor explained that they were from
enemy countries, that they had slipped into town without
notifying the authorities, and that they had called a
public meeting without a permit, all in violation of the
law, the women relented and paid the bill in full. They
knew that they should have notified the governor and
that they should have asked for permission to hold their
meetings. Their justification for evading the law is a
rich bit of Quaker history:

> We were content in not having done
> so because compliance probably would have
> prevented the meeting.

> We distributed many books amongst
> them and had divers opportunities to
> explain our principles to them: which
> they allowed to be good. So upon the
> whole we have no excuse to feel sorry we
> fell into their hands.[20]

This squared the violation of the law with their
conscience, but it was the Lord who had directed them to
visit Friends in the Southern part of France, and now
they were turning back from that objective. How could
they adjust to that?

To make sure that this nuisance-loaded carriage
would start in the right direction, the governor sent an
escort of mounted troops to accompany these intruders on

the first two days of their retreat from Friedberg. The
women ministers still would not forget that they were
heavily charged with divinely sanctioned concerns, nor
would they remain dormant packages in the carriage
during the two days of their well guarded retreat.
Their weakness in allowing human authority to change
them from a course sanctioned by their Eternal Commander
to visit Friends in France weighed heavily on their
minds. When the mounted troops turned back they
revealed their decision to the two men in their party.
As one of the women related the story:

> Two days after we were discharged
> from prison, notwithstanding their
> threat, we believed it right to pursue
> our first prospects, being under appre-
> hension that we had submitted to command-
> ments of men . . . we were willing to
> make another trial if either of them
> would go with us.21

God had protected them through their past trials,
and they had complete faith that He would continue to do
so even as they penetrated the land of the greatest
military power in the world.

When neither of the men would agree to go with
them, the valiant three were forced to give up the bold
venture, but they felt that God would understand that
they wanted to go. As Sarah Harrison put it: ". . . we
felt comfortably released not doubting that the will
was taken for the deed."22 Their summary of their
expedition into war-ridden Germany is a gem:

In the course of the journey, forty-
five meetings were attended, besides
paying a visit to most of the families
in Pyrmont Monthly Meeting (which
included all the particular meetings in
Germany) and holding several religious
conferences. About six hundred and
seventy-five books (and pamphlets) were
distributed and we travelled by land and
water nearly sixteen hundred miles.[23]

Upon landing in England, Charity Cook and Mary
Swett, her companion, continued their mission of
visiting Friends in meetings along the route to London.
On the sixth of First Month, 1799, Charity preached in
an appointed meeting in Gracechurch Street Meeting House
to a large assembly which included many of the "richest
trading men in London." Here again Charity was able to
attract a large crowd and to speak acceptably to this
social and intellectual class of English society."[24]

Charity Cook must have remained in England during a
good part of the year 1799, but it is known that she was
in Ireland during the months of November and December of
that year. On the sixteenth of November she was struck
down by dreaded smallpox. On November 29th Sarah
Stephenson wrote in her diary from the little village of
Rathfriland, thirty miles south of Belfast:

Dear Charity Cook (of South
Carolina) is confined here with smallpox,
they have been out for three days and
not a large burden.[25]

Her report for November 30th was a different story:

> We returned from Quarterly Meeting
> held at Lurga, (eighteen miles southwest
> of Belfast) and found Dear Charity very
> ill, the doctor doubting her getting over
> the night . . .[26]

On December 11th, nearly one month after the beginning of her illness, Sarah Stephenson wrote from Dublin:

> We left Charity with the appearance
> of favorable recovery.[27]

On January 6, 1800, writing from her sick bed, Charity said she had "a thankful heart that looks likely I shall recover and be spared a little longer."[28] This is all that is now known about Charity's battle with smallpox which must have lasted for more than two months. On December 14, 1799, Henry Hull, a New York Friend visiting within the limits of Bush River Monthly Meeting, wrote in his Journal: "We rode to Isaac Cook's whose wife Charity was on a visit to Friends in Europe."[29] It must have been several weeks, perhaps months, after Charity recovered before Isaac Cook learned that his wife had had this struggle for her life in a little Irish village, cared for by Irish Friends now unknown to us.

In 1801, Charity made a second visit to Ireland and attended Dublin Yearly Meeting a few months before beginning her return trip to America. The two Irish journeys must have covered several months: sufficient time for her to visit all the monthly meetings and most of the homes of Friends in Ireland. From tradition comes the account of her interview with Patrick O'Brian, an eight foot giant whom we might call the "Paul Bunyan of Ireland." He is said to have "respectfully received her testimony."

It seems a striking coincidence that Charity's return to New York was in company with Martha Routh, one of her close associates on the Severn four years earlier. Martha Routh's husband, Richard, was with her, but Charity's husband did not even know that she was contemplating her return home. After a stormy voyage, they reached New York on December 16, 1801; four years after leaving that port for Liverpool; five and one-half years after leaving her South Carolina home.

Five and one-half years after leaving her family, the travel-hardened Charity Cook rode into her home community on a Sunday morning, too late to reach her home before the family would leave to go to meeting for worship at Bush River Meeting House. She went first to the meeting house for the meeting for worship. It was a typical Friends meeting house with separate meeting rooms for men and women. However, by opening the large shutters in the partition wall a joint meeting for worship could be held with the women assembled in their room and the men in theirs. Charity, a minister, would sit in the gallery facing the body of women worshippers; and Isaac, an elder, would be similarly located on the men's side. From their respective positions they could not see each other, and Isaac did not know that Charity was on this side of the Atlantic Ocean until he heard her voice in prayer. He waited patiently for the prayer to end, then rose, went through the partition door to the women's side to Charity, stooped and kissed her and returned dutifully to his place on the men's side. At the conclusion of the meeting one of the elders reprimanded Isaac for disturbing the meeting in that "unseemly manner." It is not difficult to see Isaac point his finger at the stern elder and give his quick reply:

> If thee had not seen the wife in
> five years I think thee ought to kiss her
> as soon as thee could.30

It was probably soon after Charity's return that she and Isaac attempted to ford Raburn's Creek in a two-horse wagon after a heavy rain. When they reached the middle of the stream they found the current too strong for fording. The current carried them down stream, capsized the wagon and drowned the horses. Isaac was able to reach the bank of the stream by catching hold of a floating log. In spite of heavy clothing and without assistance from man or nature, Charity swam to safety. Her swimming skill was probably acquired in Cane Creek; her childhood home had been within several hundred yards of the stream.

In Fourth Month, 1802, only a few weeks after her return from England, Charity was given a certificate by Bush River Monthly Meeting to visit all the meetings in South Carolina and Georgia. She had a story to tell which these Friends, most of whom were from backcountry meetings, were eager to hear. In 1804, she was given a certificate to visit Friends in some of the northern states. On this journey she had as her travelling companion her husband, Isaac Cook. It was the first time he had accompanied her on a religious journey. At that time, Keturah, the eleventh child, was eighteen years of age, and Isaac was now free to accompany Charity on her religious visits.

Isaac and Charity were caught by the stream of emigrants to the Middle West, and on 10-26-1805 Bush River Monthly Meeting granted them a certificate to Miami Monthly Meeting in the southwestern part of Ohio. They settled within the limits of Caesar's Creek Meeting, a subordinate of Miami Monthly Meeting, to which some of their children had already emigrated. They were among the early settlers in that Quaker community.

From meeting records we learn that five persons of various ages bearing the name "Isaac Cook" went from meetings in South Carolina to Caesar's Creek Monthly Meeting in Ohio; some of them before Caesar's Creek Monthly Meeting was set off from Miami Monthly Meeting. As if an additional complication were needed, in 1813, Isaac Cook, a nephew of Isaac and Charity Wright Cook, married Charity Lewis, a granddaughter of Isaac and Charity Wright Cook. This means that two married couples, with the identical names of Isaac and Charity Cook, were in the records of that monthly meeting. It is not surprising that important historical treatises have garbled information about both couples in treating the deaths of members of one of the couples.

It now seems probable that Isaac and Charity Cook who went to Whitewater Meeting in Indiana in 1814 were the young couple and that in 1819 Issac and Charity Wright Cook went to Silver Creek Meeting about twenty miles south of Richmond, Indiana. There Isaac died on 1-15-1820 and was buried. Later that year Charity returned to Caesar's Creek, Ohio. The travelling ministry seems to have been in her blood. She visited several of the meetings in Ohio and Indiana. Accompanied by her son, Joseph, she visited some of the meetings in Pennsylvania and the sessions of Baltimore Yearly Meeting in August, 1820. It was in her 76th year and this was her last journey. She died on 11-13-1822 at the age of 77; probably at Caesar's Creek.

What was Charity Cook's vocal ministry like? So little is known about it that it is difficult to give even a brief answer. No evidence has been found that she ever kept a diary or journal, or that she wrote her memoirs. No one has ever left a copy of any of her sermons. Only brief references to them and two short excerpts have been found.

Tradition tells of her use of intonations in her delivery, breaking many of the words into distinct syllables with special accent on some of them; and alternating high and low pitch to produce a sort of rythmic sing-song or cadence. It is not at all surprising that she used this sort of delivery, for in that day intonation was the hallmark of good preaching, and it was widely used in some of the other denominations. This method of delivery often produced effects which some of the more irreverent auditors sometimes translated into versions of a humorous character.

Charity Cook must have belonged to the school of evangelism which was in evidence in the Society of Friends in that day. During the second half of the eighteenth century the influence of George Whitefield and John Wesley was sweeping through the English colonies of America, and their influence reached members of the Society of Friends including those in the backcountry. Stephen Grellet, a contemporary of Charity, gave this sort of ministry on his two journeys through the Carolinas in the first half of the nineteenth century. Martha Routh and Sarah Harrison, two of the outstanding ministers of that day closely associated with Charity Cook, were exponents of this type of Quaker ministry. They were alternate travelling companions of Charity in America, on the Atlantic Ocean, in England and in Germany. Thomas Scattergood spoke highly of her ministry and said she was especially effective in "public meetings" which were made up in large part of non-Quaker attendants.[31] The major purpose of public meetings was to win converts. When Charity spoke to the German crowd in Minden, she is said to have "preached Christ and him crucified" and called the crowd to repentence. Some of the brief references to her sermons and some of the short interpretations of them give evidence of an evangelical tone in her ministry.

Charity Cook's lifespan covered three-fourths of what is called in Quaker history "the Quietistic Period." In that time the itinerant ministers, both men and women, poured their hearts and minds into concerted efforts to cultivate spiritual purity in the membership of the Society and to build hedges to protect Friends from the worldly influences around them. Charity's

ministry seemed to fit this pattern. Among the
qualities which stood out in her ministry was a boldness
which characterized itinerant ministers of her day.
They had a sharp sense for detecting weaknesses in the
discipline or spiritual fiber of Friends in meetings
being visited. When abberations were detected, it was
the inexcusable duty of the minister to bluntly proclaim
it, call the members to account for their weaknesses and
point ways for immediate reform.

It is not surprising that she "eldered" some of the
English Friends for what she considered a violation of
the principle of human equality. She had grown up on
the frontier and in the backcountry of the American
colonies, the breeding ground of the democratic principles of liberty and equality. This part of Charity's
heritage supported the Quaker principle of human equality in the sight of God--that God draws no lines to
divide mankind into different social classes. The servants in the homes of some of the affluent English
Quakers did not escape the critical eye of this
experienced travelling minister. She saw a wide social
gap between some of the "well-fixed" English Friends and
their servants, and in her opinion their treatment was
often harsh. In a meeting for worship in Bristol, she
boldly challenged the treatment of servants as she had
seen it. She had already convinced one woman that she
should help her servant scrub the heavy kitchen utensils. One irate member of the Bristol Meeting wrote
into his diary, for our information, his denial that
their servants lived a hard life or were imposed upon in
any way. And then he asked the question for posterity
to answer:

Is it worth their while to come from America to inculcate principles of equality? . . . Can it be supposed that they are sent for no higher errand than this?32

Perhaps it was such pricking of the conscience of another English Friend which caused him to refer to Charity Cook and Mary Swett's exercising" . . . their little gifts in the ministry." While Elizabeth Fry seemed to grumble at the frequency of their visits in her home she was led to say: "What they had to say was kind and affectionate." Though some expressions of dissatisfaction are found, English and American Friends frequently referred to her as "Dear Charity." The few of her many letters which are available clearly indicate that her correspondence was with numerous Friends on both sides of the Atlantic Ocean, many of whom were prominent leaders in the Society.

Something of her spiritual power may be indicated by a story reputed to have been told by President Isaac Sharpless of Haverford College. As her sister, Susannah Hollingsworth, was about to leave Charleston, South Carolina, on a religious visit among Friends in England, the two sisters sat on shipboard for a few minutes in prayer and meditation. Suddenly Charity told her sister that she should not take passage on that ship. Susannah respected Charity's warning and left the ship with her luggage to wait for another ship. The vessel on which Susannah had first booked passage sailed and was never heard from again.

Nereus Mendenhall classed Charity Cook among the "valuable ministers" in the history of North Carolina Yearly Meeting. Of these he named her as one of eight who were called" . . . to labor for the Lord in foreign lands."[33] If this tribute by the outstanding Quaker leader and scholar of North Carolina Yearly Meeting in the last half of the nineteenth century is a surprise to anyone, a glance at Charity Cook's long and wideranging itinerant ministry may remove it. The course of her travelling ministry covered forty-six years, and it took her into most of the local meetings and into the homes of members of these meetings on both sides of the Atlantic Ocean. To her a rich part of this phenomenal experience must have been becoming acquainted with many, and perhaps most of the ablest men and women in the society of Friends in America and Europe. Very few Friends were able to have such an extensive course in Quakerism.

Charity Cook seems to have lived under the compulsion that her ministry must reach all Friends and their neighbors, wherever they might be on either side of the Atlantic Ocean. Though conscious of her weaknesses, she seemed at home with Friends of all levels of learning and all degrees of spiritual nature. John Belton O'Neall must have characterized her correctly when he said that she was a "gifted woman."[34] Her life's story corroborates this evaluation. She was widely known, greatly respected and held in affectionate esteem for her outspoken ministry. While she was not a revolutionary minister, she was one of a wandering host of "publishers of truth" who gave a good part of their lives to preserve and strengthen the widely scattered Society of Friends.[35]

Notes

1Thomas Clarkson, A Portraiture of Quakerism
(Indianapolis: Merrill and Field, 1870), p. 453.

2This conjecture on the time of arrival is based on the
dates and places of birth of the seventh and eighth
children: the seventh born at Monocacy, Maryland, on
12-12-1748 O.S., and the eighth born at Cane Creek
North Carolina 12-23-1749 O.S. Between the two births,
Third Month (May O.S.) would be the logical time for
the journey.

3Cane Creek Monthly Meeting, Birth and Death Records,
1:3.

4Ibid

5Catherine Payton Phillips, "Memoirs of the Life of
Catharine Phillips," Friends Library, 14 vols.
(Philadelphia: Printed for the editors, 1837-1850),
11:212-213.

6The complaint against Jehu Stuart reached the Cane
Creek Monthly Meeing Of Men Friends on 1-1-1761.

7Western Quarterly Meeting, Minutes, 8-8-1761.

8William Wade Hinshaw, Encyclopedia of American Quaker
Genealogy, 7 vols. (Ann Arbor: Edward Bros., 1936),
1:1015.

9Bush River Monthly Meeting, Birth and Death Records,
p. 14.

10Bush River Monthly Meeting, Minutes, 12-26-1771.

11This story was acquired in Prairie City, Oregon from
Aaron Macy. He acquired it from material collected on
the Cooke family by B.F.Cooke, a great-grandson of
Joseph and Mary Herbert Cook.

[12] In Liverpool, England. See Charity Cook's letter to Jonathan and Ann Dawes in Friends Miscellany, 12 (4th month 1839): 149-150.

[13] "Memoirs of Abel Thomas," Friends Library, 13: 476.

[14] "Memoirs of Martha Routh," Friends Library, 12: 468.

[15] Letter from Charity Cook to Jonathan and Ann Dawes, Friends Miscellany, loc. cit.

[16] Memoirs of the Life and Travels of Sarah Harrison," Friends Miscellany, 11 (3rd month 1838): 154.

[17] Ibid.

[18] Ibid., 155

[19] Ibid., 158-159.

[20] Ibid., 163.

[21] Ibid., 164.

[22] Ibid.

[23] Ibid.

[24] "Memoirs of Thomas Scattergood," Friends Library, 8:160, 163.

[25] "Life and Travels of Sarah Stephenson," Friends Library, 4:204.

[26] Ibid.

[27] Ibid., 205.

[28] Charity Cook's letter to George and Ann Miller, quoted by Norman Penny in Bulletin of Friends Historical Association, 19 (Autumn, 1930):86.

[29] "Memoirs of Henry Hull," Friends Library, 4:267.

[30]To this tradition the Aaron Macy's unpublished manuscript on the Cook family adds: "I am thankful to God for allowing my wife to return to me after all these years."

[31]"Memoirs of Thomas Scattergood," Friends Library, 8:149.

[32]From the Diary of Samuel Dyer, 11 mo. 25, 1800, quoted by Norman Penny in "Life and Travels of a Southern Quaker Minister," Bulletin of Friends Historical Association 19 (Autumn 1930):86-87.

[33]Nereus Mendenhall, "Historical Sketch of North Carolina Yearly Meetings," Nereus Mendenhall Papers, The Quaker Collection, Guilford College, Greensboro, N.C.

[34]John Belton O'Neall, Annals of Newberry (Newberry, S.C.: Aull and Houseal, 1892), p. 30 and Willard Heiss, "Quakers at Bush River," part 2 of Quakers in the South Carolina Backcountry (Indianapolis: Indiana Quaker Records, 1969), p. 2

[35]In 1981 a book-length version of this paper was published as Charity Cook, A Liberated Woman by Friends United Press, Fuller bibliographic and manuscript sources are cited in that publication.

EVANGELICAL RELIGION AND WOMEN'S LIBERATION
IN THE NINETEENTH CENTURY
Winthrop S. Hudson

As I understood my assignment for this project it was to discuss the religious ferment of the nineteenth century and its bearing, if any, on women's self-understanding and leadership activities. The topic I suggested in response--"Evangelical Religion and Women's Liberation"--indicates that I believe that the evangelical religion which produced the ferment had a liberating effect upon women.

To place the topic in perspective, one may make the following preliminary observations.

1. Evangelical religion is the religion associated with the revivals of the eighteenth and nineteenth centuries in Britain and America. These revivals stood in continuity with one another whatever they were called--the Evangelical Revival, the Wesleyan Revival, the Great Awakening, the Second Great Awakening, the great Kentucky Revival, the Finney Revivals, Methodist revivalism, or "new measures" revivalism. They were linked both in space and in time, being a trans-Atlantic phenomenon and bridging the turn of the eighteenth to the nineteenth century.

2. The evangelical revivals of the eighteenth and nineteenth centuries stood in succession, with an interval of three-quarters of a century intervening, to the great "revival" commonly referred to as Puritanism

or the Puritan movement. This is the point made by Alan Simpson in his book, Puritanism in Old and New England, when he raised the question: "How does one define Puritanism?" He responded by saying that, first of all, Puritanism must be defined as a religious revival, a revival similar in kind and character to the evangelical revivals of the eighteenth and nineteenth centuries, passing through the same cycle of new vitality, energy, growth, declension, and decline. He answered the question of the definition of Puritanism, in the second place, by summarizing the general consensus of mid-twentieth century scholarship that the scope of the Puritan movement--the range of Puritan types--covered a broad spectrum extending as one continuous whole from those willing to accept a primitive or reformed episcopacy on the right through a whole galaxy of forms and groups in the middle and ending with Quakers, among others, on the left. Puritans were people in motion, possessed of peculiar restlessness, which often led them to embark on "spiritual pilgrimages" from form to form and group to group until some of them ended their pilgrimages as Seekers, Happy Finders, Quakers, or some other such type of expectant faith.

3. What was normative both for the Puritans and for the evangelicals was the experience of conversion, a preoccupation with the workings of the Holy Spirit (e.g., Richard Sibbes, John Cotton, and other members of William Haller's "spiritual brotherhood"). This preoccupation with the Spirit was accompanied by a millenarian fervor of which numerous examples could be cited from members of the Westminster Assembly through Jonathan Edwards to Lyman Beecher. A major burden of George Fox's message was "the terrible day of the Lord,"

with Christ already rising up in sons and daughters to bruise the head of the Serpent and inaugurate the new age of the spirit when all creation would be renewed.

4. A further feature of this religious fervor, whether in its puritan or evangelical form, is that it was never contained within denominational boundaires. Just as the restless energy of Puritanism ranged over a broad spectrum of otherwise differing religious groups, so the revivalist thrust of evangelicalism penetrated and was expressed within most denominations. By the mid-nineteenth century, even Unitarians at Harvard had been touched by the pervasive enthusiasm of evangelicalism. Nor were Quakers or Friends immune to its influence--J.J.Gurney being one name which comes readily to mind in this connection.

5. A final conspicuous feature of revivalist evangelicalism, even in its earlier Puritan form, was the predominance of women among converts and church members. And of these women, even in the early period, a number were thrust forward into prominent roles. When one thinks of Puritanism culminating in a period when tinkers preached and women prayed, one thinks of John Bunyan, but one also thinks of women who might be called proto-Quakers or crypto-Quakers--such women as Elizabeth Hooton, Dorcas Erbery, Anne Hutchinson, and Mary Dyer, who were pre-Foxian publishers of truth. With Quakers in mind, it is interesting that in the latter part of the eighteenth century when Quaker "quietism" was disturbed by evangelical excitement, two notable prophetesses emerged from the ranks of the Friends-- Jemima Wilkinson, the Great Universal Friend who established her Jerusalem on a hill above Keuka Lake in

the wilderness of western New York, and Ann Lee (Mother Ann of the Shakers) whose followers were brought together to form the United Society of Believers in Christ's Second Appearing. In both instances, Christ was appearing in female form to complete the revelation of God and to bring the old age to an end.

So much for the preliminary observations placing evangelical religion in its larger context. What of the relationship of evangelical religion to the liberation of women in nineteenth century America?

I.

No one has dealt as perceptively with the relationship of evangelicalism to women's liberation as Donald G. Mathews in his book <u>Religion</u> <u>in</u> <u>the</u> <u>Old</u> <u>South</u>.[1] Mathews notes the predominance of women among church members and suggests that the reason for this was the fact that evangelical religion conferred upon women a new sense of psychological and social space. This liberating effect upon women was related to several features of evangelical religion which, though interwoven, may be isolated for the sake of enumeration.

First of all, central to evangelical religion was the conversion experience. For a women, conversion became something of a declaration of independence. This may be inferred from the negative response her conversion occasionally elicited from parents and more often from the way in which a conversion experience would bring her into open and sometimes violent conflict with her husband. Conversion involved a break from the past. It brought a sense of release from prior constraints of a women's customary role and cultural stereotype. "The release," Mathews comments, "was from a sense of psychological dependence upon others--either parents or spouses--and provided a sense of social distance from the matrix of group relationships previously valued. The New Birth was just what it was represented to be, a new entry into a new kind of life. It was a renunciation of the old life."

For a woman, conversion may be described as analogous to a declaration of independence, not simply because it freed the convert from psychological dependence upon those nearest to her and from accustomed patterns of life. It was a declaration of independence because in the conversion process God had given her a vision of her place and role in life and had generated a resolute determination to pursue an independent course of action to that end. The pursuit of holiness, of sanctification, or perfection, it came to be called.

A second aspect of evangelical religion which contributed to a woman's sense of self-confidence and thus of liberation was the ritual following conversion and preceding church membership. Women as well as men were expected to stand alone before the congregation to make a public profession of faith by relating their conversion which began with a conviction of sin and a surrender to Christ, and ended with a flooding sense of forgiveness, acceptance, release, and assurance. Except for the church, public gatherings were primarily gatherings of men. Even though present women, like children, were supposed to be seen and not heard. For a woman to become the center of attention before a mixed assembly and to engage in the act of public speaking to an attentive and receptive audience was for her a novel experience. It conferred upon her a sense of rough equality and was a symbol of her claim to respect and honor. Reports Mathews of the experience: "She had stood up in meeting on her own . . . and expressed some of her most private thoughts which were accepted by the community as significant and praiseworthy." This did much for her self-esteem and was a further step in the process of liberation.

A third step toward equality was church membership. Although hedged by male authority, church membership conferred status and at least a type of equality. More important than symbolic status was the supportive role of the church. Some women found within the intimacy of the church the concern, care, companionship, and sense of worth they did not receive from their husbands. Other women found within the church and its disciplinary procedures protection from abuse by husbands. Moreover, "without understanding the interpersonal dynamics involved," women could "employ the pastoral relationship to create a sense of space between them and the people who lorded it over them." They could cite opinions expressed by the minister and Biblical texts from his sermons to counter authoritative pronouncements by other males and thus find room for independent maneuver.

A more subtle aspect of evangelical religion in fostering a sense of psychological space for women was "the repressed sensuality of a religion which emphasized love, care, and intimate companionship with Christ." This could and did lead to a confusion of "sacred" with "profane" emotions and to an escape from sexual repression. When mixed with the "perfectionism" of much evangelical religion the escape from sexual repression could lead to the "spiritual wifery" which swept through some perfectionist circles, or it could find expression in the perfectionist "complex marriage" of John Humphrey Noyes' Oneida Community. Departures from the accepted code of sexual morals, however, were not common. What was common was for sexual feelings to find expression within conventional modes of behavior. A degree of sexual excitement seems to have been a component of at least some female conversion experiences. The sensuous overtones of revivals and camp meetings impressed many observers, but they may have missed the sexual element in the conversion experience itself. The reports do describe how women under conviction of sin would fall to the ground where they would toss and turn and writhe, moaning and crying out, until as their bodies grew tense an overpowering feeling of release would overcome them accompanied by burst of tears and sobs of joy. It is likely that this intimate and never-to-be-forgotten encounter with Christ's tender love and compassion was as much a sensual as a spiritual experience, although ignorance of sexual feelings may have given the convert little reason to suspect that mixed emotions were involved. What she did know was that the experience was profoundly satisfying and gave her a new sense of well-being. Donald Mathews suggests that an even more common form for the release of sexual feelings was the "attraction of women to the young men who led the evangelical movement." Unaccustomed as many of them were to "compassionate, impassioned, and even passionate men, such as the clergy seemed to be," it is not surprising, when one reads between the lines of their letters, that women often experienced emotions toward the young preachers that "they could not quite fathom, but which they knew excited and fulfilled them."

II.

Even more important than these primary aspects of evangelical religion in creating psychological and social space for women was the development of exclusively female organizations through which women could participate more freely than in the church itself in affairs outside the home. Hedged about by male authority in the church, women formed auxiliaries-- groups and societies of their own--which provided opportunities for self-expression, assuming responsibility, and perfecting leadership skills. In the beginning, these auxiliaries were local--prayer circles, "aid" societies, and "mite" societies to accumulate funds for charitable and missionary projects. In addition to their formal objectives, these groups became the focal point of social activities for women.

It is true, of course, that occasionally a woman would burst the bonds of male authority and function in a mixed society. This occurred when a woman's account of her conversion was so profoundly moving that she would be asked to repeat her testimony with the result that she would become something of an itinerant evangelist not unlike earlier "publishers of truth." This phenomenon was most common among Wesleyan groups (i.e., groups with a Wesleyan theology--Methodists, Free Will Baptists, Christians or Disciples). At midcentury, Phoebe Palmer of "holiness" fame was the most notable example of this type of female leadership. Almost as conspicuous was Ellen Gould White, who later became the prophetess of Seventh-Day Adventists. She had an especially compelling story to tell and found her life transformed by the response she won in the telling of it. For Ellen it was a second rebirth, and a psychological assessment of the dynamics involved would make a fascinating study.

Phoebe Palmer and Ellen Gould White were exceptional women and their path to leadership was not the path pursued by most women who rose to prominence. Much more common were women who gained space for themselves and found their way to leadership through female societies. No one can understand the clustering and bonding together of women in support of common causes without an understanding of the explosive sense of mission of evangelical religion and of the instruments (the voluntary societies) that were fashioned to forward the mission.

A further word should be said about "the explosive sense of mission of evangelical religion." Mention has been made of the restless energy generated by Puritanism. This was equally true of evangelicalism. Charles G. Finney insisted that "conversion" was not the end of the Christian life, but its beginning. The effect of conversion, he said, was to put people to work for the Kingdom. Phoebe Palmer made the same point with less vivid imagery. Her slogan was "saved for service."

The mission of evangelicalism began with evangelization, the winning of converts. To this end, mission societies, Bible societies, tract societies, education societies, societies for the promotion of Sunday schools and the evangelization of seamen were formed. They were grass-roots organizations at the outset, local groups organized by individuals and focused on a single objective. Gradually the local units were pulled together to form national societies. Then the mission impulse gave birth to a reform impulse--the impulse to outwardly as well as inwardly Christianize and perfect the nation. To this end, temperance societies, anti-slavery societies, peace societies, anti-dueling societies, health food societies, municipal reform societies, societies for the aid of females who have deviated from the paths of virtue were formed. It was an ambitious vision, each society devoted to a single objective to enlist broadest possible support but all working together for a common goal.

As the most numerous and ardent of evangelicals, women banded together in auxiliary societies to do their part in providing support for the various mission and reform enterprises, whether they were denominational or interdenominational. Imbued with the sense of mission generated by evangelicalism, the enthusiasm of women readily spilled over into specific concerns of their own, the most prominent of which was forwarding the cause of female education. Few problems arose as long as women kept within their own sphere. Tension arose only when women who had gained self-assurance as effective speakers and propagandists within their own societies were not allowed to speak or participate at sessions of male-dominated national societies for which they had enlisted significant support. The most famous of these encounters took place, however, not in the United States but in London at an anti-slavery meeting attended by Lucretia Mott and Elizabeth Cady Stanton.

It was within this context that a self-conscious women's rights movement was inaugurated, symbolized by the Seneca Falls Convention of 1848. Held in the center of the Finneyite territory of upstate New York, the convention was convened by Elizabeth Cady Stanton, who had received her early impetus from evangelical reform activity.

The story and the cast of characters of the women's rights movement are familiar and need not be rehearsed. What is important to remember is the psychological and social space provided by evangelical religion as well as an accompanying ferment which generated an almost passionate sense of mission for a wide variety of causes. This was the context out of which the crusade for female education and women's rights emerged. In addition to women directly involved in this dual thrust of specifically female concern, there are other women engaged in a varied assortment of causes during the first two decades of the twentieth century who in their time were of major stature and who are worthy of much more scholarly attention than they have received. Moreover, a scholarly account of the role of the wives of evangelical clergymen throughout the nineteenth century would be rewarding in terms of the insights it would provide.

LUCRETIA MOTT
HOLY OBEDIENCE AND HUMAN LIBERATION
Margaret H. Bacon

From 1833 to 1848, Lucretia Mott nourished the
infant women's rights movement in America, providing a
community of support for such pioneers as the Grimké
sisters and Abby Kelley Foster. At the Seneca Falls,
N.Y., Woman's Rights Convention, she was the guiding
spirit. For another thirty years she was a fearless
convention leader and speaker for women's rights, while
providing comfort, inspiration, and advice to Elizabeth
Cady Stanton, Susan B. Anthony, Lucy Stone, and many
others. Her pioneering work in developing educational
and vocational opportunities for women resulted in the
establishment of several institutions of higher
education. In 1866, she was made first president of the
Equal Rights Association in honor of her long years of
leadership.

Yet, Lucretia Mott was more than a pioneering
feminist. Her dedication to the abolition of slavery
was her first and primary commitment, and she
accompanied this with a real determination to get rid of
racial descrimination in social life and public
conveniences. As the most famous of the female
abolitionists, she was called The Black Man's Goddess.
Her work for peace, for the rights of American Indians,
and for Irish immigrants was impressive. She was a
pioneer in social work, and a lifelong advocate of
freedom of thought and religion. She tried to
understand the workings of an economic system that made

the rich richer and the poor poorer. She was a spokesperson for and a practitioner of non-violence.

What motivated this small and simple Quaker woman to involve herself in so many areas of reform? Was she driven by psychological tensions? Filled with anger at the restrictions in her lot as a woman? Seeking, if unconsciously, for fame? The answers are not easy to come by, for she was not introspective. She did not keep a diary, nor write much about herself in her letters to relatives and friends. But a close study of her correspondence, her sermons and her speeches made me believe that her secret source of strength was her implicit faith in the promptings of the Divine Spirit. Although she did not call herself a mystic, she believed that God guided her to perceive her manifest duty, and strengthened her for each task. Her religious life did not involve states of ecstasy; it was as natural to her as breathing. Toward the end of her life, she wrote to her sister that she did not really need to set aside any special place or time for worship, she worshipped always.

"Those who go forth ministering to the wants and necessities of their fellow human beings, experience a rich return, their souls being as a watered garden, as a spring that faileth not,"[1] she said in one of her sermons. The Quaker concepts of a direct relationship between God and human beings and of continuing revelation have flowered from time to time in the lives of individuals. Lucretia Mott's life was such a flowering, advancing the cause of human liberation and moving the Society of Friends toward its present orientation to peace and justice.

Critics sometimes ask why she did not center down to one reform, but seemed to respond to each new demand. The answer lies very simply, it seems to me, in her sense of Divine leading. The choice to stick to abolition, or women's rights, and ignore the pressing needs of American Indians or prisoners was not hers to make, she felt. It was not women's liberation, but human liberation to which she was dedicated, although she proceeded, in true Quaker fashion, step by step as the way opened. She was a nineteenth century shaper of human space, pushing back frontiers for blacks, women, Indians and many others so that they, too, might be free to be obedient to manifest duty and the Holy Spirit.

Lucretia Mott was born on Nantucket in 1793, daughter of a sea captain and his strong and able wife. Due to an apparently incapacitating handicap afflicting her older sister, she was her mother's right hand helper and support during the long, lonely days her father was away at sea. As a result, she developed a deep attachment for her mother which lasted as long as they both lived, and appeared to be a source of great strength to her. She saw her mother as a typical daughter of the island, strong, humorous, self-reliant. While Thomas Coffin was away at sea,Anna kept shop as did many other Nantucket wives. "Look at the heads of those women, "Lucretia said proudly at a women's rights convention, "they can mingle with men, they are not triflers, they have intelligent subjects of conversation."2

Not until she was a student at Nine Partners Boarding School in Duchess County, New York, did Lucretia Mott discover that in the larger world women were treated as inferiors. The discovery came when she learned that a favorite women teacher was being paid forty percent of the salary offered a young man. "The injustice of this distinction was so apparent, that I early resolved to claim for myself all that an impartial creator had bestowed," she wrote in a brief memoir.[3]

The young man in question, James Mott, was not to be blamed. In fact, several years later he and Lucretia were married in Philadelphia, where the Coffin family had moved, and here made their home for the rest of their lives. They had six children, of whom five lived, and in time numerous grandchildren. Both were members of large, warm, extended families, and family visitation on a daily basis was an important part of Lucretia Mott's life.

The marriage appears to have been a singularly happy one; another source of Lucretia Mott's strength. She believed and frequently said that "in the true married relationship, the independence of husband and wife are equal, their dependence mutual, and their obligations reciprocal."[4] In many ways this appeared to be the pattern in the Mott family. James, who was taciturn and a poor speaker, enjoyed accompanying his accomplished wife and listening to her. She was his vocal chords and tongue. And, independent as she was in many ways, Lucretia was always strengthened when he was somewhere in the room. They shared an interest in many reforms and James was often chosen as president of societies in which they both took a part. If the world sometimes called him "Mr. Lucretia Mott" neither of them seemed to care.

For a while after the birth of her first two children, Lucretia taught school in order to help make ends meet. Thereafter she devoted herself to reforms, preaching, and lecturing. She was an accomplished housewife, known for her largesse in entertaining anyone and everyone who came to her door-escaped slaves, reformers, politicians, travellers from Europe, literati. Her system of dividing household tasks so that each member of the family had a job helped to make this possible. She also loved her housework, getting some relaxation and some physical exercise from making pies and beating rugs. Nevertheless, she believed that women should have the right to choose between housework and professional life, and supported several young women in their efforts to get started as teachers and as doctors.

The death of a young son in 1817 turned Lucretia Mott toward a deepening religious quest. A few years later she became a recognized minister in the Society of Friends, and continued to preach and travel in the ministry most of her long life. In 1827, at the time of the separation between the Orthodox and Hicksite Friends over matters of authority and doctrine, she reluctantly chose the Hicksite position, and thereafter for some years was active as Clerk of Women's Yearly Meeting (Hicksite), and on the Education and Indian committees. Her growing involvement in the anti-slavery campaign, and her growing outspokenness on the question of women's rights made her a controversial figure, while her equalitarian views led her to challenge the authority of the elders within the Hicksite fold. Efforts were made to disown her, but she clung to her place, and used her knowledge of Quaker procedures and of Scripture to retain her right of membership. It was at this time that she adopted the slogan, "Truth for authority, not Authority for Truth."3

In December of 1833, William Lloyd Garrison founded the American Anti-Slavery Society in Philadelphia. Four days later, Lucretia Mott organized the Philadelphia Female Anti-Slavery Society. This remarkable group, interacial from the beginning, gave women their first taste of political experience, and provided a support community for the pioneer women who disobeyed the taboo against their speaking to mixed audiences. As corresponding secretary, Lucretia helped to link up the Philadelphia group with several others, and to arrange for a national gathering, the American Society of Anti-Slavery Women. In 1840, when women were finally admitted to full membership in the American Anti-Slavery Society, (a large group of clergymen and others have seceded as a protest) she was made a Board member, and chosen as a delegate to the World Anti-Slavery Convention, held in London.

British abolitionists, many of them Quaker, were not prepared to admit women to membership in the convention, and Lucretia and the few other American women delegates were warned that they might not be seated. When in fact this was the case, Lucretia entered into a forceful protest that a World Anti-Slavery Convention should not eliminate half the world. She was so strong, and yet warm and gracious in her position, that she deeply influenced Elizabeth Cady Stanton, the young bride of a delegate, and Ann Knight, a British Friend who came to champion women's rights in that country.

Back in the United States, Lucretia Mott dedicated herself anew to lecturing against slavery, and began as well to speak frequently on the rights of women. A strong supporter of Garrison, she frequently mingled with "the world's people" in such enterprises as the New England Non-Resistance Society and the Anti-Sabbath Convention. This decade from 1840 to 1850 saw her almost constantly facing challenges within both the New York and Philadelphia Yearly Meetings (Hicksite). In the decade before she had developed a dyspepsia which flared up under stress. During the 1840's she was frequently "bent double" with stomach pains. The death of her beloved mother in 1844 was a severe blow.

Yet, this was in many ways the most creative period of her life. Each challenge seemed to cause her to deepen her spiritual roots, as well as to reach out to her support system of family and friends. It was at this period she established workshops for poor women, white and black, developed an exchange between the women of Exeter, England, and of Philadelphia in order to head off war in 1846 over the Oregon Territory, developed her feminist thought, and gave support to several emerging institutions: the Philadelphia Female Medical College and the Female School of Design. Earlier she had chaired a committee which laid the groundwork for the founding in 1864 of Swarthmore, second Quaker co-educational college.

From Seneca Falls to the Civil War, she was a reluctant leader of the women's rights movement, always pleading with her younger colleagues to let her "slide" but chairing the most beleaguered of the meetings with a poise and strength that was widely admired. She had the ability, as Wendell Phillips once remarked, to correct critics with "a silken snapper on her whip."[6] She had the prized Quaker capacity to "elder" without losing her composure. She could be very angry without guilt, because of her spiritual wholeness.

Yet, it was during this time that she was under the greatest stress as an abolitionist. She supported Non-resistance to the Fugitive Slave Law, and helped Harriet Tubman, William Stiff, and others. Within the Anti-Slavery Society, she struggled to heal the growing dissension, and to argue against the turn toward violence and support of Free Soil settlers with rifles. Some of her speeches about the relationship of non-resistance to liberation, and the problems posed by a violent state which upheld slavery with the bayonet still make challenging reading today. Among the Garrisonians she remained the most steadfast to the principles of non-resistance during the Civil War, supporting conscientious objectors while she baked pies for the black troops of Camp William Penn, across the road from her Chelten Hills home.

The tragedy of the Civil War caused Lucretia to devote the remaining years of her life to the cause of peace, although she continued to be active in the women's rights movement, and to work for equal justice for blacks and working people. In 1866, she took part in a campaign to integrate the Philadelphia trolleys, and in 1876, she tried to persuade the Centennial Commissioners to open the fair grounds on Sunday so that working class people might attend on their only day off. She continued to be interested in new causes and new ideas up until her death, shortly before her 88th birthday.

One of Lucretia Mott's concerns during her later years was the establishment of the Free Religious Association, an ecumenical body seeking common elements in all religions, and dedicated to freeing men and women from "the fetters of sectarian belief" which created, she believed, a false dichotomy between religion and science. In a speech before this group in May of 1873, she expressed her lifelong faith in the capacity of goodness of human beings, which could be nurtured by Holy Obedience:

> You do not hear, in any of the pulpits, a definition of what love and justice, and mercy and right are. You know and all know that they are innate, and self-defined. Therefore, I say preach your truth, let it go forth, and you will find, without any notable miracle, as of old, that every man will speak in his own tongue in which he was born. And I will say, if these pure principles have their place in us and are brought forth by faithfulness, by obedience, by practice, the difficulties and doubts that we may have to surmount will be easily conquered. There will be a power greater than these. Let it be called the Great Spirit of the Indian, the Quaker "inward light" of George Fox, the "Blessed Mary, Mother of Jesus" of the Catholics, or Brahma, the Hindoo's

God--they will all be one and there will
come to be such faith and such liberty as
shall redeem the world."[7]

Freedom of thought and inquiry for Lucretia Mott
were not simply rights as such, but sacred channels to
the will of God. The liberation of slaves, of women
from their "degraded position", of men and women from
sectarian prejudice had one overriding object.
Permitted to seek the Truth without fetters, human
beings could perceive manifest duty and through Holy
Obedience could become instruments in the realization of
the Kingdom of God.

Men and women were not always obedient to God.
Disobedience to Lucretia was sin, and sin was very real.
But in their natural state human beings were more apt to
discern the Truth. Social institutions, however, had
been developed which gave man power over women; the
slave-owner power over the slave, and power is
corrupting. It would be quite possible, Lucretia
thought for woman to be corrupted if she were given too
much power:

> It has sometimes been said that if
> women were associated with men in their
> efforts, there would be not as much
> immorality as now exists in Congress, for
> instance, and other places. But we
> ought, I think, to claim no more for
> woman than for man; we ought to put woman
> on a par with man, not invest her with
> power, or call for her superiority over
> her brother. If we do, she is just as

likely to become a tyrant as man is as
Catherine the Second. It is always
unsafe to invest man with power over his
fellow being. `Call no man master . . .'
is a true doctrine. But be sure there
would be a better rule than now; the
elements which belong to woman as such
and to man as such, would be beautifully
and harmoniously blended. It is to be
hoped that there would be less war,
injustice, and intolerance in the world
than now.[8]

To free woman from her degraded position was to
free man as well. "There is nothing of greater
importance to the well being of society at large--of man
as well as of woman--than the true and proper position
of women" Lucretia stated in a Discourse on Women,
delivered in Philadelphia in December of 1849, and
widely quoted for many years. Were woman to be allowed
to engage in many pursuits now closed to her, man would
be freed, "The energies of men need not then be wholly
devoted to the counting house and common business of
life, in order that women in fashionable society may be
supported in their daily promenades and nightly visits
to the theatre and the ballroom."

If woman were restored to her rightful place able
to develop her natural powers to the fullest, humanity
as a whole would benefit;

The question is often asked, `What
does woman want more than she enjoys?
What is she seeking to obtain? Of what

rights is she deprived? What privileges
are withheld from her?' I answer, she
asks nothing as a favor, but as a right
she wants to be acknowledged a moral,
responsible human being.9

Similarly, Lucretia Mott believed that the slaveholder was corrupted by power. The abolition of slavery
would free him and restore him to his natural self. It
was this belief that enabled her to make several extensive trips through the South, speaking not just to
Quakers, as John Woolman had done 100 years previously,
but to large public gatherings. Somehow her genuine
caring for the slaveholder, as well as her opposition to
the slave system registered, for she was heard with
respect, in one case "enchaining a normally restless
audience."

Understanding that the slaveholder and the
dominating husband were both victims of the system did
not mean in Lucretia Mott's view that either the slave
or the woman should be less militant in demanding
rights.

It was not until the slaveholder was
told `thou art the man' that a healthy
agitation was brought about. Woman is
told that the fault is in herself,in too
willingly submitting to her inferior
condition; but like the slave, she is
pressed down by laws in the making of
which she has had no voice, and crushed
by customs that have grown out of such
laws. She can not rise therefore, while

thus trampled in the dust. The oppressor
does not see himself in that light until
the oppressed cry for deliverance.

To the charge, made in the nineteenth century as in
the twentieth, that women were being too aggressive,
Lucretia answered that nothing much was accomplished by
quiet workers. "Give me noise, a real Boanerges." Once
more, her confidence that she was walking in the Light
made it possible for her to be entirely open, expressing
honest anger as well as caring love.

Lucretia's devotion to freedom of speech flowed
from the same religious base. Only if men and women
together earnestly sought the Truth, listening to one
another, would right principles emerge. At almost every
gathering she chaired, whether of women or of
abolitionists, she began with an admonition that
everyone speak forth. At the first anniversary meeting
of the New England Non-Resistance Society in September
1839, she argued that a reform society must be based on
the sacred right of opinion. She supported Garrison
when he refused to limit the articles published in his
paper, The Liberator, to the abolitionist cause alone,
but gave space to communitarians, anarchists, women's
rights advocates and many others who shared in the anti-
slavery crusade but were also involved in other social
reforms. And in the same vein, she defended the right
of radicals and extremists, such as Pearl Andrews and
Eliza Farnham, to speak at the women's rights
conventions. "Never fear for the cause," she wrote
critics, "we can `live down' all the harm that `free
love' or the maternity question can do us, only let our
faith not fail us . . "11 "Let each expound his own

creed, and then let us judge."12

Implicit in her concern for freedom of speech was Lucretia Mott's belief in continuous revelation. God did not speak only to the prophets and apostles of long ago; He speaks to men and women today. Sometimes His message is not heard because it is expressed by the poor, the outcast, the despised. Frequently, it is not heard because it is too upsetting to the power relationships on which men and women have based their lives. What is needed is a whole series of messiahs to stir men and women sufficiently so they would turn to the Light within.

Christ had been available to all men and women everywhere long before the birth of Jesus of Nazareth. He came as messiah through Jesus, but might he not come again and again? She liked to quote George Fox as saying, "Christ has come to teach his people himself," and William Channing's statement, "the messenger of the highest is now in our midst." By being wholly obedient, might one not aspire to be such a messiah? In a speech in New York in 1848, she referred to "The Jesus of the present age, on the Mount Zion of Peace, and the Jesus of the present age on the Mount Zion of Freedom."13 Denying human depravity, and therefore the necessity of a vicarious atonement, she believed Christianity to be an essentially simple religion:

It is lamentable that the simple and benign religion of Jesus be so encumbered with creeds and dogmas of sects. Its primitive beauty obscured by these gloomy appendages of man--the investigations of

honest enigmas checked by the cry to
heresy--infidelity . . . I long to see
obedience to manifest duty leading to
practical righteousness at the Christian
standards . . . the fruit of faith.[14]

It followed for Lucretia Mott that not all
Scripture was inspired. She knew the Bible as well as
most trained ministers of the gospel, but she felt free
to interpret it in light of her own religious
convictions, and to question those passages that seemed
to condone slavery, war or the subordination of women.

In regard to St. Paul's injunction that women keep
silent in the churches, she argued that this was meant
for a particular church group. Elsewhere he gave
explicit instructions on how they should appear when
speaking publicly. At any rate, many of the opposers of
women's rights who liked to quote Paul themselves
rejected his counsel, she argued. A bachelor, he
advised them not to marry![15] On a deeper vein, she
liked to quote Paul's statement that in Christ there is
neither male nor female.

In a day of evangelical revival, with its emphasis
on the atonement, Lucretia's views were considered
heretical. She did not help matters by frequently and
proudly calling herself a heretic, and refusing to
discuss theology, which she defined as "idle speculation
about the nature of God." It was the religious life,
the life of the Spirit that mattered to her. Over and
over again she stressed that it was "by their fruits you
shall know them." Men and women who did not share her
grounding in a daily experiential religious life found

her ideas unformed and exasperating. Edward Hicks, the sign painter, A Quietist but not a reformer, thought she was "wily and conniving" in creating a following. But when she preached in Quaker meeting the authenticity of her inspiration moved hearts and won converts on all sides.

Until the eve of the Civil War, Lucretia Mott was a thorn in the flesh of the more conservative wing of the Hicksites, and a person beyond the pale for the Orthodox. Thereafter a gradual shift began to take place. She was sometimes "amused" to see former opposers packing boxes for the contraband at Race Street Meeting, and gratified that the Orthodox also developed a Freedman's Association.

In 1877 her long struggle to achieve the complete equality of women in the business of Philadelphia Yearly Meeting (Hicksite) ended in success.[16] The Society, however, never supported her in her more worldly activities for women's rights, such as participation in the National Woman's Suffrage Association's convention in Philadelphia on July 4, 1876. Many individual Quaker women continued to draw their inspiration from her. At the time of her death, Susan B. Anthony said that for the past thirty years she had always felt she was right when she had the approval of Lucretia Mott. The spiritual leadership she gave the cause of 19th century feminism was recognized in 1923 when Alice Paul named the new Equal Rights Amendment the Lucretia Mott Amendment.

In other areas, the Society of Friends began to catch up with Lucretia Mott. As president of the ecumenical Pennsylvania Peace Society she had led the opposition to military training in the schools. Prodded by the Philadelphia Women's Yearly Meeting (Hicksite), under Lucretia Mott's influence, the Men's Yearly Meeting made a protest to the Board of Education in 1897.[17] Gradually the study of non-resistance retitled non-violence, once an anathema, has become acceptable to Friends.

In Indian affairs, Lucretia Mott always called for respect for the native American culture and religion, as well as land rights. This position, far in advance of her time, has slowly become part of much current Quaker work with the aborigines.

Today, American Friends are known to the public for their leadership in reforms associated with equality and peace. The groundwork for this reputation was laid in the nineteenth century by a few inspired individuals who, grounded in the basic principles of the Society of Friends, were in advance of their fellow Quakers in perceiving the call of humanity. There has always been a tension for latter day Children of the Light between living in conformity with society, and transforming society. Lucretia Mott was a transformer, willing to withstand the hostility and ostracism of many Friends for the sake of her sense of walking in the Light. Her influence as well as her spirit remain with us, I believe, today.

Notes

1"Sermon" 3-17-1850, Mott Mss., Friends Historical
Library, Swarthmore College.

2Proceedings of Woman's Rights Convention, Cleveland,
1853.

3Memoir, as prepared for Sarah Hale. Manuscript in
Mott collection, Friends Historical Library, Swarthmore
College.

4Autograph, Mott Mss. 1870. Friends Historical Library
Swarthmore College.

5Mott, Mss. Lucretia Mott to Mary P. Allen, 6-5-1877.

6Boston Public Library, Wendell Phillips to Elizabeth
Pease 3-9-1851.

7May 30, 1873, "Discourse" before the Free Religious
Association, Boston.

8Proceedings of the Woman's Rights Convention,
Cleveland, 1853.

9"Discourse on Women," 1849. Philadelphia.

10History of Woman's Suffrage, Stanton et al. Vol. I,
page 159.

11Columbia University, Lucretia Mott to Elizabeth Neall
Gay 12-9-58.

12Mott Mss. Lucretia Mott to Martha Coffin Wright 7-6-
1858.

13National Anti-Slavery Standard 5-18-1848.

14Library of Congress, Lucretia Mott to Elizabeth Cady
Stanton 3-23-1841.

[15]Woman's Rights Convention, Rochester 8-2-1848.

[16]In 1877 Philadelphia Yearly Meeting Hicksite adopted a minute proposed by a committee on discipline headed by Lucretia Mott: "That the discipline be so altered and amended that the women Friends shall have the same voice as men in all business meetings of the Society."

[17]Hicksite Yearly Meeting Minutes. May 14, 1897, page 280.

SUSAN B. ANTHONY
QUAKER EQUALITY WRIT LARGE
John H. Stoneburner

Susan B. Anthony was a radical reformer in the
temperance movement, abolitionism, and, particularly,
the women's rights movement. One should not let those
stiffly formal pictures of Anthony posing in her best
finery fool one. Susan Anthony spoke in public gatherings where women had not spoken before; she constantly
traveled on her own to lecture and to get petitions
signed, when to most people these activities seemed
unsafe and unwomanly; she was a sharp critic of many of
the dominant religious and political institutions and
movements of her time; she wore bloomers and wanted to
continue wearing them when others, such as Elizabeth
Cady Stanton, thought they were offending too many
people; she provoked and faced violent mobs as an
abolitionist speaker and organizer for William Lloyd
Garrison's American Anti-Slavery Society; she was the
publisher of The Revolution, the first newspaper which
provided a forum for the women's movement; she was an
early proponent of women being included in the labor
movement; she was arrested and tried for voting, so that
she could test whether or not women were included under
the Fourteenth Amendment; she was a key figure in a
disruption of part of the official program, of our
country's centennial celebration in Philadelphia; she
was the primary moving force in getting the first
massive volumes of the History of Woman Suffrage
written, published, and distributed, when the movement
was still very much a failure and when historians almost
universally agreed that women were not worthy subjects;

she gave the impetus to the formation of the International Women Suffrage Alliance; she was a major force in keeping the women's rights movement alive year after year. Time has smoothed the cutting edges of Susan B. Anthony's career in the American consciousness, but these are the acts of a radical social pioneer.[1]

The major thesis of this essay is that Quakerism was the first and the most important influence upon Anthony's radical understanding of human equality. There certainly were other important sources, especially the Enlightenment human rights philosophy of many of the abolitionists, but during the crucial early years of Anthony's women's rights reform activity the major religious, moral, and intellectual motivations and framework of her thought and actions came from the Quaker tradition. This thesis will be developed in three steps. The first will be a brief sketch of Anthony's life, with a special focus on its Quaker dimensions. The second step will be an exploration of some of the major features of the particular types or divisions of Quakerism in which she participated. The final step will be an interpretation of several of the speeches that Anthony wrote during the 1850s, which were strongly influenced by her Quakerism.

Quakerism in the Life of Susan B. Anthony

Susan Brownell Anthony was born in 1820 of a Quaker father and a Baptist mother on a farm outside Adams, Massachusetts. The Anthony family had been Quakers for at least six generations. Susan's father Daniel, had attended Nine Partner's School (later to become Oakwood

School). Daniel Anthony got into difficulty with the
Quaker meeting in Adams because he had married his wife
Lucy outside of meeting (Quakers were not supposed to
marry non-Quakers) and because he ran a store that sold
alcoholic beverages. He acknowledged his misconduct and
was retained in the Society of Friends. It was also in
Adams that Susan Anthony first encountered her father's
sister, Hannah Hoxie, who was a well-known Quaker
minister, that is, a person recognized by her fellow
Quakers as having a special gift for speaking in meetings of worship.[2]

When Susan was six, the Anthony family moved to
Battenville, New York, which is some thirty-five miles
north of Albany. Here she was educated in a district
school and in a home school established by her father.
Daniel Anthony joined Easton Friends Meeting, and in
1833 Susan was accepted into membership. At age
fifteen, she began to teach school to young children
during the summer. Her father, reflecting the typical
attitude of Quakers toward the education of their
daughters, thought that Susan "should be laying the
foundations for thy far greater usefulness."[3] At age
seventeen, Susan joined her sister Guelma as a student
at Deborah Moulson's Friends' Seminary near
Philadelphia.

In 1837, Daniel Anthony suffered serious economic
losses. To help the family financially, Susan left
school and began to teach at Eunice Kenyon's Friends'
Seminary in New Rochelle. During this period, Daniel
Anthony again showed his independence and was disowned
by Easton Meeting for allowing a group of youth, but not
his own children, to dance in his home, since he thought

that this was preferable to having them dance in the
local tavern.[4]

In a letter written during this period, Susan
already expressed the type of moral fervor and clarity
that was to characterize so much of her adult life. At
New Rochelle, she was outraged by the local Quaker
meeting's treatment of Afro-Americans, which did not
square with her own vision of Quaker morality.

> The people about here are anti-Abolition-
> ist and anti-everything else that's good.
> The Friends raised quite a fuss about a
> colored man sitting in the meeting-house,
> and some left on account of it. The man
> was rich, well-dressed and very polite,
> but still the pretended meek followers of
> Christ could not worship their God and
> have this sable companion with them.
> What a lack of Christianity is this!
> There are three colored girls here who
> have been in the habit of attending
> Friends' meeting where they have lived,
> but here they are not allowed to sit even
> on the back seat. One long-faced elder
> dusted off a seat in the gallery and told
> them to sit there.[5]

Another comment made in a letter written to Aaron
McLean, who was soon to marry her sister Guelma,
indicates that Quakerism was also having a shaping
influence upon her understanding of the role of women.

I attended Rose Street meeting in New York and heard the strongest sermon on "The Vices of the City," that has been preached in that house very lately. It was from Rachel Barker, of Dutchess county. I guess if you could hear her you would believe in a woman's preaching. What an absurd notion that women have not intellectual and moral faculties sufficient for anything but domestic concern!6

After the family moved because of bankruptcy to Rochester in 1846, Susan became the headmistress of the Female Department of Canajoharie Academy. Then having become dissatisfied with teaching in 1849, she returned to the family home, where she managed the small family farm while her father began to build his insurance business.

During the period Susan had been in Canajoharie, the Anthony household had become a center for liberal Quakers and other abolitionists. A group of Rochester Quakers had left the local Hicksite Friends meeting because of their abolitionist stance in 1848. For a brief period, they attended the Unitarian church, until a minister came who was also opposed to their abolitionist views on slavery. They returned to the Unitarian church after William Henry Channing was chosen as its minister. In the interval, these Quaker-Unitarians also aligned themselves with the Friends of Progress or Progressive Friends, who will be discussed below. They informally met at the Anthony home for Sunday dinner. Frederick Douglass, who by this time was a resident of Rochester, sometimes met with them. This group was visited by such leading abolitionists as William Lloyd Garrison, Parker Pillsbury, Wendell Phillips, and Samuel May, who were also among the chief early male supporters of women's rights. For instance, Samuel May, who was the Unitarian minister in nearby Syracuse and a good friend of Daniel Anthony, wrote a carefully reasoned defense of women's rights, The Rights and Conditions of Women, in 1846, two years before the first woman's rights convention in Seneca Falls.[7]

In 1853, Susan was accepted into the membership of Rochester Friends Meeting, although at the time she was apparently attending the Unitarian Church with her family and the other Quakers who were abolitionists. The reasons for this are an unsolved puzzle. She remained a member of this Quaker meeting the rest of her life, while apparently continuing to attend the Unitarian Church whenever she was in Rochester.[8] In any case, Susan had identified with a network of liberal Quakers, Unitarians, and abolitionists, who were critical of all the religious, social, and political institutions that were preventing the fulfillment of what they considered to be the God-given promise of America. During this period, she began to take the first critical steps toward her long career as a reformer. She had her family's strong support, especially that of her father. As she put it later in life: "Father encouraged my public work from the start."[9]

In the temperance, abolitionist, and women's rights movements, Susan Anthony found the public spaces to express her vision and understanding of Quaker values.

As shall be seen in more detail below, there was a direct link between her understanding of the essence of Quakerism and her commitment as a reformer. Given the fact that they had no political status, for women such as Anthony reform activity was virtually the only way to have a direct influence in the public sphere. There was a sense of satisfaction for Anthony in accepting a vocation which, in spite of its relative poverty, ridicule, and possible violence, allowed her to commit herself wholly to her religious ideals and which often provided a strong and supportive brotherhood and, especially, sisterhood of like-minded persons.

Anthony's exceptional organizational ability and political acumen quickly won the respect of the leaders in the various reform movements in which she participated. In the years prior to the Civil War, she first functioned as a temperance organizer, both because she was committed to its goals and because she was hesitant to respond in an unequivocal manner to Elizabeth Cady Stanton's appeal that she take up the work of women's rights. Prejudice against women in the temperance movement and her attendance at first women's rights conference in Syracuse in 1852 completed her conversion to the struggle for women's equality. Almost immediately, she became the prime mover in a series of state and national women's rights conventions. Then with her earlier commitment to abolitionism moving to the forefront--Abigail Kelley Foster, another Quaker, had tried to get her to join this cause as a speaker and organizer in 1851--Anthony became the principal New York agent for William Lloyd Garrison's American Anti-Slavery Society from 1854 until the Civil War. During the Civil War, in a major organizational accomplishment, she and

Elizabeth Cady Stanton initiated and developed the
Woman's Loyal National League, which gathered hundreds
of thousands of signatures on petitions calling for the
emancipation of the slaves. After the war, she went to
Kansas to be with her brothers, Daniel and Merritt (the
latter had been one of John Brown's followers in
Kansas). Repeated requests by some of her reform
colleagues then brought her back east.

Anthony faced many discouragements over the rest of
her life. Many abolitionists said after the war that it
was the "Negro's hour" and that it was senseless to work
for women's suffrage at the same time. The National
Woman's Suffrage Association, led by Stanton and
Anthony, existed in tension with the New England based
America Woman Suffrage Association, led by Lucy Stone.
Her newspaper, The Revolution, failed, leaving her with
a $10,000 debt that she paid off in six years by an
almost superhuman schedule of constant traveling and
speaking on the Lyceum tour. Women's suffrage was
defeated in a multitude of state campaigns. Through all
of these and more Anthony perserved with her hope and
determination intact. At age 74, she spoke in support
of suffrage in every one of the counties in New York
between January and April.[10] Two years later she spoke
three times a day in the California campaign. And
during much of her life, because she was the only single
woman among the first leaders of the woman's rights
movement, she was especially vulnerable to verbal and
written attacks from those who were anti-equal rights.
Large segments of the press, for much of her life,
predictably labeled her "a bitter, jealous, man-hating
spinster, whose advice to women was `startling and
disgusting.'"[11]

Of course, Susan Anthony was no saint. She had her share of weaknesses and shortcomings. She was often blunt, stubborn, and demanding. She made questionable decisions and compromises in her efforts to achieve the right to vote for women. Although she constantly gave speeches throughout her long career as a reformer, she always found speaking to be very psychologically difficult, but she also comments in her diary when someone has said she is a more effective speaker on behalf of women than someone like Lucy Stone.[12] She could often be self-effacing and sacrificial, but she also could be demanding and obstinate. The flaws should not be ignored, but they do not obscure her moral insights, fortitude, and courage.

As the years passed, Anthony became much more accepted by the American public. Wealthy and more influential women joined the suffrage movement. Focusing almost entirely upon trying to gain the right to vote for women, she believed that once women achieved this goal they would then have the leverage to make society more humane and just. Unlike Stanton, she tried to avoid getting involved with all other controversial issues, such as religion. In 1906, while she attended her last women's suffrage convention, a group of women scholars, including M. Carey Thomas, President of Bryn Mawr College and Quaker, gave moving speeches about her contributions to women's education in America. Forcing her failing body to speak, she left her famous message to the future with regard to women's rights: "Failure is impossible."[13]

Hicksite and Progressive Friends

In order to understand more adequately the types of Quakerism that provided the religious and moral milieu in which Anthony's convictions developed, it is necessary to take a brief glance at Hicksite Quakerism and the Progressive Friends. In 1827, a split took place in Philadelphia Yearly Meeting between what came to be known as the Orthodox and Hicksite Quakers. This division carried over the next year into New York Yearly Meeting. The reasons behind this division are very complex, including social and economic as well as theological factors.[14]

Influenced by evangelical English Friends and by the dominant evangelical Protestantism of early nineteenth century America, those Quakers who came to be called Orthodox placed, over a period of time, a heavier emphasis upon the authority of the Bible as God's full and unchanging revelation, the doctrine of original sin, the divinity of Jesus, the substitutionary view of the atonement, and the trinity. They also stressed such traditional Quaker affirmations as the importance of personal religious experience and moral living. For the Orthodox, true Quakerism was increasingly equated with holding these beliefs.

Hicksite Quakers were a heterogeneous response to this Orthodox development. Included among the Hicksites were both traditionists, who wanted to hold on to what they considered to be the original forms of Quaker thought and practice, and liberals, who were trying to come to terms with how Quakerism should relate to the modern world view and who were committed to making their Quaker values relevant in the larger world.

Elias Hicks, for whom this branch of Quakerism was named, fits into the traditionalist category. Born in 1746 and an old man when the split actually became formalized, Hicks was a Quaker Quietist, that is, he believed that the human mind and will should be stilled or silenced by the voice and will of God so that humans might more fully reflect His purposes. As a result, the Bible in his view was an important source of spiritual knowledge but it was not the sole or even primary rule of faith and practice--the "light" (of God) or "the divine teacher within" was the final authority. He also downgraded the importance of the divinity of Christ by affirming that it was much more significant for persons to be open to the presence of God in their own lives in the present than in dwelling upon a past historical event. And salvation comes not from imputed righteousness brought about by Christ's death upon the cross making "satisfaction" for human sin but by the self being obedient to the inward Saviour. Nor is there any original sin committed by Adam and Eve that causes a distortion of human nature: persons are capable of obeying God and of living righteous lives. Hicks also was convinced that historically Quakers had rejected all outward religious tests, such as creeds, because of the fear that they would become false substitutes for following God's will. In addition to these theological concerns, Hicks was deeply bothered by what he saw to be the increased unholiness among many of his fellow Quakers, which led to such actions as being willing to use or sell the products of slave labor, and to becoming too preoccupied with wealth. Believing that Friends should be largely separated from the world, he urged them not to join any organization or movements, such as abolitionism, which contained non-Quakers.15

In addition to traditionalists such as Hicks, there were religious liberals such as Benjamin Ferris, one of the editors of the journal The Berean, and Lucretia Mott. Influenced by streams of Enlightenment thought, Unitarianism, and Transcendentalism, these liberals had a strong belief that persons should be allowed to search freely and openly for religious truth. They believed in more democratic ways of governing the Society of Friends, which meant a reduction of the authority of Yearly Meeting and of the elders and ministers. Belief in the doctrines that were being stressed by the Orthodox were seen as outmoded and not in accord with the tests of modern reason. They affirmed the ongoing direct communion that can exist between the divine Spirit and the human spirit and the perfectibility of individuals and society. Rejecting separatism, these liberal Hicksites were dedicated to establishing a society here on earth that would be characterized by "brotherly love, freedom of conscience, and human equality."16

The Orthodox branch of Quakerism in the United States soon had another major split, this time between the Gurneyites and Wilburites. The Hicksites did not suffer any major divisions. However, in the late 1840s and the 1850s, there were small groups of quite liberal Hicksites who formed their own Yearly Meetings in Pennsylvania, Ohio, Indiana, Michigan, and New York that were variously known as the Friends of Progress, Congregational Friends, and Progressive Friends.17

Near Waterloo, New York, Progressive Friends established a Yearly Meeting in 1848. The Hicksite Genesee (New York) Yearly Meeting had been established in 1834 for Quakers in western New York, Canada, and later Michigan. In June 1848 some two hundred Friends met separately at Farmington while Genesee Yearly Meeting was in session because they were not in agreement with the Yearly Meeting. They addressed their grievances to it in a formal document, but, not surprisingly, Genesee did not respond affirmatively to the dissenting group's appeal. In a second Farmington conference, October 1848, these radical Quakers set up their own Progressive Yearly Meeting, founded on the "Basis of Religious Association," written by one of the Clerks, Thomas McClintock.[18]

There were four major reasons for the formation of Progressive Friends from the Hicksites. First of all, the Progressive Friends wanted to throw out the hierarchical authority and disciplinary power of the Yearly Meeting and return to what they saw to be the liberty and equality of early Quakerism.[19] The second cause was difference over doctrine and religious toleration. The Hicksites in Philadelphia, to emphasize that it was not developing a new type of Quakerism after its split from the Orthodox, continued to affirm that a person could be disowned who denied "the authenticity of the Holy Scriptures and the divinity of Christ."[20] New York Hicksites made similar doctrinal affirmations. In fact, doctrinal tolerance came to be practiced among the Hicksites through the efforts of persons such as Lucretia Mott, who never joined the Progressive Friends but attended many of their meetings and shared many of their views. Nevertheless, Progressive Quakers were influenced by such new intellectual and religious currents as Transcendentalism, Spiritualism, and by a strong dislike for evangelical theology in all denominations. They wanted the intellectual freedom to modernize or progress beyond traditional Christian and Quaker theological formulations.

The third reason, and probably the underlying one, was the issue of abolition.[21] After a century of struggle, Friends had wholly rid themselves of slavery and were firmly grounded by tradition and conviction as anti-slavery. During the first three decades of the nineteenth century, they practiced their rejection of slavery most frequently by using moral persuasion, which it was thought would gradually and peacefully bring about change. Less frequently, they abstained from the use of products made by slave labor. Infrequently, they were involved in the underground railroad. However, a small but deeply committed number of Friends also joined and became leaders in the abolitionist movement. Most of the Hicksite Friends, as well as the Orthodox, could not accept the abolitionists, concerned as they were about the non-Quakers in the abolitionist cause, the mobs, building burnings, and violence that seemed to follow the abolitionists, and threaten national unity and trade. (Quaker abolitionists believed that the economic reason was primary for the anti-abolitionist Quakers.) Many of the abolitionists either were disowned or left the Society of Friends because they believed that the only right stand for Quakerism was full participation in the anti-slavery crusade. One of the consequences of the official Hicksite position was that local Meeting houses could not be used for abolitionist gatherings. Progressive Friends were abolitionists and not gradualists; they thought that they were being asked to compromise and be patient with the horrible reality of slavery.[22]

A fourth reason for the formation of Progressive Friends was evidently the struggle to achieve equality for women, not only among Quakers but in the larger society. The Progressive Friends' document of grievances addressed to Genesee Yearly Meeting was signed by the two Clerks, Thomas McClintock and Rhoda DeGarmo.[23] A month later the wife of Thomas McClintock, Mary Ann McClintock, met with three other Quaker women-- Lucretia Mott, Martha C. Wright (Lucretia's sister), and Jane C. Hunt--and with Elizabeth Cady Stanton, at the Hunt home to draft the call for the first women's rights convention. Both McClintocks were among those who signed the Seneca Falls Declaration. When a continuation of the convention at Seneca Falls was held two weeks later in Rochester, Rhoda DeGarmo was one of the leaders and along with Amy Post, another Quaker, insisted, against the initial objections of Lucretia Mott, Elizabeth Cady Stanton, and Mary Ann McClintock, that a woman should be president of the convention. The view of DeGarmo and Post prevailed: Abigail Bush, still another Quaker woman, presided. Daniel and Lucy Anthony, as well as Susan's sister Mary, also signed the Seneca Falls Declaration at the Rochester convention.[24]

The "Basis" which founded the Progressive Yearly Meeting implicitly and explicitly embodied constructive responses to each of these four concerns over which they split. It stressed that the object of religious association was "the promotion of Righteousness--of practical goodness--love to God and man--on the part of every member composing the association, and in the world at large."25 The document also states that there should be freedom to pursue the truth, that each individual should answer only to the Divine Light in his or her own conscience, and that there is a progressive unfolding of truth and duty in history.26 With regards to governance, local Meetings were to govern their own affairs. Yearly Meeting only was to exist for advice and counsel and for the "promotion of the great interest of humanity--everything that concern man at large-- including the existing evils of the day. . . ."27 Meetings of Ministers and Elders were to be discontinued. The equality of women was to be recognized in a concrete way by doing away with the traditional practice of having separate Meetings for Business for men and women and instead having Meetings in which both sexes participated together.28

During the next few years, such people as William Lloyd Garrison, Gerrit Smith, Sojourner Truth, Frederick Douglass, and Elizabeth Cady Stanton spoke at Waterloo. Given the liberal principles of the Progressive Friends, it is not surprising that non-Quakers were invited to join the association. Nor is it surprising that Anthony regularly attended the Progressive Friends Yearly Meetings at Waterloo, and became the clerk of the Meeting, along with James Truman, in 1857. During that particular year, the Meeting approved Testimonies which addressed the issue of slavery, by recommending that the North separate itself from the South and that each individual should ask him or herself whether he or she could continue to support a government that was presently supporting "a covenant with death," and the issue of war, by holding that it is irreconcilable with a religion of love. It also wrote Testimonies on the subjects of intemperance, tobacco, spiritualism, authority, and inspiration. Another one affirmed co-education, because "the true and harmonious development of the race demands that the sexes be associated together in every department of life. . . ."[29] Finally, the gathering examined the status of marriage, including hearing and discussing a radical paper by Elizabeth Cady Stanton. It was resolved that the various economic, legal, and psychological abuses of marriage should be exposed and that women should be rescued from these types of oppression.[30] While the Progressive Friends may have been more radical on a few issues, such as in its interest in spiritualism and its determination not to compromise its abolitionism, than the liberals among the Hicksites, overall there was a considerable amount of agreement between the two types of Quakerism.

Most Waterloo Progressive Friends were disowned in 1849 by Genesee Yearly Meeting, but for reasons that are unclear, Anthony was not among those removed.[31] After the Waterloo Meeting came to an end at the 1857 session, she would often attend the annual meeting of Longwood Progressive Friends at Kennet Square outside of Philadelphia.

Quakerism and the Early Speeches of Anthony

The final step in uncovering the relationship between the Quakerism of the liberal Hicksites and the Progressive Friends and the career of Anthony is to explore several of the speeches that she wrote and delivered in the 1850s. Anthony, of course, had no formal training as a religious thinker. In addition, she did not like to write, and her speeches and lectures were never prepared for publication. Yet they provide an invaluable means for more adequately understanding her convictions and actions. A clear religious point of view comes out in the various speeches that she wrote in the first years that she was a reformer.

Her religion was a liberal form of Christianity, practical and civic. She explicitly stated that Christians should quit wasting energy debating theological issues, which should be left up to the conscience of the individual, and move on to what Christianity is really about, namely, the triumph of human goodness.

> Friends, the time has fully come for us to cease to waste all our precious hours in discussing questions of mystical theology and speculative faith and adopt the plain practical principles, taught by Jesus of Nazareth.[32]

Or to give another example: "The only unmistakable evidence of a man's belief in the doctrines taught by Christ, is to be found in the every day acts of his life."[33]

Anthony's view of God was that He is the source of the eternal laws of truth and goodness. Although she does not reflect in detail about the matter--in part because of her skepticism mentioned above about the fruitless quality of theological debate--she was apparently denying belief in a God who directly intervenes in the course of human affairs. The

regeneration or redemption of society takes place not by
God's supernatural acts but by human deeds that are in
accord with God's truth.

> Yes, friends we ourselves are the
> instruments by means of which God answers
> our prayers--and unphilosophical indeed
> are they who ask God to banish from our
> land the three great National scourges of
> War, Slavery, and Intemperance.[34]

Drawing upon the imagery of Matthew 25, she stated that
it is precisely those that the churches label infidels,
because they declare the Bible is written only by
humans, that are found doing the works of
righteousness.[35]

   Although God does not act in supernatural ways, He
is still present within the human soul, and humans, who
are not disabled by the inheritance of original sin,
have the ability to receive and enact new and more
adequate understandings of the truth.

> The soul that would be a true medium of
> God's Sunlight must keep itself unstained
> by cowardice,--must possess itself of the
> spirit of heroism that we dare to follow
> whenever and wherever it shall direct. .
> . . When God gives to any soul a new
> development of truth, it is not his to
> keep, but to give to the world. It is
> not his privilege to choose his time,
> even, for now is the only speck of time
> he can call his own. . . . What solemn

> folly, then, to talk of waiting for the
> world to get ready to receive a truth
> before giving it . . . . Was the world
> prepared to receive the great truths
> uttered 1800 years ago by Jesus of
> Nazareth? Certainly not![36]

Jesus was significant, not because he was uniquely divine, but because he was the highest fulfillment of human potential. And for Anthony, Jesus was a prophet and agitator against injustice rather than a superficial peacemaker. Out of this kind of thinking she could call William Lloyd Garrison, who was widely condemned by church leaders as a heretic, "the most Christlike man I ever knew."[37] Similarly, the true people of God are those who courageously strive to transform the injustices of the world. By overcoming "the selfish impulse" those who respond to the truth in their consciences break the silence which most of the so-called Christians perpetuate and speak out boldly on behalf of constructive change.[38] The "light of truth" calls humanity to new reforms.

In her early years as a reformer, Anthony applied this religious viewpoint to each of her primary areas of concern, temperance, women's rights, and abolitionism. Since the second of these became the primary focus for her reform activity, it will be useful to explore how Anthony drew in significant ways upon her religious stance in this area. She began with the above-mentioned claim that every individual has a God-given power that is capable of growth and development.

The hope of the world's realization of my

ideal of the true woman must be based on
the immutable principle that there is
indwelling in every human being
irrespective of color, or sex, or
condition, the indestructable, though
perchance from unfortunate circumstances
of birth and surrounding, scarcely
recognizable germ of immortal life,
susceptible of unlimited culture, growth
and development. This undying life germ
. . . this from everlasting to
everlasting God in the soul, is the grand
distinguishing characteristic, that
separates man from all other living,
breathing, acting existences.39

In her mind, the present was ripe with the possibility
of moving to the true type of womanhood.

What was usually considered to be the fixed nature
of women by the advocates of the cult of true womanhood,
who supported an ideology which said women are
essentially pure, submissive, and domestic, was not the
result of God's created order but of false education and
misguided convention.

If to educate woman side by side with
man, to discipline her mind equally with
his in the study of Logic, the
Languages, and Mathematics,--Theology,
Law, and Medicine, does produce a change
in what have hitherto been thought the
essential elements of her womanhood,--if
she thereby becomes strong like the oak,

> capable of intense intellectual efforts
> in their results like those of men . . .
> what then is the inference to be drawn?
> Why of course no other than that the
> present difference is not of God's
> ordaining.[40]

To illustrate her point, Anthony states that women of accomplishment, such as Elizabeth Blackwell and Antoinette Brown, were also lovely and modest women. She wrote about women in the Society of Friends:

> Are the Quaker women, who, ever since the
> organization of that religious society,
> have not only been eligible to the
> offices of Minister and Elder, but have
> quite as frequently occupied them, and
> quite as honorably discharged the duties
> pertaining to their manner, any less
> Christian in their daily lives, than are
> the women of other religious societies,
> who have ever been taught that "Woman
> should keep silence in the Church and ask
> their husbands at home."[41]

From Anthony's angle of vision, women should share with men in developing their own and society's intellectual and moral potential, while maintaining some traditional feminine qualities.

Anthony also attacked the cult of true womanhood ideology from several other perspectives. She pointed out that there were large numbers of women who do not have the luxury of being economically dependent upon a

husband, that is, unmarried women and widows. Among
married women there are, in addition, those who would
have liked to be independent--those "who sigh over
Woman's lot, that of remaining useless members of
society. . . ."42 Then there are the poor urban working
women who by the thousands "stitched their lives away"
and made almost nothing in terms of wages. On behalf of
these women laborers, Anthony consistently argued for
equal pay for equal work and for the opening of the
traditional male trades and professions to women.
Finally, Anthony states that, given the lack of genuine
opportunity to make a decent living, it was not surprising that some women became prostitutes. What they
needed, she held, was not charity but profitable work.

Why is it that persons continue to perpetuate the
notion of "women's sphere?" Why, for example, do girls
and young women as they study seldom have high goals set
before them? Why is it that women are not sensitive to
their higher God-given call that beckons them to become
active shapers of history? In answer to these questions
she asked herself, Anthony answered that governments and
religion have largely been responsible. For instance,
the latter has perpetuated a misunderstanding of
marriage which places it above what are in fact higher
ends, such as the development of the individual self and
a more just society. "See her there, in every relation
in life, even in so called `Christian homes' of wealth
and splendor, see her a helpless dependent. Though
petted and loved, aye, worshipped after the world's
fashion, a humiliated being--a captive still, though in
a golden cage."43 Anthony struggled to articulate
alternatives. She reassured her audiences that she did
not mean that in a reformed understanding of marriage a

wife would no longer be recognizable as a wife.

> She will be the genial companion of man--
> the faithful trusting wife,--the cheerful
> loving mother. She will even sew on
> buttons and cook good healthful dinners.
> She will intelligently, and wisely, and
> affectionately fill all of the kindly
> offices of the true home--earth's highest
> and holiest soul benefactions--just as
> the true man will do, and then like him,
> will do something more.44

Her model for the "something more" in marriage likely
came from her experiences with couples like James and
Lucretia Mott who combined the raising of a family,
domestic duties, and effective involvement in the public
sphere.

In these speeches there were intimations of what
today would be called a type of feminist theology.
There was some sensitivity about sexist language. For
instance, Anthony expressed skepticism about the claim
of male ministers and lecturers that when they used the
term "men" it included "women" for them. Moreover, she
observed that when she, or any religiously earnest woman
of intelligence, listens to the leading clergy and
speakers, she recognizes that they draw upon the
masculine and not the feminine experience. Using
notions about direct non-mediated experience of God and
continuing revelation that directly reflect her
Quakerism, she writes:

> She [the true woman] will hear the word

of the Lord, spoken to the ancient
prophet, "stand upon thy feet and I will
speak to thee." And obeying the word,
she will look to no man or mediator or
interpreter for she like him, if he
comply with the requisition, holds direct
communion with the All-Father.45

Although she used a sexist metaphor, "All-Father," in
speaking about God, she has articulated the basis for an
equalitarian feminist way of religious thinking, that
is, by beginning with the actual religious experience of
women.

There is a fundamental harmony between the
religious and moral views that Anthony wrote in her
speeches during the 1850s and the views of the liberal
wing of the Hicksites and convictions of the Progressive
Friends. In all three one finds a rejection of orthodox
interpretations of the authority of Scripture, a God
who acts in supernatural ways, the unique divinity of
Jesus, the saving value of Jesus' death upon the cross,
original sin, and the importance of theological
doctrines. Likewise all three affirmed freedom in
searching for a more adequate understanding of God's
truth, direct experience of God, continuing revelation,
Christianity essentially as a type of prophetic
morality, belief in human progress, Jesus as a human
model, God as a rational, moral, and loving reality,
openness to other liberal or progressive religions and
social movements, commitment to human equality, and the
strongly held conviction that authentic values should
not lead to any type of separatism among their

upholders but to the transformation of the total
society.

   After the early 1860s, Anthony, for the large
part, quit writing her speeches and began simply to use
notes. From what evidence is available, these lectures
were much more secular in their language and orientation
than the ones that she wrote earlier in her life. This
raises the question: Did Anthony significantly change
in terms of her religious standpoint?   Elizabeth Cady
Stanton wrote that Anthony became an agnostic.[46] This
seems extremely doubtful.   Except when she visited
Stanton, Anthony continued to attend church services all
of her life, and there are statements that she made in
the latter part of her career that explicitly affirmed,
though in less detail, the same type of liberal Quaker
convictions that she drew so strongly upon during the
years that this essay has focused upon.   Towards the end
of her life, she also mentioned at least twice that she
was still a Quaker.[47] Rather than describing her as an
agnostic or a secular reformer, it is more accurate to
say that reform had become the essence of Anthony's
religion. Over the years, reform had become for her the
suffrage movement, because she, wrongly, thought that
given the necessary political leverage women would
reform other areas of society. If reform had become her
faith, it was certainly consistent with the kind of
Quakerism that was so influential upon her childhood and
youth, and then upon that critical period during her
early thirties when she made the crucial decisions about
her basic life direction and identity. As a radical
social reformer Susan B. Anthony was shaped most fundamentally by liberal Quakerism which was striving, like
her, to have Quaker equality writ large in the outside
world.

Notes

1On the life of Susan B. Anthony see Katherine Anthony, Susan B. Anthony (Garden City: Doubleday, 1954); Ida H. Harper, The Life and Work of Susan B. Anthony (Indianapolis: Bowen-Merrill, 3 vol., 1898-1908); Alma Lutz, Susan B. Anthony (Boston: Beacon, 1958).

2Anthony, Susan B. Anthony, pp. 15-16.

3Harper, The Life and Work of Susan B. Anthony, Vol. 1, p. 24.

4Ibid., Vol. 1, p. 37.

5Ibid., Vol. 1, p. 39.

6Ibid., Vol. 1, p. 40.

7Anthony, Susan B. Anthony, pp. 87 and 97; Lutz, Susan B. Anthony, pp. 23-24.

8Anthony, Susan B. Anthony, pp. 113-14.

9Harper, The Life and Work of Susan B. Anthony, Vol. 1, p. 224.

10Ibid., pp. 759 and 876.

11Blanche Glassman Hersh, The Slavery of Sex (Urbana: University of Illinois, 1978), p. 110.

12Susan B. Anthony, Diary, Feb. 13, 1871, Susan B. Anthony Papers, Library of Congress.

13Lutz, Susan B. Anthony, p. 308.

14See Robert W. Doherty, The Hicksite Separation (New Brunswick: Rutgers University, 1967); Elbert Russell, The History of Quakerism (New York: MacMillan, 1942), pp. 280-328. Although not used in this essay, an insightful analysis on the Hicksite-Orthodox split is found in: Jerry Frost, "Years of Crisis and Separation: Philadelphia Yearly Meeting 1790-1860" in Friends in the Delaware Valley, ed. John M. Moore (Haverford: Friends Historical Association, 1981).

[15]See Elias Hicks, A Series of Extemporaneous Discourses (Philadelphia: Joseph and Edward Parker, 1825). The best detailed treatment of Hicks' life and thought is Bliss Forbush, Elias Hicks, Quaker Liberal (New York: Columbia University, 1956).

[16]Doherty, The Hicksite Separation, p. 86. Also see Lucretia Mott: Her Complete Speeches and Sermons, ed. Dana Greene (New York: E. Mellon, 1980).

[17]See A. Day Bradley, "Progressive Friends in Michigan and New York" in Quaker History 52 (1963), pp. 95-103; Allen C. Thomas, "Congregational or Progressive Friends, A Forgotten Episode in Quaker History" in Bulletin of Friends' Historical Society (1920),pp. 21-31; Albert J. Wahl, "The Progressive Friends of Longwood, Bulletin of Friends' Historical Society XLII (1953), pp. 13-32.

[18]Bradley, "Progressive Friends in Michigan and New York," p. 98.

[19]Wahl, "The Progressive Friends of Longwood,", p. 14.

[20]Russell, The History of Quakerism, pp. 324-25.

[21]Ibid., p. 371.

[22]For Quaker responses to slavery see Thomas Drake, Quakers and Slavery (New Haven: Yale University, 1950).

[23]Bradley, "Progressive Friends in Michigan and New York," p. 98.

[24]"Basis of Religious Association, 1848." In the Appendix of the Proceedings of the Yearly Meeting of Congregational Friends, held at Waterloo, New York, 1848 (Auburn: Oliphant's Press, 1849), p. 40.

^{26}Ibid.

^{27}Ibid., p. 42.

^{28}Ibid.

^{29}Proceedings of the Yearly Meeting of Congregational Friends, held at Waterloo, New York, 1857 (Rochester: Steam Press of Curtis, Butts & Co., 1857), p. 17.

^{30}Ibid., p. 20.

^{31}Bradley, "Progressive Friends in Michigan and New York," pp. 99-100.

^{32}Susan B. Anthony, "The Church and the Liquor Traffic," 1852, Library of Congress, Susan B. Anthony Papers.

^{33}Ibid.

^{34}Ibid.

^{35}Ibid.

^{36}Susan B. Anthony, "Expediency," 1853, Library of Congress, Susan B. Anthony Papers.

^{37}Quoted in Harper, The Life and Work of Susan B. Anthony, Vol. 1, p. 17.

^{38}Anthony, "The Church and the Liquor Traffic."

^{39}Susan B. Anthony, "The True Woman," 1857, Susan B. Anthony Papers, Schlesinger Library, Radcliffe College.

^{40}Susan B. Anthony, "Woman's Rights," 1854, Susan B. Anthony Papers, Schlesinger Library, Radcliffe College.

^{41}Ibid.

^{42}Ibid.

[43]Anthony, "The True Woman."

[44]Ibid.

[45]Ibid.

[46]Elizabeth Cady Stanton, Eighty Years and More (New York: Schocken, 1898 and 1971), p. 161.

[47]Harper, The Life and Work of Susan B. Anthony, Vol. 2, pp. 631 and 793; Vol. 3, p. 1265; Anthony, Susan B. Anthony, p. vii. For an interpretation, which I read after this essay was written, that stresses the secular side of Anthony's position, see the commentary by Ellen Carol DuBois in Elizabeth Cady Stanton, Susan B. Anthony, Correspondence, Writings, Speeches, ed. Ellen Carol DuBois (New York: Schocken, 1981).

THE CONTRIBUTION OF
SEVEN QUAKER WOMEN TO EDUCATION
Helen G. Hole and Carol Stoneburner

This paper will consider the contribution of seven Quaker women to education, and suggest the fact that their Quaker involvement was significant in the development of this contribution. Four of them were active Quakers, "concerned Friends," as the Quakers phrase it, who participated fully in the institutional activity of their meetings; the other three, who eventually separated from Friends, were nevertheless profoundly influenced by their Quaker upbringing.

The first Martha Tyson was important in the development of the movement which resulted in the founding of Swarthmore College.

Martha Tyson
1795-1873

Martha Ellicott Tyson,[1] the daughter of Quaker parents, was born in Ellicott city, near Baltimore, and lived in or near Baltimore all her life. After attending a small elementary school taught by a Friend, Joel Wright, she received no further formal education, but she must have had good tutors; we know that she read French easily and that she was considered a cultivated woman. In later life she knew Schliemann, the archaeologist, and other scientists and scholars.

At the age of twenty, she married Nathan Tyson, a son of the eminent Quaker merchant and philanthropist, Elisha Tyson. We are fortunate enough to know a little about their wedding. Martha wore a fine white mull dress with a low neck, puffed short sleeves, and a narrow skirt which fell to her ankles. Over this a white satin cape with a pleated frill was crossed in front and tied in back. Her bonnet and shoes were of white satin; her gloves of white kid. The groom wore white satin breeches, a white silk vest, a dark claret-colored coat, long white silk stockings tied at the knees with white satin bows, and black shoes. We can visualize them standing before their Meeting, saying their vows to each other in Quaker fashion without benefit of preacher:

> "I, Nathan Tyson, take thee, Martha Ellicott, to be my wedded wofe . . ."

and,

> "I Martha Ellicott, take thee, Nathan Tyson, to be my wedded husband . . ."

each promising, with divine assistance, to be faithful and loving. There was nothing said of the husband's endowing his wife, and nothing of his authority over her. They simply took each other in the presence of God, and their friends--a symbol of the Friends' attitude toward the relationship of the sexes. The reading of the certificate, to be later signed by those present, legalized the proceedings. A Meeting for worship followed.

The Tysons moved into their beautiful and gracious home where they lived out their wedded lives with the exception of twelve years (1838-50) spent in Hartford County, Maryland. Their family grew to twelve children, of whom eight lived past middle age. Their home was a center of hospitality and meetings for Quaker concerns. Some notion of the scale of the hospitality can be inferred from the fact that one of the decisive moves in the founding of Swarthmore was a meeting held in 1860 at the Tyson's home which included not only sixty members of the Yearly Meeting but also a number of visiting Friends representing New York and Philadelphia Yearly Meetings. A tea-supper was served to this large group.

Martha Tyson had many Quaker interests. She was active in her home Monthly Meeting (the smallest Quaker business unit), in the larger Quarterly Meeting, and in her Yearly Meeting, and served on committees on all of these levels. She was a minister and an elder in Baltimore Yearly Meeting; in this way her spiritual gifts were overtly recognized. After the division of Friends in 1827, she and most of her relatives and friends joined the Hicksite branch, and she remained a Hicksite Friend all of her life.

Outstanding among her interests was the appropriate education of Quaker children. In forwarding this concern, she worked through committees, often though not always, as Clerk (we would say Chairperson). Decisions in the committees were reached by consensus, and the labor of first achieving this consensus and then reporting the recommendation to a higher body where, in turn, a committee must be appointed and the process repeated, was a laborious one, but she was deeply committed and unsparing in her efforts. As a result of her concern, in 1847 she became active on the Committee of the Women's Meeting of Baltimore Yearly Meeting (at this time men and women met in separate business meetings) to promote education throughout the Meeting membership and to distribute books. In 1848, a letter from the Women's Meeting in Baltimore to Philadelphia Year Meeting, and signed by Martha Tyson, told of the appointment of a joint Committee on Education (both men and women). In 1852, a report of this joint Committee, signed by Lloyd Morris and Martha Tyson, brought the concern for the education of Friends forcibly to the attention of Friends at large. From this time on, whenever there is a report on this subject from a Quarterly Meeting or the Yearly Meeting, Martha Tyson's name appears as one of the signers. Benjamin Hallowell, a distinguished educator, and Martha Tyson became the most influential Friends with this concern. The researches of the Committee showed (1853) that out of 1,337 Yearly Meeting children of school age only 336 attended Friends schools. The following year, the subject of establishing a Boarding School was broached. This seemed desirable in part because Westtown (founded in 1799) and Moses Brown (1794), both well established schools with a long tradition, were no longer acceptable to Hicksite Friends, nor were the latter's children welcome there. Later the project was broadened to become a college. Though Swarthmore began by providing both secondary and college-level work, it did not become exclusively a college until 1892, twenty-three years after its opening. A Quaker college was needed by Hicksite Friends, since Haverford was in the hands of the Orthodox.

In 1850, the concern to create Swarthmore as a preparatory school and as a college became a joint project of Baltimore and Philadelphia Yearly Meetings. Lucretia Mott, noted preacher, abolitionist, advocate of the rights of Native Americans and women and an organizer of the Peace Movement, had played a role similar to Martha Tyson in Philadelphia Yearly Meeting.

It is obvious that from that time on the two women worked closely together. If it were not an un-Quakerly metaphor, we might say that their movements formed a kind of ballet in which first one and then the other steps out to forward the concern.

In 1858, Lucretia Mott attended Baltimore Yearly Meeting, where she presented her educational concern and the attention it was receiving in Philadelphia Yearly Meeting. We may imagine Lucretia and Martha conferring together at this time and laying further plans. The next year Martha, in turn, traveled to Philadelphia and New York Yearly Meetings in the founding of a school.

The next year, 1860, was an eventful one. There was an epistle from the Philadelphia Women's Meeting to the Women's Meeting in New York endeavoring to enlist their sympathy and support. A four-column appeal by Martha Tyson in the Intelligencer (7 mo. 28) set the subject squarely before Friends. Not long after this occurred, the gathering at the Tyson's home, referred to earlier, of sixty Baltimore Friends and a number of representatives from New York and Philadelphia,was followed by a meeting in the Meeting House the next day. In October a conference was held in Philadelphia, at which we know both James and Lucretia Mott were present, and in the same month a similar meeting was held in New York, attended by both Martha Tyson and James Mott. It was in these meetings that the foundation for Swarthmore was laid.

It is not the intention of the writer to follow step-by-step the events down to the opening of the College in 1869, nine years later. There were moments of deep discouragement as a result of the Civil War and a prolonged period of unemployment when financial backing seemed almost unobtainable. It is said that when the possibility of abandoning the whole scheme was being debated at a meeting, a small voice--a woman's-- was heard to say, "Persevere!" Probably this was Lucretia Mott's comment, although another version, placing the event in another meeting, says it was Martha Tyson's. At any rate, from then on the project went forward. In the summer and autumn of 1862, Lucretia had a minute authorizing her to visit Quarterly Meetings in the Philadelphia area. A committee for the school was appointed: both James and Lucretia Mott served on it, and we know that Martha Tyson attended some of its meetings. A constitution was set up and a Board appointed which, astonishing for that day, had on its sixteen members of each sex. The College was to be co-educational. A name was found and a site selected. Martha Tyson and Benjamin Hollowell contributed a series of counsels through articles in the Intelligencer.

In 1868, James Mott died at the age of eighty. Lucretia was then seventy-five; she was to live twelve more years. The following year, 1869, she was present at the inauguration of Swarthmore, and made a few "remarks." She hoped, she said, that the institution would never degenerate into a mere sectarian school; it should be free of theological bias and should prepare those who attended it to receive good wherever they found it. "The Voice of Truth is so plain and so universally applicable that all may hear it in their own tongue in which they were born," she said. She referred to the skepticism which may grow from the study of science when unaccompanied by religious faith, and hoped this would not be the case here.

The next day in the presence of 800 people she, assisted by her son, Thomas Mott, planted on the grounds two oaks which had been raised from seed by James Mott.

Martha Tyson was unable to attend the inauguration, but we know that she visited the college later. It is sad to note that she, unlike Lucretia Mott, did not end her association with it on a liberal note. She died at the age of seventy-eight, and towards the end she expressed anxiety about the complete co-educational freedom allowed there. This seems strangely out of character for a woman whose ideas had always been liberal, but probably we should make allowances for her age and state of health.

It should be noted that Swarthmore was most unusual, not only in having both men and women on its Board and in being co-educational, but also in offering a complete education for women. A few places like Oberlin and Earlham were doing this, but they were so few that Swarthmore felt that it was almost alone.

Martha Tyson's concern for education can best be summarized by an article she wrote for the Hicksite periodical, the <u>Intelligencer</u>, in 1860.2

> I consider a human soul without
> education like marble in a quarry, which
> shows none of its inherent beauties until
> the skill of the polisher fetches out the
> colors, makes the surface shine, and
> discovers every ornamental cloud, spot
> and vein which runs through the body of
> it. Education, after the same manner,
> when it works on a noble mind, draws out
> to view every latent virtue and
> perfection, which without such helps are
> never able to make their appearance.
> What sculpture is to the block of marble,
> education is to the human soul.

Prudence Crandall
1803 - 1890

In comparison with Martha Tyson and Lucretia Mott, Prudence Crandall is a minor figure. Her contribution was largely concentrated around the years 1831-33 when she conducted a school for girls in Canterbury, Connecticut.[3] This contribution was summarized by Ellen Larned, a nineteenth century historian of the county in which the school was located: "Miss Crandall did not succeed in educating many colored girls, but she educated the people of Windham County."[4]

Prudence came of a Quaker family, was born in Rhode Island, and moved with her parents to Connecticut. She was educated at Moses Brown, then known as "Friends

Boarding School." She afterwards became a school-mistress in Plainfield, Connecticut, near Canterbury,the site of her future school. She was handsome, though not beautiful, and her face showed firmness of character, a firmness which was later revealed in her actions. In old age, she told a visiting journalist, "My whole life has-been one of opposition,"[5] and certainly this was true of that period of it with which we are acquainted.

In 1831, backed by some prominent and affluent citizens of Canterbury and the surrounding area, who evidently respected her and thought her qualified, she opened a school for young ladies. It was a day school but there were also some girls who came from a distance whom she took as boarders. The rate for them was $25.00 a quarter, including board, washing, and tuition.

All apparently went well until, in the second year of the school, she enrolled a respectable black girl, Sarah Harris, as a day student. She was a member of the neighboring church. The town reacted unfavorably to this move, and Prudence soon realized that she had stirred up a hornet's nest. Community pressure was applied to her by parents, financial backers, and the community at large to drop the girl from the school. This Prudence refused to do, and the opposition increased. The firmness of her character now became evident. When Daniel Frost, one of her backers, pointed out to her that these leveling principles might result in inter-marriage, her answer was: "Moses had a black wife!"

She consulted William Lloyd Garrison, the abolitionist and editor, and others and when it became evident that the school could not continue in its present form another year, she inserted a small advertisement in The Liberator for March 2, 1833, announcing the opening of a "High School for Young Colored Ladies and Misses."

The community was now up in arms, and the school was harassed. No stores would sell it provisions. When pupils and teachers took walks for exercise, chicken heads, dead cats and refuse were thrown at them. Windows were broken, and manure was dropped in the well; for a time, the only water available was brought by Prudence's father from his nearby farm. The final act of vandalism was an attempt to set fire to the house.

In the meantime, the citizens of Canterbury, by petitioning the State Legislature, succeeded in getting a statute passed against anyone who boarded or sheltered colored persons who were not Connecticut residents. A month later, June 27, 1833, Prudence Crandall, twenty-nine years old, Quaker school-mistress, was arrested by the Sheriff because, "with force and arms," she had willfully and knowingly harboured and boarded certain colored persons who were not inhabitants of any town in the State. "With force and arms" was the legal jargon for "with conscious and obstinate determination."

Her friends, who included Samuel May, a Unitarian minister and prominent abolitionist who lived six miles away, hurried to her. She and they agreed that bail should not be put up for her at first, since she was to be imprisoned on a matter of principle; she was locked for the night in a cell last occupied by a murderer. Permission was, however, given to her friend, Mary

Benson, to stay with her. The next day Samuel May and
Mary Benson posted the bond.

So ended this experiment in inter-racial education.
Prudence was obliged to close her school. A year later,
she married one of her sympathizers and became Prudence
Crandall Philleo. She later joined the Unitarians and
spent a good part of her later life in Kansas.

Samuel May summarized his feelings about the
incident by saying, "I felt ashamed of Canterbury,
ashamed of Connecticut, ashamed of my country, ashamed
of my color."[6]

It may be some consolation to know that when
Prudence was 83 and a resident of Kansas, the State of
Connecticut expunged from the record her conviction as a
criminal, and even apologized for what it called "the
cruel outrages" inflicted on her. They also voted her
a life pension of $400.00 a year.

Perhaps we may say that Prudence Crandall did
something to educate the State of Connecticut as well as
the county of Windham.

Maria Mitchell
1818 - 1869

Maria Mitchell,[7] one of eight children, was born in
Nantucket into a Quaker family, as was Lucretia Mott,
and grew up in the same environment of able women whose
capacities were fully used and with the men away much of
the time. Both of her parents were at various times

Clerks of the Monthly Meeting. Her father's hobby was astronomy, and she shared his interest. At the age of twelve, when an annular eclipse of the sun was visible in Nantucket, Maria counted seconds while her father observed the eclipse. At seventeen, she was reading Bridge's Conic Sections and Bowditch's Navigator. At sixteen, she taught in a private school, and later opened a school of her own. The student body, all girls above six, included some Portuguese children. She charged $3.00 a quarter, and gave them a thorough grounding. The girls sometimes rose before dawn for bird walks, and they were out after sunset to observe the stars. Maria was a qualified surveyor as well as an astronomer; we may be sure that surveying and astronomy had their influence on the curriculum. We may also be sure that the three "R's" were carefully taught.

This school she gave up to become librarian for about twenty years of the Nantucket Athenaeum. During this time she continued her study of mathematics and made astronomical observations. In 1847, when she was 29, she discovered a comet and was awarded a gold medal by the King of Denmark. This discovery made her famous. She traveled abroad, attended meetings of Scientific Societies, and above all continued her studies. By 1865 she was recognized in Europe and the United States as a scientist of high standing.[8] She became a member of several learned societies and a receiver of medals; also the possessor of a fine telescope, the gift of American women. After the death of her mother, she moved with her father to Lynn, Massachusetts, where she could be near an observatory. From 1849 to 1868 she was employed by the United States Almanac Office.

In 1865, when she was forty-seven, a great change came into her life. Vassar College, a newly opened institution of learning for women only, asked her to become director of their observatory and professor of Astronomy. This was female education in the experimental stage; it appealed strongly to Maria who believed that women's education should conform to the same high standards as men's. Taking her father with her, she moved into the observatory, where she had living quarters. Here she was to stay for twenty-three years. Her salary was $800.00 a year, with room and board included for herself and her father.

Teaching, rather than research, now became her life work. Dealing with women students who, in many cases, were academically poorly prepared, she persisted nevertheless in demanding careful, accurate work of a high level, individual observation and independent thought. She believed that the study of Astronomy could be a means of producing well educated and useful women. "Did you learn that from a book, or did you observe it yourself?" was a frequent question of hers.

She was not partial to lecturing, then the accepted method of teaching. "Why," she wanted to know, "should Professor X--or anyone else--lecture on that which can be found in books?"

She was gentle, quiet, and dignified in manner, her personality almost over-powering to some, but genial when she became known. A breakfast given to her students in her observatory apartment was an annual event; each guest received an individual verse of eight to eleven lines in length written by Maria. On one occasion, she told them, "I have written you each a poem, and I have told you you are all angels. We shall see whether you are so foolish as to believe it."[9]

She hated the "police work" of teaching--marking, compulsory attendance, etc.--and some said jokingly that she graded in inverse ratio to the marks given in other classes. In order to be perfectly objective in her evaluations, she got her students to sign assumed names to their papers and examinations. She expected a great deal of them, and most of them made a strong effort to live up to her expectations.

She was no man's (or woman's) rubber stamp, and had decided ideas of her own. Women, she felt, were "underestimated, under-educated, underpaid."[10] She observed the injustice of lower salaries for women teachers, and waged a long battle against it at Vassar; the practice was ended there in 1872. Women's education, she believed, should be controlled by women; she wanted women on the Vassar Board of Trustees. In 1887 three were appointed, one year before her retirement.

She was a strong advocate of Women's Suffrage. This right, she felt, was as clear to her in its correctness as that "the shortest distance between two points is a straight line."[11] When a man in Europe had taken her to the opera, calling for her in a carriage, she, a few days later, called for him in the same way and took him to the theater. In general, she was impatient of the slowness of the conservatives. In her diary she notes:

Our faculty meetings always try me in this respect: we do things that other colleges have done before. We wait and ask for precedent. If the earth had waited for a precedent, it would never have turned on its axis.[12]

Maria Mitchell had national and even international recognition. She was the first woman elected to membership in the American Academy of Arts and Sciences, and one of the nine founders (also twice its president) of the Association for the Advancement of Women. Her thirteen years as chair-person of its Science Committee were distinguished. She belonged to a number of other outstanding learned societies. Important papers were read by her at large conferences on such subjects as "The Higher Education of Women" and "The Need of Women in Science," and her influence was great.

As we have seen, Maria was brought up in a Quaker home under strong Quaker influences. At the age of twenty-five, however, she was disowned as being unsure of her religious beliefs.[13] Her search for truth was apparently too outspoken and fearless for her Meeting. Eventually, she became a Unitarian.

There were, however, many evidences of the continuing influence of her Quaker upbringing. She always wore clothes which were in the tradition of Quaker simplicity; one of her students remembers her wearing Quaker-like garments and dainty lace, either black or white, over her curls.[14] Ostentation of any kind she avoided. Plain directness of speech and a complete lack of polite formulas were characteristic.

Her students she called by their first names, instead of saying, "Miss So-and-So" as the other professors did. Her lack of interest in theology and theological argument was marked, and she was not fond of ritual observances: "I do not pray to order," she protested when she was asked to reform her lax attendance in chapel. She was, however, deeply religious, and, like the main historic stream of Quakerism, saw no antagonism between science and religion. Most of all, her attitudes toward women, their potential and their rights, obviously stem from her early upbringing.

There is a tradition that when she was dying, she was heard to say in a kind of amused wonder, "Well, if this is dying there is nothing very unpleasant about it!"[15]

A recent exhibit at the Smithsonian Institution on Nineteenth Century Women of Science featured Maria Mitchell's work. The centerpiece of the exhibit was the telescope she used in teaching her Vassar students.

Emily Howland
1827 - 1927

Emily Howland, born in Sherwood, New York, in 1827, was the granddaughter of Benjamin and Mary Howland, two of the earliest Quaker settlers in Cayuga county.[16] By the time she was born, the Friends meetings in the area had taken the queries about the education of their children seriously, and there were numerous small schools for Quaker children held in various homes in the area. One was led by David Thomas, a naturalist and very early geologist. Another was held in the country home of Asa and Ruth Potter and was later moved to Aurora. This one became a select school for girls and two of the students who attended this school were daughters of Judge Miller of Auburn. One of these daughters, Frances Adelaide, was the future wife of Secretary of State William Seward. This may well have been the school that Anna Folger Coffin, mother of Lucretia Coffin Mott and Martha Coffin Wright, taught in--starting in 1827. That was the period along Cayuga Lake when there was considerable migration from Nantucket Island, and Anna Coffin may well have come to be near family or friends from Nantucket during her widowhood. This school is also most probably the school that Emily Howland attended where the English Quaker, Susanna Marriott, was teacher.

Susanna Marriott was an abolitionist, as were Emily Howland's parents. There was thus included in both her formal and her informal education an exposure to the issues of slavery in this country. To quote from Judith Colucci Breault's biography of Emily Howland:

> In all these ways, Marriott was trying to teach Emily to recognize `the voice of God speaking to the soul of man,' to bear witness for what she felt was right. Throughout this period the picture remains that of a solitary child immersed in concerns beyond her years. Emily herself tells us: `In the dawn of my reading days the <u>Anti-Slavery</u> <u>Standard</u> entered our house. It has colored all the texture of thought and principle and

swayed the course of my life more than
any other influence; it has been "the
University" for me. Surely no paper can
be to me what this has been: the love of
my youth, the inspiration and the culture
of mature years, worthy of immortal
classic fame.'17

Another glimpse of this important teacher comes from
Emily Howland's Historical Sketch of Friends in Cayuga
County.

The coming of this rare teacher and
remarkable women was an event in the
history of this part of the county, from
which few persons now living here do not
derive benefit, either directly or
indirectly. Indeed the importance of the
event extended to a wide circle beyond
the county; one might say it marked an
era in Western New York. . . . The
salient trait of her character was
strength; but she was much besides; she
was large-hearted, philanthropic, just,
loving, though often stern. She gave the
rare opportunities her school afforded
for higher education, to many who could
not have otherwise enjoyed them providing
both board and tuition for such
assistance as they could render in the
household, "which" as one of her
beneficiaries remarks, "was not more than
I needed for exercise." . . . She
espoused the anti-slavery cause at its

beginning with ardor, and was a reader of the _Liberator_ for years. By most careful abstinence, she bore her testimony against the products of slave labor. She once told the writer she was implicated in the wrong only in the use of paper; this was unavoidable, and being made of cotton which had done one work, cost no increase in unrequited toil.18

Several of the traits to be found in Susanna Marriott become critical in the design for education that is later pursued by Emily Howland.

Her next formal education was in the school of Friend Wamser, in Poplar Ridge. It was while she was at the school that Emily Howland first expressed her interest in feminist issues. When there was considerable debate in the area about the extension of slavery into Texas, Emily Howland and three of her friends attempted to enter the discussion. She wrote to the gentlemen of the district this message:

> Although some think the ladies of the vicinity evince too much enthusiasm in the politics of the day, yet we cannot understand why we are to be debarred the privilege of participating in that which we feel to be of vital importance and which affects our happiness and welfare as much as yours; for certainly we as warmly wish the continuation of our country's glory, and that the lustre of its fame may not be dimmed, as any of your warmest partisans.19

Some time after this, Emily Howland was sent to the school of Mary Grew in Philadelphia. Mary Grew was a noted abolitionist and feminist. This part of Emily Howland's education was very crucial in both its formal and informal sense. Here her expectations about her abilities as a woman were heightened. Here, also, she met a group of strong, independent women who were to serve as a support group and important friends for the rest of her life. One of the popular activities for women in this group was to attend lectures on anatomy and health at the Pennsylvania Medical College for Women. Lucretia Mott was a major figure in the establishment of this series and the women doctors and medical educators were important models for Emily Howland and her friends. Periodic trips to visit with all of these women and many letters of correspondence kept the ties strong between Sherwood, New York, and Philadelphia.

Here then was a young Quaker woman, exposed to the issues of the world around her, encouraged by a feminist support group, inspired by Quaker women ministers in her own family and by two notable women teachers in her own experience. She came from a family of considerable wealth and the question clearly was--what should she do? In fact she did many things and we shall explore these. Her letters and diaries also show that some doubt about this question lingers throughout her life.

One thing she did not do was to marry and become absorbed in family life. She did, however, live at home in Sherwood much of her adult life and cared for her parents until their deaths. Emily Howland wanted to immerse herself in the issues of the day--the issues that had been her daily fare all of her life. The way to do this was through education. It was not only a very important concern within the Society of Friends, it was increasingly an important way for women to expand the area of their influence. It was through her contacts in Philadelphia that she learned that Mytilla Miner, well known teacher of free black girls in Washington, D,C., was ill and needed a replacement for herself as teacher and principal. In keeping with all of the radical influences in her life but in direct conflict with all of the more conservative aspects of life in rural New York among strict Quakers, Emily Howland volunteered to do her part. In a letter she writes to a friend from India many years after the fact, she attempts to explain her actions.

> Miss Miner accepted my proposal to take
> her school, and a year after my visit to
> Philadelphia, without the approval of any
> of my friends, I left home for the
> untried work. My words give no idea of
> what this step cost me, even at this
> distance from it. I realize the diffi-
> culties so profoundly, that I cannot
> understand how I had the strength to do
> it. It was as though I was impelled, and
> could not do otherwise. My spiritual
> vision being clear in regard to my own
> need, and in regard to the work to which
> I was sent, I was able to lay aside all
> hindrances from without and within, and
> go forward.[20]

Ill health on the part of her mother called Emily
Howland back from this venture in the second year. She
was at Tanglewood, the family home, for a period of time
and then during the Civil War she went to Virginia to
assist in the work with the newly freed slaves. A
drawing made at Camp Dodd, Virginia,21 shows something
of the conditions under which she worked. It does not,
however, show the mud which apparently was very
bothersome. She established a school for children, but
ended up teaching adults as well in the evenings. She
used all of her contacts in Washington to get supplies
for the persons in the camp. Apparently she was somewhat patronizing in her approach to the free slaves but
no one seemed to fault her on the amount of work she
did. She wrote many letters to Quakers, abolitionists
and friends begging that clothes and other supplies be
sent and then she distributed these. When it became
clear that there was not going to be land made available
to the former slaves, she persuaded her father to buy
400 acres of land in Virginia. She assisted the process
of getting a group of persons settled on this land.
Gradually the land was sold to them and a settlement was
established there.

From this time forth, a major interest in Emily
Howland's life was the education of Negroes in the
South. She gave very generously of her considerable
wealth. She was a trustee of six different schools, and
she had a particular interest in Tuskegee Institute. In
1916 Emily Howland made one of several trips throughout
the South to see these schools.

However, Emily Howland again returned to New York
State to live. She took over the running of the house

after her mother's death and was a close companion to her father until his death. It was during this period that she really took on the work of being a philanthropist.

In 1871 the Quakers of Cayuga County area had decided to start a select school in Sherwood. Hepsibah Hussey, a well known teacher from Nantucket, was hired to teach and administer the school. It was an active school when Emily Howland settled back into life in Sherwood. From then until the end of her life, she became the financial backbone of this school. She gave the money for a major addition to the school and it was customary for the teachers at the school to have room and board in her home. Her home was also the visiting place of many suffragists, Susan B. Anthony being a very frequent guest. Emily Howland gave very generously to the cause of women's rights and to the Temperance movement as well as to the education ventures already mentioned. She is said to have been influential in persuading another Quaker, Ezra Cornell, that Cornell University should be coeducational. And she gave many young women interest-free loans for Cornell.

In 1927, at the age of 99, she was awarded an honorary doctorate from the New York University for her work in education. Just before her death she saw to it that the Sherwood Select School would be made into a much needed public high school. In 1972 when this same school was rebuilt as an elementary school, it was named for her and a picture of her graces the main hall of the school.

Mary Mendenhall Hobbs
1852 - 1930

Mary Mendenhall was born in 1852 in North Carolina. Her parents, Nereus and Orianna Wilson Mendenhall,22 were deeply engaged in Friends education at New Garden Boarding School. This North Carolina Yearly Meeting (Orthodox) school which was established in 1837 and became Guilford College in 1888. Nereus Mendenhall and Orianna Wilson had both attended New Garden School and all five of their daughters attended it, went on to further education and carried on Friends' concern for learning throughout their lives.

There is a much loved story (at Guilford College) of the importance of the Mendenhall family in the survival of New Garden Hall during the tensions preceding and during the Civil War. Like many other Quakers, the Mendenhalls had a desire to migrate westward because of slavery and the threat of war. The Mendenhalls prepared to leave the teaching and administrative work of New Garden and go to Minnesota. The following description from Mary Mendenhall Hobbs' biographic account of her father captures the dilemma:

> . . . the household goods were packed in boxes and home-made trunks and carried to the station at Jamestown and the family ready to leave on the morrow. The conviction grew stronger that it was the will of the Lord for him to remain at New Garden and stand by the school, come what might. He was obedient to the holy vision, and after assuring himself that

such a course would meet the approval of his wife, ordered the boxes brought back and himself went again to the old school room.[23]

Mary, the oldest child, would have been a young girl when this decision and the move into a farmhouse on the land at New Garden occurred. It must have had a profound effect on her feelings about the school and the Yearly Meeting which carried through the testing of the Civil War days.

New Garden had had other times of severe testing. When it was proposed and approved, a gift of $1,000 from a New Bedford, Massachusetts, whaler, George Howland, had allowed construction to begin.[24] At its beginning New York Yearly Meeting had sent cots and bedding to furnish New Garden. Thus, it is not surprising that when this same George Howland, a distant cousin of Emily Howland, started a seminary for girls, Howland Institute, in Union Springs, New York (near Emily's home), Nereus and Orianna urged Mary to complement her New Garden schooling by attending it.

An incident at Howland Institute extended Mary Mendenhall's familial endorsement of the importance of education. As she remembers it--

> The next step along this line came when I was a pupil at Howland School at Union Springs, New York. There things were conducted for the education of women as human beings and not simply as females, and our ideas were stimulated to make the most of ourselves in every way.

In English literature we had a most
remarkable teacher, Miss Caroline
Comstock. She was an intense personality
and was always trying to develop the
personality of pupils and draw out strong
characteristics. Once she gave each of
us this subject to write an essay upon:
"If I should give each of you ten
thousand dollars, tell me what you would
do with it." She knew there were girls
in the class who would, in all human
possibility, have many more thousands at
their command, and she wished them to
understand values and possibilities.

There was Elizabeth King, daughter of
Francis King of Baltimore, and Carey
Thomas, later President of Bryn Mawr
College, and several girls of more
wealth. I was the only girl in the class
who was obliged to economize, who never
had and was never likely to have money to
spend as I wished, and so I thought
earnestly what use I would make of such a
vast sum as that. I decided I would
build a school here in North Carolina
where girls whose fathers were less able
and far less willing to educate their
daughters than my own dear father was,
might have as good an opportunity as I
was then having in that lovely school on
Cayuga Lake. I put my soul into that
consideration.25

This is exactly the kind of project that Mary Mendenhall did put her soul into. After attending Howland, she returned to New Garden as a teacher. She married Lyndon Hobbs, and then like her mother before, supported her husband in many informal ways, as he took over the leadership of New Garden Boarding School. As New Garden moved through the process of becoming Guilford college (1888--Lyndon Hobbs, first president) she remembered the earlier challenge. She was convinced that there were young women who should be at Guilford but whose parents either placed too little emphasis on their education or that they could not afford to pay their expenses at the college. Mary Mendenhall took this concern to the Women's and the Men's Yearly Meetings and a fund was started to create a cottage where these young women might stay. By doing the work for their maintenance cooperatively, they were able to cut their educational costs considerably. Gradually the need for this grew and Mary Mendenhall Hobbs dreamed of the building which would more permanently serve this need. After many years, in 1907, New Garden Hall was dedicated.

Mary Mendenhall Hobbs was also concerned about the education of other North Carolina girls and she was an advocate and avid speaker and letter writer in the project to insure that the Normal School in Greensboro was made into a college for young women. Thus, North Carolina's Women's College, now the University of North Carolina at Greensboro, was aided by her efforts. For this work in women's education she was granted an Honorary Doctorate from that institution in 1921. Late in Mary Mendenhall Hobb's life, old New Garden Hall was named for her and Hobbs Dormitory still offers coopera- tive living for Guilford women students.

An equally important part of the education of women in Mary Hobbs Hall is the philosophy of the woman whose vision was turned into brick and mortar. She wrote to one of her protegees who was being trained for the education of women at Guilford:

> I think the way to do is to have some
> idea of making something of yourself as
> an individual human being. I do not
> believe one ought to marry as an end--
> that is, to make up your mind that `I
> must have a husband whether or no.' Go
> and do your work. Make yourself a valued
> member of society--be able to take care
> of yourself--and then, if someone whom
> you respect and love comes into your
> life, you will be ready to do your part
> in making a lovely home as an equal
> partner in the firm. . . . Women need to
> be in a position to command a place of
> respect and equal authority in the home.
> . . . We need better educated, better
> trained women with a broader outlook on
> life for the future homemakers in this
> country, and that is why New Garden is
> built--to help toward that.[26]

Martha Carey Thomas
1857-1935

Another young woman who was attracted to Howland School was M. Carey Thomas of Philadelphia.[27] She was particularly pleased that this was "no mamby-pamby" cherishing of young ladies. Her father had not been convinced that this level of education was necessary for his daughter but with her fervent efforts and her mother's helpful influence, he was finally persuaded to allowed Carey to attend Howland. At Howland, she was an exceptionally able student and as she was about to graduate, Miss Slocum, the teacher of philosophy and political science, called her in. "She had watched Minnie carefully and discovered that she could go to the roots of things and understand them. In a word, Minnie was the only girl she had seen with the 'power of mind' to advance women's positions in the world." "What we want in the cause of women are not doctors and lawyers (there are plenty of those). We want scholars. You have, I think, as fair a start as any boy of seventeen in the country and now I want you to be a great scholar. I don't think you will be content to merely receive and not originate. . . . I want great things of you."[28]

Minnie, or Carey as she called herself later, then persuaded her family to let her go to Cornell University, open to women only in 1878. At Cornell she continued to be a brilliant student, and at one point was instrumental in opening a literary group on Swinburne to a younger woman student, Florence Kelley (a Quaker and later an important social reformer).

After graduating from Cornell, Carey Thomas chose
to go to graduate school in Europe, as there was at that
time no American university which would grant women a
doctorate. Upon completion of that she became involved
in the creation of Bryn Mawr College, through the
assistance of her father who was active in the
beginnings of that Quaker College (Orthodox) for young
women. She would have been willing to be the college's
first president but she was instead its first dean.
Some few years later she became president and continued
in the deanship for several years. Most of the young
women at Bryn Mawr came from wealthy homes. Clearly the
emphasis on excellence of standards for women was a very
strong part of M. Carey Thomas' thrust in education.
She wanted no special courses for women and she was not
an advocate of protective legislation for women any more
than she was for a watered-down curriculum. In fact,
her determination to maintain rigid standards of
curricular excellence, based on the educational standard
of the men's colleges in the Northeast and European
models of her own education, meant that her
administration at Bryn Mawr was lacking in creative
alternatives and flexibility. She did, however,
demonstrate that women had equal ability in learning, in
teaching, in scholarship and in administration. Unlike
Prudence Crandall, Mary Mendenhall Hobbs and Emily
Howland, M. Carey Thomas was not particularly concerned
for young women from less wealth or from different
racial or ethnic groups. A summer institute for such
women was established at Bryn Mawr during her
administration, however. There was also an experimental
school employing the progressive tenets of John Dewey,
but the emphasis for the college was on the
establishment of a graduate program for scholarly

excellence. M. Carey Thomas was continually active in the cause of woman's rights, and the Deanery (her home) was frequently a visiting place of suffragists. She also was talented in finding ways to finance the construction of major buildings at Bryn Mawr, priding herself on raising over a million dollars for the construction of educational space for women. The library at Bryn Mawr is named in her honor. She also served as trustee at Cornell and Johns Hopkins Universities and she and her friend Mary Garrett were instrumental in opening medical education for women at the latter.

Jane P. Rushmore

1864 - 1958

Jane Rushmore, a prominent Friend whose death took place in the middle of this century, is our next subject.[29] We know less about her, and her impact was largely either within the Society of Friends or as an interpreter of it. She is included to show that the same tradition continues into our times.

She was born into a Friends family in a small rural community, Preston Hollow, in Albany county, New York, within view of the Catskill Mountains. Her parents were strong members of a tiny Hicksite Meeting; the family attended it regularly and went to Quarterly Meeting, even when it was held in Albany. Jane's father was especially important in encouraging her eager, curious mind and teaching her independent ways of thinking.

Jane followed her brothers to Swarthmore, entering at the age of fifteen. English was her favorite subject, though she enjoyed mathematics, taught by Susan J.Cunningham, trained by Maria Mitchell and recommended by her when Swarthmore needed an astronomer. An observatory was later built for her there. Jane referred to her as a "professor of gumption and common sense."[30] Jane took no notes in her courses, but her retentive mind was stored with much she never forgot. She stayed two years at Swarthmore. One of her important memories was of a visit to the college by Lucretia Mott , then in her eighties; Jane spoke of the aura which seemed to surround her. It was during this period while she was attending Swarthmore Meeting that Jane became a true, convinced Friend.

Jane Rushmore is now chiefly remembered for her work in Friends organizations. She was active in the Friends General Conference, and particularly in promoting the unity which now exists between the two branches of Friends, then known as the Orthodox and the Hicksites. She instigated and planned Biennial conferences and the formation of Friends Central Bureau in 1911. In many ways, she helped to bring Friends organizational thinking into a modern context. Her contributions to religious education were many, and for years she was a vigorous and effective member of the Religious Education Committee. She had a keen interest in George School, a co-educational Friends boarding school near Philadelphia. For two years (1922-23) she had the responsible position of Clerk of the Women's Meeting of the Yearly Meeting--those were still the days when the business was conducted separately by the two sexes--and when the two combined in 1924 to become one

Meeting, she was chosen Clerk for three years. For twenty-seven years she was a member of the Yearly Meeting Representative Committee, the body in which decision-making powers were lodged between Yearly Meetings, and for nineteen of those years she was its Clerk.

In all these activities she was basically an educator, and for most of her life she was a practicing teacher. In 1882, when she left Swarthmore at the age of eighteen, she became the public school teacher in her home town. She had forty pupils, who had run out the last two teachers. Three big boys who were impressed by her and wanted to learn took over the discipline for her, and she had no problems. After teaching there and later at a private school, she was asked to take over London Grove school, thirty miles outside of Philadelphia. She was the only teacher for twelve children; her salary was $40.00 a month, later increased to $50.00. She accepted a black student, but was able to cope with the objections of some parents and neighbors. She was an extra-ordinarily good teacher; when a class was reciting the other students found what was going on so interesting that they listened, too. She taught Bible, produced plays, and had individual assignments for pupils. By 1900, thirty-six years later, there were fifty-two students and the school was a two teacher school.

A story shows how she handled her students during the early days of her time there. One of them wanted to leave before a piece of work was done. Jane (she was always known as Jane), standing with her back to the only door, said to him quietly but firmly:

"Thee can go if thee wants, but I'd like
thee to think about something first. If
thee goes, which thee may do, thee'll
never come back. Think it over."

The student stayed. By the time his work was
done, he had become much more cheerful. As he left,
Jane said to him: "Goodbye, I'll be very glad to see
thee tomorrow."[31]

From London Grove she went on to Martin Academy in
Kennett Square, and later for a year to Friends Central.
We are told that she encouraged original thinking among
the students, and gave them considerable participation
in school government.

During her teaching career, her incredible energy
poured out in all sorts of ways. She read a paper in
Yearly Meeting, she chaired committees, she attended
institutional conferences in Philadelphia and classes at
the University of Pennsylvania; she concerned herself
with the Y.W.C.A., she took her turn in sitting up with
a sick neighbor, she stayed overnight in the homes of
her students to get to know them, she spoke frequently
to large audiences. For many years she contributed
labor and oversight to a center which distributed coal
and milk at reasonable prices to distressed families and
served meals for undernourished children.

In closing this abbreviated account of a remarkable
woman, it might be well to mention in her own words some
of her educational principles:

We think that a man is educated not
when he is replete with knowledge of many
things, but when he has full use of all
his potential possibilities, and knows
how to put these into effective and
altruistic action. . . .[32]

Education has among its main
objectives the development of a capacity
for vision, skill in organizing, and
ability to make adaptations to unforseen
conditions. . . .33

The business of education is to help
develop people, not merely to train their
minds. . . .34

THEIR CONTRIBUTIONS

We have seen a parade of Quaker women engaged in
almost every facet of education for girls and women in
the nineteenth and twentieth century. Formal and
informal, private and public, rural and urban, primary,
secondary, undergraduate and graduate. All of them,
even those in female single-sex schools, believed in and
attempted to provide an education for all facets of
life. All of them had been educated on a generally
equal basis with men and they were determined to carry
forward and to extend this work.

Notes

1For the biographical details of Martha Tyson's life, I
have relied on William I. Hull, A History of Swarthmore
College, Vol. I (Typescript in the Friends Library at
Swarthmore).

27 mo. 28, 1860.

3My chief sources on Prudence Crandall are: 1) three
letters in the Connecticut College Library, New London,
Conn., describing the difficulties of her school in
1833. They form part of the Library's American Woman's
Collection MS 71-1608. 2) Edmund Fuller Prudence
Crandall, an Incident of Racism in Nineteenth Century
Connecticut, Wesleyan University Press.

4Fuller, p. 96.

5Fuller, p. 21.

6Fuller, p. 95.

7Especially helpful have been Dorothy J. Keller, Maria
Mitchell, an Early Woman Academician; and Mary King
Babbit, Maria Mitchell as her Students Knew Her.

8Caroline Herschel and Mary Somerville preceded her.

9Babbitt, p. 24.

10Babbit, p. 130.

11Babbitt, p. 140.

12Babbitt, p. 14.   Oct. 31,, 1866.

13Keller, p. 19.

14Mary King Babbitt, who graduated in 1882 when Maria
Mitchell was 64.

[15] Wright, p. 238.

[16] Primary sources are: 1) Judith Colucci Breault, _The World of Emily Howland: Odyssey of a Humanitarian_ (California, Les Femmes, 1976); 2) Emily Howland, "Historical Sketch of Friends in Cayuga County" (Cayuga County Historical Society, _Collections_ No. 2, 1882) and "Letters" collected in manuscript collection Cayuga County Historical society; 3) Lucy Jacobs, "Historical Sketch of Sherwood School: 1871-1964."

[17] Breault, p. 10.

[18] Howland, "Historical Sketch of Friends in Cayuga County."

[19] Breault, p. 12.

[20] Letter to Pundita Ramabai of India, April 1888.

[21] Breault, p. 58.

[22] Algie I. Newlin, "Orianna Wilson Mendenhall: In a Family Picture," _Guilford Review_, Number Seven, Spring 1978.

[23] Mary Mendenhall Hobbs, "Nereus Mendenhall," _Quaker Biographies_, Series II, Volume V: pg. 267.

[24] Dorothy Lloyd gilbert (Thorne), _Guilford, A Quaker college_ (Greensboro, N.C.: Guilford College,; 1937), p.

[25] Gilbert, p.

[26] Mary Mendenhall Hobbs, "Letters to Rachel," manuscript collection, Friends Collection, Guilford College, Greensboro, North Carolina, p. 31.

[27] Resources are: M. Carey Thomas, _The Making of a Feminist: Early Journals and Letters of M. Carey Thomas_ (edited by Marjorie Housepian Dobkin, Kent State University Press, 1979), and article by Clifton J. Phillips on "Martha Carey Thomas" (_The Dictionary of_

Notable American Women, 1607-1950, Vol. III.

[28]Dobkin, p. 92.

[29]Sources on Jane Rushmore: Emily Cooper Johnson, Under Quaker Appointment, the Life of Jane Rushmore, and Jane P. Rushmore, The Quaker Way, and Further Steps Along the Quaker Way.

[30]Johnson, p. 19.

[31]Johnson, pp. 38-39.

[32]The Courier, Jan., 1951, quoted in Johnson, pp. 146-7.

[33]Jane Rushmore, The Quaker Way, p. 33.

[34]Ibid., p. 34.

QUAKER WOMEN AND MEDICAL PRACTICE
IN THE NINETEENTH CENTURY
Margaret Sery Young

Not many nineteenth century American women healers were physicians. Medical practice was male territory. Certainly there were other professions in which women were unwelcome, but in no other were women regarded as so out of place, in no other were barriers to them so strong and boundaries so clear. But this had not always been so.

"Domestic practice" rather than medical practice was considered the appropriate health occupation for women in colonial America. Women called domestic practitioners looked after community health. They were part-time healers often relying on herbal remedies and folk-medicine. They attended at birth and death, doing the manual work necessary to make the sick comfortable. They came from the same social class as their patients, they understood their patients' lives and were often able to give them emotional help conducive to healing.

The European forerunners of these domestic practitioners had been the female healers of the 15th, sixteenth and seventeenth centuries. Frequently these earlier female healers had been the only "doctors" for the poor and for women. They were often from the lower class and felt at ease with the poor. These female healers learned from other female healers; frequently mothers taught daughters. Physicians, on the other hand, were males from the upper class and treated members of the upper class almost exclusively. Physicians studied under other physicians in order to learn to heal and frequently had university educations. The dual practice system of domestic practitioners vs. physicians can be traced to the fourteenth century, when the church decreed that anyone who could heal without having studied under a physician was a witch and that witches must die. From the late fifteenth through the eighteenth centuries about nine million people were executed as witches. Most of them were women and many of these women were healers and midwives. Witch-midwives were believed to "surpass all witches in their crimes." It was feared that they would steal placentas and umbilical cords for use in witchcraft rites or that they would kill children before baptism or offer them to the devil.1

Although highly suspect, midwives were necessary. The Church sought to control them through licensing (an attempt at boundary maintenance) which eventually limited their ability to compete with physicians.

In colonial America, however, there were no medical institutions and few full-time physicians; wives and mothers were responsible for medical care. Female midwives and healers reigned supreme although they, like everyone else in the colonies did not know the basics of anatomy and physiology and lacked formal training. The presence of men in the birthing chambers was regarded as inappropriate. Male physicians were called upon only as a last resort. In the early eighteenth century several women went to Europe especially France and Germany to study midwifery. Some returned to set up flourishing practices.[2]

At the same time significant changes took place in British medicine: a new field, obstetrics, developed borne of a greater understanding of the mechanics of birth and the use of obstetrical instruments, especially forceps. By 1760, the new obstetrics began to spread to America. Traditional midwifery began to change.[3]

Shifts in technology tend to squeeze women out of formerly central roles.[4] With the inventions of forceps and speculum, the social space for women constricted: midwifery changed from an art practiced by untrained women to a legitimate branch of medicine. The role of midwife declined. The popularity of the general practitioner as "birther" grew. Some women continued to use midwives. However, upper class urban women (especially in Philadelphia, Boston, and New York) felt that a physician-attended birth would be a safer and shorter delivery. By the end of the 1820's those who could afford a general practioner employed him rather than a midwife.[5]

Despite this, at the time few physicians specialized in obstetrics. Most upper class deliveries in northern cities were attended by general practioners. These men realized that although physicians earned higher fees for delivery than had midwives, midwifery was not a very lucrative specialty. However, these men also perceived, quite accurately, that midwifery fed general practice. The physician who worked well in the birthing chamber earned the gratitude of the patient and her husband. This insured a varied practice with a range of ailments. Midwifery was a way of securing patronage. Consequently, most physicians eagerly added the more common normal deliveries to the infrequent abnormal ones to which they would be called anyway.[6]

In order to do this, they reinforced the idea that a woman's best safeguard against the hazards of childbirth was employment of a general practioner who could assist at birth: "a birthing specialist."

However, it was not necessarily true that the general practioner was a birthing specialist. Even in the better medical schools where midwifery and the diseases of children and women constituted a separate department, no courses in the area were required. Young practitioners began their careers with less practical knowledge in obstetrics and diseases of women and children than in any other branch of medicine. Many of them never attended a delivery during medical school.[7]

Then as now, most obstetric cases were normal and a knowledgeable physician had to do little more than a competent midwife. However, these men with poor training and no experience in midwifery were equipped with obstetrical instruments. And they tended to interfere with instruments to the disadvantage of mothers and infants.[7]

A contemporary development in medicine complicated matters. In the mid-eighteenth century a medical elite had begun to form in the colonies. Full-time medical practice developed among the men who had served in the Continental Army's medical services or who had studied in the medical centers of Europe became full-time physicians.

They began to encourage laws that excluded unlicensed practitioners from medicine and licenses were granted only to allopaths. Allopaths believed that disease was an imbalance of body fluids. They bled and purged their patients to restore the balance. Allopaths were members of an exclusively male medical sect. Women were rigidly excluded. They belonged to the same social class as most of the legislators making the licensing laws. They became known as "regular" physicians.[9]

Several types of "irregulars" also existed, many of whom played a significant role in the Popular Health movement of the nineteenth century.

1) Thomsonians, many of whom were feminists insisting females had a right to be treated by members of their own sex, prescribed herbal cures. Women attending Thomsonian meetings formed "Ladies Physiological Societies" with the goal of health information with each other.

2) Homeopaths were another group of irregulars. They emphasized treatment of the patient rather than the ailment. The homeopathic physician sought to build up the patient's strength and resistance to illness through a regimen of rest, healthy food, very small doses of medicine, and the power of suggestion.

3) "Eclectics," adopted what seemed the most sensible modes from the various other sects.[10]

In what was essentially a social class struggle, "irregulars" and proponents of the Popular Health Movement worked to repeal the licensing laws of the early nineteenth century. This enabled non-allopathic medical groups to establish their own schools and obtain charters for them. Most nineteenth century women physicians were irregular physicans; for a time it appeared that women would regain their role as healers.11

However, there were a few other barriers. Industrialization and urbanization led to a separation of women from the labor force and the workplace. The places men worked were separated from the homes where women were supposed to care for their families. Factories were considered unfit places for women.

Victorian morality, fostering the image of women as angelic, fragile, pedestaled, sickly and most suited to mastering the arts of homemaking and child-raising grew out of this division of labor. Previously a man's place had also been at home--as farmer and as artisan. Now, women were isolated and the scope of their functions dwindled. The occupation "housewife" spread to include a larger portion of the female population and constricted further their social space. Those who were too poor to be housewives, lived, bore their children, watched them die and died themselves in the squalor of the urban slum.12

Into this imbroglio came women who wanted to be physicians. They came for many reasons. Some (including the first woman physician in the United States, Elizabeth Blackwell) saw the effort to participate in a male-dominated profession as an expression of women's rights. Others saw it as an important health reform, while still others saw it as essential for Christian modesty.

Despite their reasons, it was difficult for them to gain access to medical schools. Regular physicians had only recently wrested from female midwives the domain of the birthing room. They were reluctant to share it with female medical practitioners.[13] They feared that the former domestic practitioners would weaken the purity of the allopathic medicine with the notions of the many irregular medical sects. They feared also that females were too angelic and fragile for the rigors of the profession.[14]

Indeed, Elizabeth Blackwell's acceptance was a bit of a fluke. She had applied to Geneva Medical College in 1847. The 150 male students attending the college were so "rude, boisterous and riotous" that neighborhood residents threatened to have the college indicted as a nuisance. There was so much noise during lectures that it was difficult to hear. The faculty, unwilling to take action on Blackwell's admission, referred it to the students and required a unanimous affirmative vote for her acceptance. Jokingly, and to the dismay of the faculty, the rowdy group voted for her acceptance. In the words of a fellow student, "Her entrance into that Bedlam of confusion acted like magic upon every student . . . For the first time a lecture was given without the slightest interruption, and every word could be heard as distinctly as it would if there had been a single person in the room.[15] Blackwell graduated ranking with the best students in the class. She was awarded the title "Domina," the only feminine form for "Doctor" which could be found.[16] Immediately after her graduation, Geneva Medical College closed its doors to women applicants.[17]

After completing medical training, Blackwell desired to set up a practice, but could find no clients, a common problem for early female physicians. Dismayed, and ready to quit, she turned to writing and speaking about health and physiology. Quaker women were strongly represented in her audience.[18] Eventually these Quaker women ignored popular opinion and sought Blackwell as their physician, very subtly but definitely creating a space in which she could practice.

A few women were accepted into male medical schools but obstacles were so great that eventually women had to establish their own schools. When they succeeded in doing this, they were unable to find places to complete internships and residencies. Many completed internships and residencies abroad, often with medical training superior to that available in the United States. Frequently, they were forbidden from entrance into private practice and had to establish their own alternative forms of medical practice and networks among women-physicians.

Quaker women were important in establishment of the networks of medical education and practice. Their importance in providing a support-system for female physicians has already been alluded to in the case of Elizabeth Blackwell. However, they also played a very active function in encouraging women to seek medical degrees and establish practices. Quaker women appear to be overrepresented among notable nineteenth century American women-physicians.[19] Quite likely this has been due to the fact that Quakers encouraged education of women and emphasized science as an important component of education. However, Quakers and especially Quaker women facilitated the entrance of many Quaker women into medical practice by establishing and funding schools,internships and residencies, as well as clinics in which women could practice. This ability to establish organizations in which to carry through plans and programs may well have been due to the early training of Quakers in Meeting to speak, organize and carry through plans and programs. And, true to Quaker tradition, there was nothing monolithic in their approach. Quaker women entered and supported schools for both regular and irregular physicians.

The process and product of these support networks and varied views of medicine are made evident in focusing on two networks of Quaker women of great importance in nineteenth century medical practice. One is well known. In a way this group is a professional family with one woman fostering several others. The group includes Ann Preston and the Female Medical College of Pennsylvania, later the Women's Medical College of Pennsylvania. There are several Quakers in this lineage and many fictive or adoptive offspring. This is a lineage of regular physicians. There is another. That of the energetic homeopath, Clemence Lozier, founder of the New York Medical College and Hospital for Women.

Ann Preston and the regular physicians
of the Women's Medical College of Philadelphia

Ann Preston (1813-1872) was of Quaker parentage
and a lifelong member of the Philadelphia Friends
Meeting. Members of her family were active
abolitionists and women's rights supporters. She began
her education in Quaker schools but returned home to
care for her invalid mother and run the household. In
addition, she was active in the local anti-slavery
society, writing its reports, and petitions, and also
took active part in the local temperance movement.
Later she turned to teaching school. To support herself
she continued her own education informally and was part
of the audience when speakers such as Lucy Stone,
Elizabeth Cady Stanton and Susan B. Anthony addressed
the lyceum.

Her concern for the need for enlightened attitudes
toward female physiology grew. By 1840 she was
teaching physiology and hygiene to women and girls.

Lucretia Mott who had been her friend since
childhood and the Philadelphia Quakers, many of whom
were physicians encouraged her to study medicine. In
1847 she became a medical apprentice with a Philadelphia
physician. After two years she applied for admission to
four Philadelphia medical colleges - and received four
refusals.

In 1850, a group of Quakers led by William Mullen,
a businessman who had studied medicine, founded the
Female Medical College of Pennsylvania. They did this
because of several concerns:

1)   That women should have the right to practice medicine,

2)   That in the interest of modesty women should treat women,

3)   That in improving the lot of working class women, more medical help was needed.

At age 36 Ann Preston entered the first class. (There were seven members; four of them were Quakers.) Almost immediately, the state medical society voted to expel any member who taught at the college or consulted with a female physician. It became impossible for women students to be admitted to any teaching clinics in Pennsylvania.

Unable to obtain practical experience in a hospital, Preston accepted a teaching job in physiology and hygiene. To provide her students with the bedside clinical experience she had not been able to obtain, she founded a women's hospital in connection with the college, traveling and doing much of the fundraising herself.

When the college was closed during the war between the states, she encouraged local Quaker women to sponsor Dr. Emeline Cleveland (a friend of Friends) to do post graduate work at the School of Obstetrics and Maternite in Paris. Cleveland did so, completing her work with honors, touring the wards and lecture rooms of London and Paris. She returned home to open the Women's Hospital of Philadelphia, administer it capably, inaugurate with Ann Preston nurse's training, and training for beside nursing for laywomen,[22] and clinical training for medical students.

In 1866 Ann Preston became dean of Women's Medical College of Philadelphia as the Female Medical College came to be called. She was the first woman to hold the position.

In 1868 she applied for her students to attend general clinics at the Philadelphia Hospital and Pennsylvania Hospital. Male students rebelled, hooted, jeered, and spat tobacco juice on them while instructors looked on.

The presence of Ann Preston and her students was protested also by the boards of medical colleges and hospitals and many individual doctors because it was considered immodest and immoral to educate men and women in medicine together. Her reply that "wherever it is proper to introduce women as patients, there it also is but just and in accordance with the instincts of truest womanhood for women to appear as physicians and students" has become a classic argument in favor of women in the medical profession.[23]

Preston continued as dean and professor of physiology until her death. Emeline Cleveland her former student and close friend and colleague, succeeded her. Two other classmates in Ann Preston's class at Women's Medical College of Pennsylvania were Hannah Myers Longshore and Hannah's sister-in-law Anna Longshore. Both apprenticed themselves to Joseph Longshore, an eclectic physician who drafted the charter for the Women's Medical College and served on its faculty. After completing their medical education, both became successful physicians.[24] A later Quaker student, Anna Elizabeth Broomall joined the faculty and held the chair in Obstetrics. She was devoted to the development of preventive medicine, insisting on prenatal and postnatal care in the home. She led the movement to provide the poor of Philadelphia with high quality obstetrical care. Her efforts greatly reduced maternal mortality rates in the Philadelphia area. Although barred from membership in the Philadelphia Obstetrical Society because she was a woman, a male colleague was permitted to read her papers.[25]

Rachel Bodley, a chemist and the school's third dean, was also a Quaker. She had encouraged Anna Broomall and Clara Marshall who later became the fourth dean. Clara Marshall, from the same farming community in Chester County as Ann Prescott, specialized in pharmacy and broke the barrier as the first woman appointed to the Philadelphia Hospital staff.[27]

Thus for years, Quakers dominated the board, the administration and, to a lesser extent the student body of the Women's Medical College of Pennsylvania. The school was a pioneer in medical education for women. The college opted for orthodox medicine, eventually accepting only allopaths or regular physicians on its faculty. It became a respected medical school, opening the domain of regular medicine to women.

Clarence Lozier[28] (1813-1888) was another prominent woman-physician of the nineteenth century. Unlike Ann Preston the women of the Women's Medical College of Philadelphia, Clemence Lozier practiced homeopathic

medicine and had little respect for "regular" physicians and their medicine. She worked to carve a respectable place within medicine for homeopathy.

Although a devout Methodist, Lozier was first introduced to medical practice by her Quaker mother, a domestic practitioner whose healing skills were so well known that she was frequently consulted by physicians.

Orphaned at age eleven, widowed after only seven years of marriage and having lost all but one of her children, to accidents or harsh medical treatment, Lozier was very interested in medicine and reform. Supporting her family by opening a school when her husband's health failed, Lozier quickly introduced physiology, anatomy and hygiene into the curriculum. She studied her brother's medical books and entered an eclectic medical school at age 40, graduating with highest honors. She set up an extremely successful practice while Blackwell and Preston were still attempting admission into "regular" medical schools.

Her lectures to women patients became so popular that she decided to found a medical college for women. With the help of Elizabeth Cady Stanton, the New York Medical College and Hospital for Women, a homeopathic institution and the first woman's school of medicine in New York, was chartered. The school was co-educational. Lozier was president and professor of diseases of women and children. She pioneered in this specialty after touring european hospitals. The school became nationally known and recognized with over 200 graduates (including her son) before it was absorbed into the New York Medical College.

Like Ann Preston, Clemence Lozier was adamant about her students' right to attend lectures in public hospitals and did not hesitate to call a "public indignation meeting" in order to rally public opinion to their cause when her students were rudely treated at a local clinic lecture.[29]

While practicing and teaching, Lozier attended meetings of the County Medical Society and became the first woman to read a paper before the state homeopathic society. Devoted to patient education, she also wrote several popular works.

Like Preston, Clemence Lozier was strongly committed to reform. Her involvement in reform movements led to a close friendship with Elizabeth Cady Stanton. With earnings from her private practice she helped support Susan B. Anthony's suffragist weekly. She opened her home to reformers of all types, participating not only in health reform but also in prison reform, abolition of slavery, humane treatment of Indians and international arbitration. Her reform programs were never for the benefit of women only. Because of this, Clemence Lozier became an outspoken critic of women who failed to challenge the health care standards of men in order to be accepted by "regular" physicians.

Her health and medical education reforms questioned the basis of an elitist medical system. Her school was not a separate but equal women's medical school; it was coeducational from the very beginning. She never sought acceptance in the allopathic medicine of the regulars;

she challenged other physicians to question the
assumptions of allopathy.

Clemence Lozier's lineage did not survive as long
as Ann Preston's. Her students were not as widely known
as Preston's. They belonged to the "wrong" medical
group, the irregulars. Her school did not survive into
the mid-twentieth century as did the Women's Medical
College of Pennsylvania. Apparently, this was not
because it taught a less effective form of medicine, but
rather because it challenged mainstream regular
medicine.

The Flexner report of 1910 brought to a close the
irregular schools, condemning them as inferior.[30] This
meant opportunities for medical education for women
decreased markedly. It also meant the demise of a
strong voice for preventive medicine and ancient "arts"
of healing. The Women's Medical College of
Pennsylvania, on the other hand, continued into the mid-
twentieth century as a women's medical school before it
became coeducational. Other women's schools closed or
merged with men's medical schools soon after the Flexner
report. This further decreased opportunities for women
in medicine.

However, the existence of the Women's Medical
College was unusual for other reasons than that it
continued as a women's school longer than the others:
Women's Medical College of Philadelphia worked within
regular medicine and kept its dedication to preventive
medicine and patient education even while it was purged
of some of its irregular roots in order to survive in a
world of allopathic medicine. Because the college

needed to establish its own clinics and hospitals in which its students and graduates could practice it kept close to its patients to a greater extent than other schools. The continued involvement of administrators of the school in social as well as medical reform movements may well have been the reason for this.

Thus Quaker women shaped the space of medical practice. They provided active support systems for women physicians in two ways: by being their patients, and referring others as their patients; and by sponsoring their medical education.

They literally shaped spaces. When medical schools were closed to them they built their own. When medical internships in the United States were closed they widened their spaces. They went abroad. When more women needed space to practice they built their own clinics and hospitals.

They shaped more human spaces for their patients. They crossed class lines to minister to lower class women in the urban slum. They improved obstetrics and pediatrics. They challenged the roots of the male-dominated profession by questioning the values of a male-dominated profession with male health-care standards.

In breaking boundaries while shaping space for full and healthy lives they questioned the values for which they broke them and questioned the compromises which had to be made.

Notes

¹Gena Corea, The Hidden Malpractice: How American
Medicine Treats Women as Patients and Professionals
(New York: Harcourt Brace Jovanovich, 1978), p. 26,
and Jane B. Donegan, "Man-Midwifery and the Delicacy of
the Sexes" in Remember the Ladies: New Perspectives on
Women in American History, edited by Carol V. R. George
(Syracuse: Syracuse University Press, 1975) pp. 90-
109.

²Corea, op. cit., p. 27.

3Donegan, op. cit., pp. 90-91.

⁴Elise Boulding, The Underside of History: A View of
Women Through Time (Boulder, Colorado: Westview Press,
1976), p. 2.

⁵Donegan, op. cit., p. 90.

⁶Ibid., p. 92.

⁷Ibid., p. 92.

⁸Ibid., p. 92.

⁹Corea, op. cit., p. 27.

10Ibid., pp. 27-28.

11Ibid., p. 29.

¹²Carol Lopate, Women in Medicine (Baltimore: Johns
Hopkins University Press, 1968), p. 1, and Donegan, op.
cit., p. 95.

¹³Jean Donnison, Midwives and Medical Men: A History of
Inter-Professional Rivalries and Women's Rights (New
York: Schocken Books, 1977), pp. 42-61.

14Donegan, op. cit., p. 109.

[15]Stephen Smith, "The Medical Co-education of the Sexes," in Pioneer Work in Opening the Medical Profession to Women: Autobiographical Sketches by Elizabeth Blackwell (London: Longmans, Green, and Company, 1895), pp. 256-7.

[16]Blackwell, op. cit., p. 259.

[17]Corea, op. cit., p. 54.

[18]Elizabeth Thomson, "Elizabeth Blackwell," in The Dictionary of Notable American Women, p. 163.

[19]Of the 53 physicians included in Notable American Women, 13 (25%) were Quakers or had one or both Quaker parents.

[20]Unless otherwise noted, Guielma F. Alsop "Ann Preston" in Notable American Women is the source for biographical information about Ann Preston.

[21]Philip S. Benjamin, The Philadelphia Quakers in the Industrial Age, 1865-1920 (Philadelphia: Temple University Press, 1976), p. 107.

[22]Patricia Spain, "Emeline Horton Cleveland," in Notable American Women, pp. 349-50.

[23]Alsop, op. cit., p. 97.

[24]Patricia Spain Ward, "Hannah E. Myers Longshore," in Notable American Women, pp. 427-428.

[25]Patricia Spain Ward, "Elizabeth Anna Broomall," in Notable American Women, pp. 246-27.

[26]Guielma F. Alsop, "Rachel Littler Bodley," in Notable American women, pp. 186-187.

[27]Guielma F. Alsop, "Clara Marshall," in Notable American Women, pp. 501-502.

[28]Unless otherwise noted, Milnor Cantor (pp. 440-441) in Notable American Women is the source of biographical information for Clemence Lozier.

[29]Corea, op. cit., p. 58.

[30]Rosemary Stevens, American Medicine and the Public Interest (New Haven: Yale University Press, 1971).

THE AMERICAN QUAKER PRESENCE
IN LATE NINETEENTH CENURY CHINA
James C. Cooley, Jr.

Evangelism was an important aspect of Quaker
activity when George Fox founded the sect in England in
the seventeenth century. At that time Fox exhorted his
followers to publish Christian truth to the far corners
of the world--even including China.[1] Quaker immigrants
to America, however, shelved evangelism when they
crossed the Atlantic. The more immediate concerns of
carving a place for themselves as Quakers in new
surroundings engrossed their energies. Not until wide-
spread revivalist sentiment in the latter half of the
nineteenth century had reawakened general interest in
evangelical work did some groups of American Quakers
develop renewed interest in carrying the gospel to
foreign lands.[2] At that time evangelism among American
Quakers attracted supporters largely from midwestern
meetings of the Society of Friends. Eastern Quakers
were as yet unwilling to squander resources on foreign
ventures which they regarded as having dubious merit
and lacking in respectability.[3] Even among midwestern
Quakers the evangelical impulse grew slowly.[4] At last
in 1881 after Eliza Cox, a shrewd-eyed matron from
Butlerville, Indiana, observed money and labor flowing
from Quaker hands to those of rival religious groups,
the idea struck her that there should be visible Quaker
representation in the movement to Christianize the
heathen of the world. With the aid of other determined
Quaker women, Eliza Cox set in motion a campaign to
support Quaker missions abroad.[5] Some years later as a
result of that campaign a Quaker meeting at Damascus,

Ohio, established a mission in China at the city of Nanking. The Damascus meeting chose China for the site of its missionary operation because China was in vogue as a place to send missionaries and because Esther H. Butler, a member of the Damascus meeting, had found a missionary position for herself in China and wanted to fill it.[6]

When Esther Butler accepted the appointment to China she became the first of three women missionaries who were to provide substance and direction to American Quaker enterprise in late nineteenth century China. Along with Esther Butler were Lenna M. Stanley and Lucy A. Gaynor. Although many other individuals made outstanding contributions to the Nanking Mission, in its early years the American Quaker presence in late 19th century China is essentially the story of these women. Esther Butler became superintendent of the mission and guardian of its evangelical purpose. Lenna Stanley shaped educational policy and designed school facilities while Lucy Gaynor, M.D., developed the medical services of the mission.

Like many other women who went into missionary work during this period, these three were seeking a sense of personal worth and achievement beyond the more narrow limits of their American lives. They were shrewd, ambitious and intelligent. And although their missionary impulses were sincere, so was the desire to strike out on their own and to combine the tradition of female independence within the Quaker heritage with perhaps such contemporary examples as Jane Addams and Carey Thomas who urged socially active women to give as free rein to their talents as possible.[7] In a later age providing a wider range of choice, none of these three women of purpose might have left their native soil. Esther Butler could have won a place for herself in politics or business. Lucy Gaynor might have concentrated her energies in public health or hospital administration. Lenna Stanley would most likely have remained in education but she would not necessarily have been confined to a classroom. That the triumvirate of Butler, Stanley and Gaynor failed to make Quaker converts of the Nanking population is testimony more to the staying power of Chinese society than an indictment of their abilities and strategy.

Esther Butler determined to become a missionary in 1884. At that time she was in her early thirties and had been teaching school for sixteen years in her native state of Ohio and in North Carolina. Probably by choice she had remained single, but she was unwilling to accept the role of spinster schoolmarm as her lot in life. Participation in a series of local revival meetings suggested an acceptable alternative career in mission work abroad and she began to search for a post. Butler's search coincided with one by a Methodist Episcopal hospital in Nanking for a missionary nurse and with the decision of her home meeting in Damascus, Ohio, to support the first American Quaker missionary in China.[8]

In preparation for her new career Butler completed a missionary training course at the recently opened Lucy Rider Meyer's Chicago Training School for City, Home and Foreign Missions. The school is an example, one among many, of the sort of business ventures being supported by the expanding of missionary enterprise. The curriculum of the Meyer's school was impressive. There, in approximately one academic year young women undertook to learn Biblical interpretation, church history, techniques of teaching religion, effective methods of visitation in heathen homes, the care and management of children, the rudiments of medicine, nursing, and finally how to preach and run a revival meeting. The teaching staff was made up of volunteer professionals from the Chicago area. According to the operator of the school the methods of instruction were simulation and practice through doing in addition to ordinary classroom teaching. Students like Esther Butler who endured, graduated.9

Esther Butler arrived in Nanking in December 1887, travel worn from a perilous voyage on a vessel already slated for the scrap yard but exhilarated by the prospects of a new lifestyle. During the next three years while Butler worked as a hospital nurse she made preparations for establishing the independent Quaker mission the Damascus meeting had determined to build. Her first task was to acquire facility in Chinese, for she soon discovered that although the Meyer's school had provided valuable training in general mission work, carrying the gospel to Chinese heathen required learning to speak and read some Chinese. In her second task which was to secure land for a mission compound and to become knowledgeable about the management of a missionary establishment she enlisted the aid of her accommodating Methodist Episcopal employers. Thus, in 1888 she purchased two acres of land and by 1890 she had erected an imposing two-story brick structure in Italianate style boasting a bi-level wraparound gallery supported by large brick columns, complete with a complement of outbuildings. A high brick wall enclosed the compound and the effect of the whole was of being aloof and removed from its Chinese neighbors. It was soon identified as the "Quakerage."

From the acquisition of the land to the design of the mission's programs Esther Butler, now superintendent Butler, followed well-established patterns of late 19th century missionary enterprise in China. These patterns were shortly to become the subject matter of Hampton C. Dubose's book, Preaching in Sinim, published in 1893. Butler had a methodical turn of mind. She was a goal-oriented individual who depended on careful planning for the success of her undertakings. She understood that her principal task was to carry the Christian gospel to heathen Chinese. Secure in her own belief of the rightness of Christianity for all peoples, she was unconcerned with such questions as whether Christianity was fitted to Chinese society or if missionaries had social or intellectual responsibilities beyond preaching Christian truth. Cross cultural awareness was never her forte. Neither innovative nor contemplative by nature, Butler's saving grace and reason for success as an administrator was that she readily accepted advice from those whose opinions she respected. According to missionary practices current when Butler was outlining the work of the Quakerage, there were three major areas of missionary activity--evangelical, educational, and medical. Evangelical activities were to take precedence over all others. Educational and medical projects were undertaken to support evangelism. With these priorities in mind Butler began the work of the Quaker mission.[10]

In order to begin the evangelical operation of the mission Butler needed native assistants known as Bible women to carry the gospel initially into Chinese homes in Nanking and eventually into the countryside as well. Bible women, in fact, were the essential support staff of a mission. In addition to evangelical work they were nurses, cleaning women, language teachers, provisioners and cultural advisors to the missionaries.[11] They did everything but cook. To acquire Bible women Butler opened a training school for Chinese women at the Quakerage in the spring of 1891. There the women would learn some English, techniques of home visitation, and some knowledge of the Bible. In spite of generally hostile local feeling toward missionaries, candidates were usually not hard to find because of the fringe benefits that went with the job. Room and board were often part of the package and a knowledge of English which would be gained from the training program had already become an economic asset. Butler started her school with five students and soon increased the number to nine. Her need for help was acute because her only American assistant had returned home to recover her health.

The opening of the training school for Bible women and its subsequent success in providing adequate support staff for the Quaker enterprise was an achievement on which Esther Butler looked with pride. Throughout her sojourn in China the school remained one of her special concerns.[12] There is little indication that the Quaker superintendent thought of the school as much of a means to improve the lot of Chinese women through education except that in general the work of the school furthered the process of Christianizing China. Butler almost

certainly did not see her work with women's education
and as governing authority in the mission as a source of
role models for those students who would defy the
authority of Chinese tradition in later years.

The anti-missionary riots in the summer of 1891
closed the Quakerage for several months. Butler was
forced quite literally to pack her bags and flee to
Shanghai and the safety of the foreign settlements.[13]
But while in exile she continued to lay plans for
additional programs. At that point her special focus
was on expanding the educational facilities. To oversee
educational development at the Quakerage she sought the
help of her cousin, Lenna M. Stanley. Stanley accepted
the post Butler offered without hesitation. Until then
Stanley had earned a reputation for excellence as a
teacher in public schools in Michigan and Nebraska but
at age thirty-five and single the parameters of her
future in education seemed fixed or at least
predictable.[14] The post at Nanking, on the other hand,
promised opportunities for professional growth and a
broader sense of personal fulfillment through
evangelical work. Moreover, the possibility of becoming
surrogate mother to Chinese orphans in a Quaker
orphanage appealed to Stanley's maternal instincts.
Life in Nanking held out rather more variety than home
in America. Lenna Stanley arrived in China in late 1891
even before Butler was able to re-open the Quakerage.

Although Stanley was committed to the task of
converting Chinese to Christianity, her primary interest
from the outset seemed to be directed toward developing
educational facilities for Chinese females of all ages.
The course of her educational endeavors over the years

indicates that she had some idea that in the long run the greater impact of Quaker influence in China would derive from changing Chinese values rather than from publishing the gospel in the streets of Nanking or elsewhere.

Stanley's first major undertaking was to set up an orphanage for Chinese infant girls. After a little more than a year of service at the Quakerage she was prepared to accept the first charges. Esther Butler had misgivings about opening an orphanage so soon after the riots, but Stanley, although she understood that Christian orphanages were often a source of friction with local inhabitants, was determined that from such programs would come educated, Christian leaders for a different China. The orphanage succeeded and continued as an important part of Stanley's work in the remaining years of the century. She exercised care in selecting orphans and gradually won grudging acceptance from local Chinese for the service the orphanage provided.[15]

Having established a functioning orphanage, Stanley began experimenting with a day school for girls. She had done her homework on Chinese culture and believed that the high value Chinese placed on education could be used to support missionary educational programs--even for girls. In late 1893 Stanley started such a school. The purpose of the school was twofold. It was first to provide the rudiments of Christian education and second to increase contacts with local Chinese families whose members both male and female might thus come to view the work of the mission favorably. When her first attempt to attract students by offering free lunches failed, Stanley introduced instruction in English for a small fee. The English classes drew a plentiful supply of ambitious students from merchant families and the school began to succeed. By 1896 it had blossomed into a boarding school known as the Friends Seminary for girls and was on its way toward becoming self-supporting. The curriculum in addition to instruction in English included a variety of Bible courses, but some training in geography and science was also being offered by the end of the century.[16]

Stanley also helped to plan and direct the opening of day schools for boys and girls in conjunction with the street chapels which the Quakerage operated. Street chapels were located in rented buildings in some busy sections of Nanking and served as important centers of contact between missionaries and Chinese. Most Protestant missions maintained one or two. Preaching, prayer meetings, hymn singing and scripture reading were the stock and trade of the street chapel. To those offerings Stanley helped to add day schools. One of her most important contributions to those schools was in helping to train Chinese teachers to staff them. The teacher trainees Stanley selected came from the ranks of the Women's Bible Training School and from among the few adult Chinese she had been instrumental in converting or at least winning over to support mission work.[17]

By 1900 the educational facilities of the Quakerage were a testament to Lenna Stanley's efforts. In addition to the Women's Bible Training School, the orphanage, and the girls' boarding school there were five day schools in operation. The successful development of the educational wing of the Quaker enterprise had been a coopertive effort involving much

of the mission staff at one time or another and steady
financial support from America. Overall, however, it
bore the mark of Lenna Stanley's quiet determination to
introduce western culture to China through Christian
education.[18] Like Esther Butler, Lenna Stanley was
oblivious to the possibility that her work might help to
fuel rapid change in China in the twentieth century or
that her orphans and students might become more
revolutionary than Christian.

While Esther Butler wholeheartedly supported
Stanley's endeavor to develop the educational services
of the Quakerage, she knew from experience in the
Methodist Episcopal hospital that providing medical
services was the most efficient means for introducing
the gospel to the greatest number of Chinese in the
shortest time. Thus, as Stanley and others labored with
educational projects superintendent Butler focused her
attention and many of the resources of the Quakerage on
building a medical program.[19] For that purpose she
secured the services of a young physician from Chicago,
Lucy A. Gaynor. Gaynor had been born in Ireland in 1861
and reared in Chicago. Becoming a physician had been
her ambition since girlhood, and although she had
achieved that ambition by the time Esther Butler first
contracted her, she was also already becoming frustrated
by the constraints placed upon her as a woman in a man's
profession. Gaynor was then unhappily employed in an
eye and ear infirmary in Chicago and pursuing a post on
the missionary field through her own Methodist Episcopal
Church, as an opportunity of escape and opportunity.
Butler offered Gaynor the post at Nanking whereupon the
latter speedily converted to Quakerism and took passage
for China.[20]

On arrival in late 1893 Gaynor discovered that her plan to spend a year studying Chinese language and culture before attempting to organize the mission's medical services was unworkable. The demand for her skills as a physician was constant and left her little time for study. As soon as she could manage the language with the aid of an ubiquitous Bible woman she opened a clinic in the Quaker compound. In less than a year her clientele of Chinese women exceeded five hundred patients and Gaynor had begun to campaign for a separate hospital building. She enjoyed her work as a general practicing physician hugely and was a willing if not very articulate servant of the Christian faith as well.[21]

Ever mindful of the drawing power a hospital would provide as a source of Chinese contacts, Butler encouraged Gaynor in her plans to expand medical services. Meanwhile the superintendent campaigned for funds to build a hospital in the mission compound and to extend missionary activities to a major suburb of Nanking named Lu ho. The two projects were related because the major facility at a station at Lu ho was to be medical service. In less than two years Butler had collected enough money to build a hospital for women and children at the Quakerage.[22] The station at Lu ho would come later.

About the size of a large house, the hospital building Butler and Gaynor erected was well designed for missionary purposes. The focal point in the building was the chapel which also functioned as a waiting room and as an admission room. There were in addition various wards, an operating room, drug dispensary, a kind of bookstore for selling religious tracts to patients, and even space for a classroom or two. The hospital could normally accommodate forty bed patients (in an emergency double that number) and numerous out-patients as well. About a year after opening the hospital Gaynor and the two Chinese assistants she was training as physicians's aides were handling over three thousand outpatients per year.

The procedure for managing patients indicated the priorities and the purpose of the hospital--to publish the gospel and treat the sick. On arrival patients were herded into the chapel-waiting room. While they waited Bible women circulated among them distributing scrip-tures, delivering sermonettes, and finally engaging their captive audiences in discussions about Christian-ity. Such was the prerequisite for seeing Doctor Gaynor. After receiving treatment the departing patients received more religious tracts and invitations to missionary functions. Ward patients received more careful attention. Bible women or missionaries visited these patients twice daily reading scriptures, singing hymns and leading the patients in prayer. The hospital staff discovered as much as they could about patients' families, their source of livelihood and their place of residence. On leaving the hospital the staff reminded the cured patients of their continuing obligations to Christ for the gift of health, obligations which they could meet by becoming Christians and supporting the activities of the Quakerage. Follow-up visits to homes of the discharged patients were the last step of the treatment procedure. During those visits missionary workers solicited converts and encouraged cured patients to give testimony to their friends and relatives about the good works the Quakers accomplished at the mission.[23]

Butler's ambition to expand gospel enterprise through medical service included extending medical care outside the mission compound. The instruments of such expansion were street clinics in Nanking and at missionary stations set up by Bible women in nearby villages. In Nanking the street clinics were usually attached to the street chapels. At the mission stations the procedure varied but the essential combination of health care tied to evangelism remained the central feature. Thus in addition to treating patients and overseeing the hospital, Lucy Gaynor helped to establish such outside clinics. Butler placed increasing emphasis on medical services because as she wrote, "It is a herald and opener of doors."[24]

Toward the end of 1898 Gaynor advised opening a medical station at Lu ho on a permanent basis. An attempt by another Protestant group to establish a mission there was failing for lack of sufficient missionary personnel and home support. Gaynor had undertaken successfully several open air clinics in the area and she believed that it was an appropriate location in which to expand Quaker mission enterprise. Opportunities for converts abounded. The population of Lu ho was approximately thirty thousand; moreover, it was the urban center for a much larger population from the surrounding area.[25] The arrival of an additional physician, Dr. Mary Isabella French, the previous December was also a factor in Gaynor's advice to expand and gave additional support for Esther Butler's long range plan for a greater mission focus in the Lu ho area. For sometime Butler had been casting covetous eyes on Lu ho. Because there was less competition from other missionary enterprises in Lu ho she believed a carefully run Quaker Mission station promoting the gospel through medical service could expect large success. Superintendent Butler, thus, sent the recently arrived Isabella French and a veteran missionary educator, Margaret Holme, to manage activities at Lu ho. In such fashion did the American China Quakers expand the area of their operations.[26]

Lucy Gaynor had found in China what she had lacked in her homeland--the opportunity to explore her talents as a physician. As in the case of Esther Butler and Lenna Stanley, Gaynor thought that "the lines of her life had fallen in pleasant places."[27]

On the eve of the Boxer Rebellion which they would later describe as the high point of "persecution and martyrdom of Christians" in China[28] the three women who had done the most to develop an American Quaker presence in China felt that they had made a substantial beginning. From the Quakerage at Nanking and the new center at Lu ho they were publishing gospel truth in China. The Chinese might not appreciate the difference between Quaker gospel and other Christian gospel, but that point the three Quaker planners recognized as insignificant compared to the greater task of Christianizing China. Moreover, Chinese hostility toward missionary "good works" had apparently begun to subside. Indeed in the five years since the Sino-Japanese war the Chinese themselves were visibly moving toward a general acceptance of "things western" which surely could not omit Christianity.[29] To the inmates of

the Quakerage at Nanking, the apparent prospects of the
new century offered a continuing challenge to individual
creativity and a measure of personal satisfaction not
likely to be attainted at home.

Notes

This paper was presented at the 1980 Southwest conference for Asian Studies in New Orleans and appears in The Proceedings of that conference.

[1] K. S. Latourette, A History of Christian Missions in China, Second Edition (New York: Russell and Russell, 1967), p. 209.

[2] Frederick B. Tolles, Quakers and the Atlantic Culture (New York: Macmillan, 1960), Chapters I-IV.

[3] Phillip S. Benjamin, The Philadelphia Quakers in the Industrial Age 1865-1920 (Philadelphia: Temple University Press, 1976), pp. 4, 18, 112-120.

[4] Anna B. Thomas, editor, Foreign Mission Work of American Friends (American Board of Foreign Missions, 1912), p. vi.

[5] Eliza A. Cox. Looking Back Over the Trail (Women's Missionary Union of Friends in America, 1927), pp. 13-20.

[6] Blanche U. Ratcliff, "Work of the Ohio Yearly Meeting" (Friends Missionary Advocate, Vol. V, No. 5, May, 1899), pp. 66-68.

[7] See Mary P. Ryan, Womanhood in America from Colonial Times to the Present (New York: New viewpoints, 1975), Chap. V. and Nancy F. Cott and Elizabeth H. Pleck, A Heritage of Her Own (New York: Simon and Schuster, 1979), Chap. VIII.

[8] See R. W. Williams, Ohio Friends in the Land of Sinim (Mt. Gilead, Ohio: Friends Foreign Missionary Board of Ohio Yearly Meeting, 1925), pp. 7-30; and Ratcliff, op. cit., pp. 66-68.

[9]See V. H. Rabe, The Home Base of American China Missions 1880-1920 (Cambridge, Mass.: Harvard, 1978), pp. 86-87; and L. R. Meyer, "The Chicago Training School for City, Home, and Foreign Missions" (Friend's Missionary Advocate, Vol. IV, No. 2; Feb. 1888), p. 17.

[10]Thomas, op. cit.,, pp. 196-298; and P. A. Varg, Missionaries Chinese and Diplomats (Princeton: Princeton University Press, 1958), Chap. II.

[11]See E. M. Jenkins, "American Friends in China" (Friends Missionary Advocate, Vol. XXX, No. 12: Dec. 1899), pp. 132-134; and M. Holme, "Home Department-- Ohio" (Friends Missionary Advocate, Vol. XII, No. 12: Dec., 1899), pp. 136-37.

[12]Esther Butler, "Esther Butler Report," in Minutes of the Ohio Yearly Meeting of the Friends Church, 1891 (Damascus, Ohio: Aden Pim and Son), p. 27.

[13]Esther Butler, "Esther Butler Report," Minutes of the Ohio Yearly Meeting of the Friends Church, 1891, 1892, 1893, 1899 (Damascus, Ohio: Aden Pim and Son), 1891: p. 27, 1892: p. 36, 1893: p. 44, 1899: p. 48.

[14]R. W. Williams, The fifty Years with Ohio Friends in China (Damascus, Ohio: Friends Foreign Missionary Society of Ohio Yearly Meeting, 1940), pp. 49-50; and "Stanley" in Dictionary of Quaker Biography, Haverford Library Collection, Haverford, Pa.

[15]Lenna Stanley, Annual Report of Lenna Stanley, 1892 and 1893," Minutes of the Ohio Yearly Meeting of the Friends Church, 1892 and 1893 (Damascus, Ohio: Aden Pim and Son), 1892: pp. 34-35, 1893, p. 42.

[16]Lenna Stanley, "Annual Report of Lenna Stanley," Minutes of the Ohio Yearly Meeting of the Friends Church, 1897 (Damascus, Ohio: Aden Pim and Son, pp. 41-46.

[17]Esther Butler, "Annual Report from Nanking," Minutes of the Ohio Yearly Meeting 1898 (Damascus, Ohio: Aden Pim and Son), pp. 38-44.

[18] E. Lupton, "Eleventh Annual Report of the Corresponding Secretary of the F.F.M.S.," Minutes of the Ohio Yearly Meeting of the Friends Church, 1895 (Damascus, Ohio: Aden Pim and Son), pp. 41-42.

[19] Esther Butler, "Annual Report from Nanking," Minutes of the Ohio Yearly Meeting of the Friends Church, 1898 and 1899 (Damascus, Ohio: Aden Pim and Son), 1898: pp. 39-42, 1899: pp. 45-46.

[20] Anna Thomas, op. cit., p. 198, and R.W. Williams, op. cit., 1940, pp. 53-54.

[21] "Gaynor" in Dictionary of Quaker Biography and "Extracts from Report of Lucy A. Gaynor, M.D. in Charge of Medical Work," Minutes of the Ohio Yearly Meeting and the Friends Church, 1893 (Damascus, Ohio: Aden Pim and Son), pp. 43-44.

[22] R. W. Williams, op. cit., 1925m pp. 39-44.

[23] Esther Butler, op. cit., 1898, p. 126; Williams, op. cit., 1940, pp. 53-54, and Gaynor, op. cit., 1897, pp. 157-58.

[24] Esther Butler, ibid., p. 126.

[25] R. W. Williams, op. cit., 1940, pp. 57-59, and Butler, ibid., p. 156.

[26] R. W. Williams, op. cit., 1925, pp. 50-52.

[27] Lucy Gaynor, op. cit., p. 44.

[28] R. W. Williams, op. cit., 1925, p. 63.

[29] R. W. Williams, ibid., pp. 61-63, and J. K. Fairbank, ed., The Missionary Enterprise in China and America (Cambridge, Mass.: Harvard, 1974), pp. 270-273.

"NO GENTLE SAINT"
FLORENCE KELLEY AS A SHAPER
OF SOCIAL SPACE
Susan S. Forbes

On May 1, 1900, Florence Kelley began a new job as
Secretary of the National Consumers' League. During the
thirty years that followed, Kelley was a moving force in
the fight for improved working conditions in American
industry. A tireless campaigner for child labor laws,
she did not live to see ratification of a federal Child
Labor Amendment, but she did leave a strong legacy in
the form of state enactment and enforcement of age, hour
and wage legislation. As the Consumers' League's chief
inspector of factories and produce safety, she alerted
thousands of women to their rights as consumers and the
laborer's right to a decent working environment.
Through the League's issue of a consumer label of
excellence to those items produced in healthy
surroundings by adequately paid and reasonably worked
adults, Kelley influenced the practices of many manufacturing concerns. Finally, as a pacifist, feminist and
member of the settlement house movement, she joined with
other prominent women in a myriad of social reform
organizations that included the NAACP, the Anti-
Preparedness Committee (which protested President
Wilson's Defense Bill and, later, the American entry
into World War I), and the Women's Suffrage Association.
In fact, Felix Frankfurter's remark that Kelley "had
probably the largest single share in shaping the social
history of the United States during the first thirty
years of this century" may not be too great an
exaggeration.[1]

When Kelley accepted her post with the National
Consumers' League, she reached the terminus of a journey
that had led her into the first ranks of Progressive
social, political and labor reform. The path which she
had followed, however, was by no means a straight and
narrow one. She had made side trips, as she later saw
them, into radical socialism and domesticity; these
detours helped her to define her goals but other
influences were at work that showed her the means with
which to accomplish these goals. I should note here
that my choice of metaphor in describing Kelley's career
is a very deliberate one: for Quaker women, the concept
of space leads to questions of mobility of a symbolic
and literal nature--mobility in human development,
mobility in social interaction and, in the most literal
sense, mobility as physical movement. It is the purpose
then of this paper to explore the road which Kelley
traveled to make her an influential force in the
shaping of American society.

Florence Kelley was born on September 12, 1859, in
Philadelphia, Pennsylvania. Her father, William Darrah
Kelley, known in political circles as Pig-Iron Kelley,
served in the House of Representatives for almost thirty
years. There he received a reputation as a strong
supporter of high tariffs to protect American industry.
Strongly committed to industrialization as a practical
solution to many of America's problems, William Kelley
was nevertheless concerned with the accompanying evils
of the industrial life. Throughout her childhood, he
tried to share with his daughter this sense of concern.
He took Florence on trips to factories and mills so that
she could see the technological marvels of modern
manufacturing and observe, first hand, the working

conditions. On a trip to western Pennsylvania in 1871, for example, they visited steel mills which used the then newly discovered Bessemer process. While all of the adults gazed in wonder at the monstrous machinery of the process, Florence as she later recalled the incident, was far more interested in the number of children, no older than she was, who were busily at work at two o'clock in the morning.[2] Her father had no easy answers to her questions about the ethics of child labor, but he continued to educate her about this practice. Florence remembered that in her first reading lesson, she used a book which pictured the poor working children of England. Her father, when rebuked for giving his child so depressing a book, explained that "life can never be right for all the children until the cherished boys and girls were taught to know the facts in the lives of their less fortunate contemporaries."[3]

Despite his concern, though, Kelley was not optimistic about the chances of early reform of working conditions. He even justified the inequities of the capitalistic system by arguing that the duty of his generation was to build up great industries in America so that more wealth could be produced for the whole people. He did imbue his daughter with a sense of future mission, however, when he told her that "the duty of your generation . . . will be to see that the product is distributed justly. The same generation cannot do both."[4] It was a lesson that Florence took to heart.

It was not just at her father's side that Florence learned of the need for societal change. Through her mother, she was heir to a tradition of Quaker reform. Caroline Kelley, great-great grand-daughter of the

famous botanist, John Bartram, remains a shadowy figure
in much of Florence's writings; there is little beyond
descriptions of her mother's grief at the death of a
number of her infant children. After the death of her
own parents, though, Caroline had been adopted by a
family with strong interests in reform, and of this
family there is a great deal of information. Of most
importance to Florence's development was great-aunt
Sarah Pugh: a committed Quaker, Sarah was active in the
abolitionist and feminist movements. Even at the age of
seventy-one, Sarah attended meetings of the National
Woman Suffrage Association. A life-long friend of
Lucretia Mott, Sarah Pugh introduced her niece to some
of the most important reform figures of the nineteenth
century.

Most important, Sarah also taught Florence that
beliefs must be translated into some form of action. A
young Florence observed, for example, that her aunt
never used sugar or products made of cotton. Florence
asked her aunt about this and later recorded her
impressions of the conversation:

> `Cotton was grown by slaves, and sugar
> also,' she replied, `so I decided many
> years ago never to use either, and to
> bring these facts to the attention of my
> friends.'

> Not meaning to be impertinent, I said:
> `Aunt Sarah, does Thee really think any
> slaves were freed because Thee did not
> use sugar or cotton?'

> Perfectly tranquil was her reply: Dear
> child, I can never know that any slave
> was personally helped, but I had to live
> with my own conscience.'[5]

Sarah Pugh's activism and overt feminism placed her outside of the fellowship of many Quakers, but she did reflect many aspects of nineteenth century Quaker reform. Sarah gave voice to a generalized sense of benevolence that had its basis in a universal love of mankind and a strong sense of inner light. Sydney James, in his study of the origins of Quaker humanitarianism, has suggested that philanthropy became the altruistic expression of the religious convictions of Friends. During the period of political and social withdrawal of Friends in the years after the French and Indian, and Revolutionary Wars, benevolence also permitted Quakers to maintain a bond with the outside world.[6] Despite the emphasis on altruism, however, the final measure of one's responsibility to others was not the opinions or needs of others, but one's own conscience. As in the case of Sarah Pugh's boycott of slave products, the importance of her act was not its effectiveness but its conformity to the dictates of her conscience.

The importance in Quaker benevolence, then, was attached to the actions and salvation of the donor as opposed to the benefits to the recipient or the reform of conditions that led to the need for charity. This concern for the donor could sometimes deteriorate into an excessive concern for the reputation of the Society of Friends as a religious group that provided benevolence. Philip Benjamin, in his examination of the

Philadelphia Quakers of Kelley's youth, has described the complex set of motives that characterized Quaker reform efforts:

> Image building and self-congratulation were no doubt among the motives which prompted the Orthodox . . . to publish a little book which listed all the charities they sponsored in Philadelphia. Yet these philanthropies quite often gave expression to vital religious conviction frequently fostered by `refreshing seasons' of corporate worship in the Meetinghouse.[7]

Whatever the motives, however, these philanthropic activities did provide material help for many needy individuals.

Florence Kelley was thus heir to two distinct traditions: the ethical humanitarianism of her Quaker forebears and the commitment to an industrial future of her father. Both traditions exposed her to the ills of her society; both transmitted an optimism that solutions to these problems would be found, neither though provided her with practical and effective answers. As Dorothy Blumberg, Kelley's most recent biographer, has suggested, Quakerism seemed more appropriate to an earlier, simpler time when concern for the individual could lead to a relief of individual problems. On the other hand, William Kelley's belief that his generation must build industry while her generation makes it more equitable in distribution of awards, exacted too great a price in human suffering.[8] An interest in reform had

certainly been stimulated in her childhood, but Florence
was still in search of a comfortable and effective road
to social change.

The next stage of Kelley's journey took her to
Cornell University. She had discovered the recently
opened college in 1874 when she retrieved a brochure
about its plans for a co-educational program from its
resting place in William Kelley's waste bin. Impressed
with the rhetoric of equal intellectual opportunities
for both sexes, Florence determined to prepare herself
for admission. Because there was no school in
Philadelphia that could prepare a woman for college,
Florence began a course of study on her own until, in
1876, she was able to pass the entrance requirements.
At Cornell, her course of study included French, German,
Latin, algebra, literature, natural history, and
astronomy; it was a course of study designed to develop
a liberally educated person. Florence, though delighted
with the academic environment, was surprised at the lack
of interest in politics and current events. Coming from
a politically active household, she longed for that type
of intellectual stimulation at Cornell. She did join a
literature group headed by M. Carey Thomas, later to be
president of Bryn Mawr; then a sophomore, Kelley shared
in the founding of the first Social Science Club at the
university.

Florence's stay at Cornell was interrupted,
however, by a bout with diphtheria, and when she was
well enough to travel, she was forced to return to
Philadelphia to recuperate. The interruption in her
education was by no means a new experience for Florence;
she had been required to leave a number of elementary

schools because of ill health. She decided to put the months of convalescence to good use, however, and began to collect materials for a senior thesis. In choosing a topic for her thesis, Florence returned to a concern of her childhood, and wrote on "Some Changes in the Legal Status of the child since Blackstone." Meticulously researched and well analyzed, in part because of her study of the law with William Kelley, the thesis looked at three areas--custody, protection, and education--and in each examined the child in the family and the child without a family. Well above usual undergraduate standards, the thesis was published in International Review in 1882.

After graduation from Cornell, Kelley once more returned to Philadelphia but was denied admission to the University of Pennsylvania for graduate work in advanced Greek. Ironically, the official reason for her rejection was because of the Board of Trustees' expressed repugnance at the idea of men and women in the same classroom, but the unofficial and apparently real reason was because no advanced Greek was taught at the university.9 Denied the opportunity to do graduate work, Florence looked for other outlets. She joined the New Century club, a group established "to create an organized centre of thought and action among women, for the protection of their interests and the promotion of science, literature and art . . ."10 Florence worked with a group of other members to set up a program of evening courses for working women; the classes which she taught gave her her first direct exposure to the working class and a new understanding of the needs and aspirations of workers.

Kelley's interest in the activities of the New Century Club reflected not only her continuing interest in the plight of workers, but also a growing interest in the woman's movement. Through her aunt Sarah, she had been exposed to feminism at an early age. Through her father, though, Florence learned of the intricacies of the suffrage movement. William Kelley was the sponsor of the Suffrage Amendment in the House of Representatives and became a close friend of Susan B. Anthony. Their friendship did not prevent Anthony from calling him to task, however, when the Representative failed to show the respect for suffrage that Anthony demanded. Florence recalled attending one suffrage convention which met the same evening that a House subcommittee on tariffs was to hold hearings. Although William Kelley was scheduled to be a speaker at the convention, he never made it there because of the hearings. Anthony, disappointed in her friend's absence, announced to the gathering that "this is a new and painful illustration of the lack of respect for the vote even among men who are convinced advocates of suffrage. Even Judge Kelley considers the tariff on vinegar of greater importance than votes." Florence returned home after the convention anxious to learn of her father's response to this ridicule when he read of it in the morning newspaper. To her surprise, William Kelley laughed and said, "The good old Major! I'm afraid I deserved that."[11] The incident is important and worth re-telling because Anthony's behavior became a model for Florence Kelley in her later dealings with political figures. Understanding that her father, a powerful and important political figure, respected Anthony's steadfastness to her cause and show of independence, Florence displayed an equal strength of character with similar results.

Florence's experiment with education in the New Century Club came to an abrupt halt when her brother took ill and needed a traveling companion during a recuperative trip to Europe. The European travel proved important to Kelley's future. She was exposed to new ideas about the direction of industrial growth as she listened to conversations between her father, who joined his children in England, and the American Consul in Manchester. Her father had always argued that high tariffs were necessary as a protection, not only of American profits, but as protection for the American worker. He reasoned that European workers were paid less and worked harder than Americans, and, if European goods were allowed to flood the American market, the wages of American laborers would fall. Mr. Shaw, the Consul, demonstrated, however, that in some English industries hours were shorter, equipment in factories were better, and the worker's purchasing power was greater despite the free trade system and the competition from continental manufacturers. Yet, as Florence was to discover on a trip to the Black Country, in other industries, particularly ones with a sweating system and homework, the working conditions were abominable and wages were at the lowest possible level. It appeared to Florence that neither high tariffs nor free trade provided much of an answer to the problems of the workers though each could, and did, contribute to the welfare of the employer.

An equally important source of stimulation during her European travel was a visit from her college friend, M. Carey Thomas, who met the Kelleys in France. Thomas had been studying at the University of Zurich, the first European university to permit co-educational classes.

Upon hearing of the possibilities of graduate study in Zurich, Florence determined to attend the university. After she was admitted, she began a course of study which included readings in history, economics and politics. Far more important than her formal study, though, was her first serious exposure to the ideas of socialism. Florence had first learned of Marxist ideas during a visit home while she was at Cornell. A young man who was staying at the Kelley home had shown her pamphlets which he had found at the headquarters of the First International in Hoboken, New Jersey. Florence was impressed with the ideals expressed in the pamphlets, but her return to school prevented further discussion. In Zurich, however, she attended meetings addressed by such socialist luminaries as Eduard Bernstein, one of the heads of the German Socialist Party. At her first meeting, she heard Bernstein discuss the subject of tariffs. While most of the arguments against tariffs were now familiar to her, one new idea stood out--the responsibility of workers to and for each other, a responsibility which should cross national boundaries. As she listened to this presentation of Marxist doctrine, Florence grew excited. She associated the sentiments of the Internationale with the ideals of Quakerism, writing of this first meeting: "this might well have been a Quaker meeting. Here was the Golden Rule! Here was Grandaunt Sarah!"[12]

In 1884 Kelley joined the Socialist Party with the hope that socialism, by stressing the common bonds of all workers, could be the means through which the economic benefits of industrialization could help all persons. In her attempt to reconcile the demands of her Quaker conscience with the practicalities emphasized by her father, Florence had searched for a program in which equity could accompany development and the concerns of the individual would become the concern of society. Socialism appeared to be that very program.

Kelley described her years in Zurich as her novitiate. She plunged into her new movement with the zeal of the convert and sought out every major work by or about socialists. She must have been particularly attracted to the works of Friedrich Engels because, in 1884, she requested permission to translate The Condition of the Working Classes in England. Permission granted, Kelley began the translation and a lengthy correspondence with Engels, a correspondence that was to continue for many years.[13] Kelley's commitment to socialism may have been strengthened further through her contacts with a young Russian physician, Lazare Wischne-wetsky, who was a dedicated member of the party. Despite Florence's initial ambivalence because of the many differences in background and outlook, they were married in June 1884.

The years of Kelley's marriage are described in her autobiography as an almost total blank. She ended the third installment of the memoir, which appeared in the Survey magazine, with a curiously misleading statement:

> I was, however, not to turn directly from my novitiate in American and European universities to a part in the intellectual life of my generation, nor the political, nor the economic life. Instead, having married a Russian physician, I returned to America in 1886

with him and my elder son, and the
ensuing five years were devoted to
domestic life.14

In actuality, as Dorothy Blumberg has reconstructed
these years from Kelley's correspondence and published
writings, the work on the translation of Engels
continued; Florence actively participated with her
husband in the New York section of the socialist Labor
Party, and she became involved in bureaucratic and
personality-induced squabbles in the party. Most
important, though her friendship with Engels went
through cycles that ranged from mutual admiration to
near enmity, and she was eventually expelled from the
Socialist Party because the German-born leaders
distrusted her American background and obstinence in the
face of their criticisms, Kelley continued to think and
write about Marxist themes.

Two works were particularly important in Kelley's
development. In a somewhat bitter article on
philanthropy, published in 1887, Kelley contrasted two
types of benevolence. Bourgeois philanthropy, which was
supposedly based on altruism, she characterized as
actually designed to maintain the status quo for the
ruling classes: "Our bourgeois philanthropy, whatever
form it may take, is really only the effort to give back
to the workers a little bit of that which our whole
social system systematically robs them of, and so to
prop up that system yet a little longer."15

She believed, on the other hand, that working class
phlanthropy permitted workers to help each other better
their working conditions through organizations such as

trade unions and sick benefit societies. In the paper, addressed to a meeting of the Association of Collegiate Alumnae and later printed, she urged the members of her audience to refrain from participating in the patch-work efforts of the bourgeois philanthropists, and turn their attention, instead, to the real needs of the workers:

> To cast our lot with the workers, to seek to understand the laws of social and industrial development. . . to spread this enlightenment among the men and women destined to contribute to the change to a higher social order, to hasten the day when all the good things of society shall be the goods of all the children of man, and our petty philanthropy of today superfluous--this is the true work for the elevation of the race, this is the true philanthropy.[16]

Despite the rhetoric, Kelley's lecture left something to be desired in terms of concrete proposals. While she offered a devastating critique of the forms of "altruistic" philanthropy accepted by most Americans, she did not really provide an alternative, aside from a general call for class struggle, to charity organizations.

In her second major work of this period, however, Kelley did begin to develop some alternatives. In this article, "Our Toiling Children," Kelley returned to the themes of her Cornell thesis and the subject which was to continue to be her primary interest--the plight of working children. After offering persuasive evidence, again based on meticulous research, of the seriousness of the problem of child labor, Kelley proposed several solutions: Compulsory education laws which would keep children in school, minimum age laws which would keep children out of work, and a government stipend for dependent children so they could afford to go to school. Understanding that American society was far from ready to pass such laws, Kelley also suggested that women of all classes organize in support of children. Working women should organize in trade associations which could also work for protection of women workers. Middle class women should organize and use their economic power as consumers to boycott businesses which employed child labor and support businesses which improved working conditions. In this way, rather than by offering charity to individual families, philanthropists could effect changes in the entire system of child labor.17 The method which Kelley urges, the combination of union and consumer activity, reflects the new influences of socialism and the old influence of Quakerism. Here again was Aunt Sarah with her boycott of slave products. Only in the writings of her niece, Florence, the boycott was perceived not as an expression of conscience but as an effective tool for change. Kelley believed that industrialists would see selective buying as an exercise of economic power and would respond to such sanctions.

Despite the importance to the historian of this period of Kelley's life, we are still left with her dismissal of its impact upon her in all but its domestic aspects.

All of her biographers agree that her reticence to
discuss her life in New York is by no means evidence of
a repudiation of her socialist beliefs. She continued
to identify herself as a socialist and even in the days
of the Red Scare when groups such as the DAR attacked
her ties to Marxism, Kelley reaffirmed her commitment to
the ideals of the International. If the explanation of
her silence does not lie in her attitude towards socialism,, it may lie in her experience with marriage.
Kelley had been ambivalent about marriage to
Wischnewetsky from the very beginning. She had feared
that the differences in their backgrounds would likely
conflict although mutual friends wrote that they were
two congenial spirits. Wischnewetsky was in fact a
charming man with a frank and cheerful air. Unfor-
tunately, he was also a poor businessman; yet, during
their residence in New York, he invested in a number of
get-rich-quick schemes that failed to bring the success
which he envisioned. Faced with mounting debts and the
responsibility for three young children, Florence eventually decided that separation from her husband would be
in everyone's best interest. Her marriage was a bitter
disappointment to Kelley, and she discussed it with few
friends. Her silence may therefore merely reflect an
unwillingness to share with strangers what was very
definitely the most disappointing experience of her
life.

Kelley's description of her life as domestic,
however, does require further examination. It may be
fair to infer that the experience of motherhood had an
effect upon her future work that she does not explicitly
describe. Her earlier interest in the rights of
children came from a sincere but removed concern--the

concern of a privileged child of a privileged family. During her marriage, however, she came to see the needs of children from a different perspective--the perspective of a beleaguered parent trying but failing to keep a household intact. She in fact came to see that the needs of children and the needs of parents, particularly mothers, might not be one and the same. Kelley believed, throughout the rest of her life, that mothers of young children should not work, partly because of their obligations to their children but also because they tend to depress wages and "they are a fearful drag upon the men in . . . industry."18 For a feminist, socialist, and supporter of trade unions for women, these are seemingly strange sentiments. Yet, for a mother who assumed full responsibility for the support of her children, avenues of support other than employment, such as government stipends, may have seemed to be a more desirable solution to the economic needs of women. It was not, however, the solution that she sought for herself.

Once Kelley decided to seek a divorce from her husband, she ascertained that the State of Illinois offered reasonable grounds upon which to obtain both the divorce and custody of her children. Her first concern, though, was to find suitable employment. After offering her services to a number of reform organizations, such as the WCTU, and finding that they could not offer her recompense for her labor, Kelley joined the settlement house workers at Hull House. With Jane Addams' help she found temporary quarters for her children at the home of Henry Demarest Lloyd, a kindred spirit who was then at work on Wealth Against Commonwealth. Kelley was then able to join fully in the life and activities of Hull House.

Coming from the squabble of the socialist Labor Party and the distrust with which she was viewed by other socialists, Kelley must have found the environment of the settlement house a refreshing change. Now she was surrounded by women who shared much of her background and her beliefs. Addams, for example, shared something of her Quaker upbringing and early exposure to reform politics. Despite the similarities in background, however, Kelley differed from the other settlement house workers in motivation and by temperament. Unlike many of the single women who saw Hull House as a substitute for boredom or less constructive uses of leisure time, Kelley needed a job in order to support herself and her children. Furthermore, for Kelley, unlike other residents, the experience of Hull House was not one in which she learned for the first time of the ills of the industrial life. As we have seen, she already had a strong grounding in social theory and had had first-hand exposure of working class conditions in New York. But perhaps the most important difference was the one of temperament. While Addams, in particular, has been described as a proper, reserved lady, the adjectives used to describe Kelley evoke a different type of personality and demeanor. Frances Perkins described Kelley as "explosive, hot tempered, determined . . . no gentle saint." Felix Frankfurter suggested that of her settlement house contemporaries, she had "the most salient, salty character of them all."19 If Kelley then found a refuge at Hull House in the years after her divorce, Hull House found a fighting spirit who instilled in her friends a passion for reform and the skills necessary to cause change.

During her first year at Hull House, Kelley was appointed special Agent of the Bureau of Labor Statistics. Under a pay schedule based on piece work, Kelley visited sweat shops in order to compile statistics about the conditions of work. This study led to her appointment as an agent of the Department of Labor to prepare a study of Chicago slums. In her report, Kelley offered evidence of the pernicious effects of the sweating system of homework upon the health and welfare of women and children. After the circulation of her report, filled with statistical data, the Illinois legislature appointed a commission to investigate the working conditions. Kelley and her staff conducted tours of the neighborhood around Hull House, and were able to show the commission graphic proof of the allegations presented in the report. The commission gave a strong recommendation for legislation to eliminate the worst aspects of the sweatshop system. The final bill included a minimum age requirement, a maximum eight hour day for women, and initial steps to be taken to reduce the public health hazard of sweatshops. The bill, passed in 1893, also created a department of factory inspection; upon the recommendation of Henry Lloyd, Florence Kelley was appointed Chief Factory Inspector.

With a staff of twelve persons, six men and six women, Kelley began thorough investigations of the use of child labor. Her department set up procedures, including medical examinations, for judging affidavits of age. When the district attorney refused to prosecute cases which Kelley presented, she took a law degree at

Northwestern University so she could bring her own cases to court. Ever the pragmatist, Kelley found the most effective means of enforcing the law. She may, in fact, have been too successful at her job; when a new and more conservative governor was elected in 1897, Kelley was dismissed and replaced by an inspector who was more in tune to the interests of business.

In the years after her work in government, Kelley supported herself by writing, lecturing and working as an assistant to the periodical clerk of a library. Her interest in politics and reform did not decrease, however. In 1898, Kelley, along with other Hull House residents, fought for the reform of the Chicago political machine by opposing the re-election of Johnny Powers, boss of the 19th Ward.

After Powers won the election, most of the Hull House reformers decided to cut their losses and accept the realities of Chicago politics. In a rare triumph of idealism over her sense of practicality, Kelley urged a continuation of the fight. She believed that to admit defeat would be equivalent to accepting the conventional ethics of politics.

Kelley's most important work towards reform, though, came not in politics but in organizing resistance to child labor. Returning to the suggestions of her early article on working children, Kelley involved herself in the founding of a Consumers' League in Chicago. The League asked women shoppers to adhere to self-imposed restrictions designed to better conditions for workers. The first consumers' league had been formed in New York in 1891 as the result of a meeting between a young working woman, Alice Woodbridge, and a prominent civic reformer, Josephine Shaw Lowell. Woodbridge described the working conditions in retail stores as they affected saleswomen and cash girls. She asked that the patrons of these stores interest themselves in the welfare of the workers. Although it is unclear whether either woman was familiar with Kelley's work, their solution closely followed the tactics outlined by Kelley in "Our Toiling Children." At first, the new consumers' league addressed itself only to the conditions in retail establishments, and pressed for higher wages, shorter hours, more breaks, and healthier working conditions. By 1898, though, the responsibility of consumers to the producers of their purchases was also recognized. Because these goods were made in many states, however, a national organization would have to fight for effective controls. Florence Kelley represented Illinois at a convention of state and local leagues which formed the National Federation of Consumer Leagues, later to be called the National Consumers' League.

One of the main areas of discussion at the national convention was development of the tools necessary to influence both consumers and manufacturers. Kelley and others favored the issuance of a consumer label which could be placed in goods produced under proper working conditions. The League could investigate factories, make sure that the labor of neither children nor women was exploited, and also check on the sanitary conditions in order to insure that no products were contaminated. Kelley was particularly interested in this last aspect since she had seen the effects of a smallpox epidemic while she was factory inspector in Illinois. Products

which had been made in sweatshops had been contaminated
during the epidemic and led to isolated cases of
smallpox in areas to which these products had been
shipped. Kelley persuaded others that the consumer
label could be an effective impetus for change, and the
plan was adopted at the convention. The following year,
Kelley was appointed Secretary of the League and was
employed, on a fulltime basis, as factory inspector and
organizer. In 1900, Kelley left Hull House, her home of
eight years, to settle in New York City, headquarter of
the National Consumers' League.

Under Kelley's leadership, the National Consumers'
League began a program through which its policies could
be implemented. The League at first concentrated its
activities in one area of manufacturing, the production
of undergarments. Those garments which were
manufactured in healthy surroundings and without the
employment of children under the age of sixteen were
awarded the Consumer Label. By the close of her first
year as inspector of factories, Kelley had identified
fifteen which conformed to her standards of excellence.
The number rose to 38 in 1904 and 70 in 1914. Very
often, however, the garments which were produced under
acceptable circumstances were made of coarse material
and simple design. The League, then, had to mount a
publicity campaign in order to convince affluent
consumers that they should buy the products even if they
offended the customer's aesthetic standards. Kelley
had hoped to appeal to the consumer's self-interest as
the most effective source of support. She argued that
considerations of health should come ahead of considerations of taste; garments produced in tenements were
more likely to be contaminated and spread disease than

those manufactured in clean factories. By buying goods with consumer labels, the purchaser could protect her own and her family's health. In actuality, though, the appeal to self-interest was not strong enough to persuade consumers to opt for what appeared to be inferior products. The consumer in effect remained the best judge of her own self-interest.

Kelley, as the leader of a philanthropic organization, added a more traditional argument to her arsenal—one based on altruism, the responsibility of the consumer to those who were less fortunate in their economic situations. That argument had been the basis of Alice Woodbridge's original appeal to Josephine Shaw Lowell, and benevolence-minded women could still be swayed by their sense of humanitarian concern. Kelley in an essay, "Modern Industry and Morality," described the League's ethic:

> For nearly a quarter century the Consumers' League has been bringing to bear upon industry the intelligence of consumers in the interests of their own consciences and of the life, health, intelligence and well-being of wage workers . . . The League holds that consumers are entitled to a clean conscience if they act as conscientious people; that they can, if they will, enforce a claim to have all that they buy free from the taint of cruelty.[20]

In developing an argument based on altruistic concern and the dictates of conscience, Kelley moved away from her earlier socialist critique of bourgeois philanthropy. While she retained her conviction that piecemeal efforts directed at individuals would lead to no fundamental change, she no longer argued that the bourgeois philanthropist was necessarily motivated by a desire to maintain the status quo. Instead, she recognized the sincere desire of some women to subject their own desires to the needs of others because of a strongly developed moral sense. Aunt Sarah proved a far stronger influence upon Florence than Marx or Engels. Interestingly, Kelley's affirmation of altruism brought her closer to the very Quakerism from which she derived many of her ideas about responsibility. In 1927, she made formal application to join the Society of Friends.

Kelley, while basing her arguments upon the idealism of humanitarian benevolence, nevertheless remained a pragmatist in her evaluation of methods of reform. She realized that arguments based on altruism might attract supporters to the League, and economic measures of consumer action might be effective against some manufacturers, but the working conditions and level of pay would remain unchanged for most workers as long as industrialists were asked to make voluntary improvements. Far reaching reform of industry could come, however, through legislative action if accompanied by effective governmental implementation of laws which set standards for all employers.22 Kelley's earlier experience as Chief Factory Inspector of Illinois had taught her that well-drafted legislation could lead to change if the right officials were called upon to enforce the laws, and unions and reform societies oversaw their actions.

From the beginning of its existence, the NCL supported all efforts to pass laws establishing minimum age standards that would eliminate child labor. In 1910, though, after attending an International Meeting of Consumers' Leagues, Kelley presented the idea of a minimum wage law to delegates of her organization. She suggested that the League address the needs of women workers, in particular, because of the generally lower wages which women received and the failures of the labor movement to offer union protection to women. In addition, she saw support of minimum wages legislation as a statement of sisterhood that would transcend class divisions. The delegates voted to study the subject and prepare for a legislative campaign to begin in 1910. In 1912 the campaign bore its first fruit when Massachusetts passed a weak but still innovative version of a minimum wage act. During the next year, eight states followed the Massachusetts example. After these successes, the campaign ground to a halt, partly because of some legal questions about the consitutionality of both the wage laws and maximum hour laws. The NCL turned its attention to a series of court battles; Kelley asked Louis Brandeis to represent the League and file briefs in defense of the laws in both state and federal courts. After Brandeis was appointed to a seat on the supreme court, Felix Frankfurter took over his role. In general, the courts upheld the maximum hour legislation but declared the minimum wage laws to be unconstitutional until 1937 when the court reversed its earlier decisions.

Kelley's support of legislative methods of reform did not extend to support of the Equal Rights Amendment proposed by the Woman's Party in 1921. Although in sympathy with the general sentiments of equality as expressed in the amendment, she feared the practical ramifications of such a measure. In particular, Kelley feared that passage of the amendment would nullify the legislation which gave women special protection in industry. Describing the language of the amendment as ambiguous, Kelley argued that the courts would have to spend years in determining the exact meaning of the legislation. In the meantime, many efforts directed at the relief of specific problems facing women would be blocked. In her words, "This would be a new subjection of wage-earning women. . ., and to the subjection we are opposed on principle and in practice . . . The acid test of the quality of legislation is the extent to which women benefit from it."[23] Thus, when faced with what she saw as real threats to the interests of working women, Kelley the pragmatist put aside the idealism of feminism. The Golden Rule, the sisterhood of all women, might be an effective call to action, but the measure of success must be the benefits derived from the specific measures taken.

The central tension of Florence Kelley's life, then was the tension between idealism on the one hand and pragmatism on the other. That tension, as we have seen, can be traced back to the twin influences of her childhood, the Quaker humanitarianism of her greataunt, Sarah Pugh, and the practical reliance on industrialization of her father. In middle years, Marxism replaced Quakerism as the central ideal only to be itself replaced by a form of Humanitarian Socialism with the reappearance of heavy Quaker undertones in the last years of her life. These ideologies were powerful throughout Kelley's life in the shaping of her long-

range goals and the rhetoric with which she so
effectively called others to action. They never,
however, provided her with the necessary means to
accomplish her goals. Quakerism led to philanthropy
but, despite the sincere altruism of the consumers'
leagues, their economic actions resulted in piecemeal
reforms. Socialism, in her experience, led to
bureaucratic squabbles and utopian visions of revolutionary change. Only legislative and judicial action
offered possibilities of overall reform. It is fitting,
then, and perhaps inevitable, that the daughter of Pig-
Iron Kelley, champion of protective legislation for
industry, became champion herself of legislation to
protect the interests of women, children, and workers.
It was her legislative victories in particular that
helped Florence Kelley reshape the social space of
America. It was a journey well worth taking.

Notes

[1]Josephine Goldmark, _Impatient Crusader:_ _Florence_
Kelley's Life Story (Urbana: University of Illinois
Press, 1953), p. v.

[2]Florence Kelley, "My Philadelphia," _The survey_ (October
1, 1926), p. 56.

[3]_Ibid._, p. 9.

[4]_Ibid._, p. 8.

[5]_Ibid._, p. 54.

[6]Sydney James, _A People Among People_ (Cambridge:
Harvard University Press, 1963), pp. 315, 324.

[7]Philip Benjamin, _The Philadelphia Quakers in the_
Industrial Age, 1865-1920 (Philadelphia: Temple
University Press, 1976), p. 101.

[8]Dorothy Blumberg, _Florence Kelley: The Making of_
Social Pioneer (New York: Augustus M. Kelley, 1966),
pp. 40-1.

[9]Florence Kelley, "When Co-education Was Young," _The_
Survey (February 1, 1927), p. 600.

[10]Blumberg, p. 30.

[11]Florence Kelley, "My Novitiate," _The Survey_ (April 1,
1927), p. 31.

[12]_Ibid._, p. 35.

[13]See Blumberg, pp. 44-121 for full discussion of
Kelley's interaction with Engels.

[14]"My Novitiate," p. 35.

[15]Florence Kelley Wischnewetzky, "The need of theoretical preparation for philanthropic work," reprinted in Helen Hiscock Backus, "The Need and the Opportunity for College trained women in philanthropic work," Sociology (SB pv 41 - New York Public Library), p. 16.

[16]Ibid., p. 26.

[17]Florence Kelley Wischnewetzsky, Our Toiling Children (Chicago: Woman's Temperance Public Association, 1889), pp. 25-26, 36.

[18]Florence Kelley, "The Problem of the Married Woman in Industry," typescript, 1918(?), National consumers" League Manuscript Collection, Library of Congress.

[19]Perkins' remark reprinted in Notable American Women (Cambridge: Harvard University Press, 1971) v. 2, p. 319; Frankfurter remark in Goldmark, p. ix.

[20]Florence Kelley, Modern Industry (New York: Longmans, Green and co., 1914).

[21]Goldmark, p. 209.

[22]For an expression of Kelley's views on legislation, see her work Some Ethical Gains through Legislation (New York: The MacMillan Co., 1905).

[23]Goldmark, p. 185.

EMILY GREENE BALCH
AND THE TRADITION OF PEACE
New England Brahmin and Convinced Quaker
Barbara Miller Solomon

In this study of Quaker women as the shapers of human space, Emily Greene Balch (1867-1961) deserves a special place. Social investigator, economist, college professors and worker for international peace, she was in 1946 the second American woman to receive the Nobel Peace Prize (the first being Jane Addams). Balch was not a Quaker by birthright but by conviction: she joined the Society of Friends of London as a mature woman of 54 years. Balch's decision to become a Quaker was an important affirmation of her personal and social development, and it is this growth which I will discuss here. This paper does not examine in depth the signifi-cant contribution Emily Balch made to the international peace movement during the 1920's and 1930's. I will examine firstly the personal route Balch took to Quaker-ism and secondly the individual relation she made between her pacifism and her Quaker membership. These two elements provide an understanding of Balch's career in the peace movement from World War I to World War II and afterward.

A well known anecodote about Jane Addams' introduc-tion of Emily Balch at a meeting in the 1920's evokes Balch's personality. Miss Addams stated that of all the hundreds of people she had known in every part of the world, she knew "none that was as good as Emily Balch." The story goes on that Miss Balch walked forward with a slight smile on her face and, as if taking the audience into her confidence, she began. "You know," she said, "when I was very young, I decided to be beautiful." A slightly suppressed titter ran through the hall. "And then," she went on, "I discovered that God did not intend that I should be beautiful, as you all can see. So, then I decided I would be intellectually brilliant. But, alas, I soon discovered that God did not intend me to be brilliant. So I just decided to be good."[1] In recalling this anecodote Dorothy Detzer concluded "Any attempt to praise Emily Balch was always countered by some oblique sally of self-mockery."[2] It seems to me that this story also documents the frame of mind and spirit which Balch had reached. Let us treat separately the three qualities that Balch listed: beauty, brilliance, and goodness.

Emily Balch was a plain, lean woman. In girlhood she had felt painfully self-conscious about her looks. Shy, awkward, and bespectacled, she had been mortified attending dancing classes in Boston society. Her joking about her looks in public was an expression of the acceptance of herself, a sign of her security in later life. In fact, there was then a spiritual beauty in her face noted by many. Upon first meeting her in 1950 Edith Hamilton thought of the verse "'They took knowledge of them that they had been with Jesus.' She looks like that."[3]

The other qualities, brilliance and goodness, require more consideration. Balch's comment that she was not brilliant was misleading because she was intellectually very able and must have known it. She was a leader in her class at Miss Catherine Ireland's School in Boston where the teachers encouraged independence of thought. She had advanced standing as a freshman at Bryn Mawr. A member of the first graduating class there in 1889, Balch received the first award of the Bryn Mawr traveling fellowship. Her characteristic reaction was to inform the authorities that someone else, "Jim" Smith (Emily Smith, later a classicist) deserved the award. The faculty disagreed. Their perceptive assessment of Balch appeared in the Faculty Minutes: "She is twenty-two years of age, a woman of unusual ability, of extra-ordinary beauty of moral character, of great discretion and balance of judgment, very unselfish and in every way fit to be representative of the college and to engage in study in Europe."4

Balch in mature life still denied her brilliance because she believed that character should be the primary value for human beings. She would have thought it conceited to consider herself brilliant. The compulsion to deprecate oneself was not unusual for the early generation of college-educated women. Balch carried this tendency to an extreme. It is explicable in the light of her upbringing. Her New England Brahmin parents, Francis Vergnies Balch, and Ellen Noyes Balch, had stressed selflessness, derived from Puritan disinterestedness. In childhood Emily had been taught by her mother to distrust the purity of one's motives; after her death when Emily was seventeen, her father, (known for his goodness) became her model of unselfishness.

As liberal Unitarians the parents also had sought to give their children an honest exposure to religious precepts. Emily was sent to a private bible study class, and later, like her parents, became a

devoted member of the Reverend Charles Dole's congregation in Jamaica Plain, Massacusetts. At age fourteen,
Emily, under the minister's guidance, pledged herself to
"goodness." Yet as a young adult she still felt that
"egotism" was her "besetting sin."[5] Recognition from
others seemed only to make Emily demand more of herself
in quelling presumed selfishness and in finding ways to
be more useful. The practice of goodness took on
several meanings for Balch: honesty with oneself,
service to society, and acceptance of the points of view
of others. This last component became the most distinctive element in Balch's ideal of goodness.

The collegiate experience fed both Balch's
intellectual and moral growth. Somewhat reluctantly
she became a convert to women's suffrage. At Bryn Mawr,
Balch discovered the new field of economics under the
stimulating instruction of Franklin Giddings. She used
the year abroad to study in Paris, and, immersing
herself in French social statistics, produced what might
have been a Ph.D. thesis, a study of Public Assistance
of the Poor in France, published in 1893.[6]

But Balch was dissatisfied with purely academic
studies; it bothered her that she had written about the
poor but had met not one. Returning to Boston, she
assisted Charles Birtwell of the Boston Children's Aid
Society and prepared a Manual for Use in Cases of
Juvenile Offenders and Other Minors in Massachusetts.[7]
From 1891 to 1895, she associated with Brahmin reformers
and trade union leaders and, at Felix Adler's summer
school of applied Ethics, she met three young women,
Jane Addams, Katharine Coman and Vida Scudder, who
became important friends for life. Balch was soon one

of the small group who started the Boston settlement, Denison House; she agreed to be its first non-resident head worker for a year before her Bryn Mawr classmate, Helena Dudley, took over.

Soon rejecting a career in social work (it seemed to smack of philanthropy), Balch decided to prepare for college teaching and hoped that she might "awaken the desire of women students to work for social better-ment."[8]   After a semester at the Harvard Annex and another term at the University of Chicago she accepted her father's offer to send her for further study at the University of Berlin.   Study with Professors Adolph Wagner and Gustaf Schmoller and attendance in London at the meetings of the International Socialists Workers and Trade Unionists Congress broadened Balch's knowledge of theories of socialism.   On the ship home to America Katharine Coman offered her a place at Wellesley as an assistant, grading papers in economics.   Balch readily accepted as a way of beginning an academic career.   She was eager to teach and to share new ways of thinking with students.

Gradually Balch moved into a faculty position and from 1900, she was a member of the new Department of Economics and Sociology at Wellesley.   Professor Balch introduced courses on socialism (assigning Karl Marx), and on the history of American immigration, and the economics of consumption.   She sent students to Denison House and to public hearings in Boston.   While teaching, Balch continued her own activities in public service, with membership on various state commissions, such as factory inspection, minimum wage, and immigration.   In 1903, as President of the Boston chapter of the Women's

Trade Union League, she not only supported strikes of shoe and candy workers but lent money to a shoe union. These activities slowed her academic promotion.

For her primary research on immigration, Balch took a two-year leave from 1904 to 1906, first living in American immigrant communities and then with families at European places of immigrant origin and produced her major work, Our Slavic Fellow Citizens in 1910. In this work, Balch gave the viewpoints of the foreign-born and their children, repudiated the racist attitudes prevalent among Boston Brahmins and expressed faith in the assimilation of the newcomers.[9]

Throughout this period, Balch moved increasingly to radical ways of thinking about the problem of poverty. Wherever she went, socialism was under discussion. It was a fluid principle having religious, social and economic connotations. Socialism appealed to young academics, men and women, troubled by the magnitude of poverty in the cities.10

What were the attractions of socialism for Emily Balch? The emphasis on cooperation and the repudiation of self-interest were criteria that fit with her scale of values. She saw no justification for the motives of selfishness in individuals nor could she understand the motives of self-interest either for businessmen or for political leaders. Also, socialism provided a solution to her guilt about being privileged by family and education. Still it took Balch a long time to embrace socialism because of its radical associations. She disagreed with Marx's theory of surplus value and the class struggle. It was in 1906 (after ten years of thinking) when she was living in Prague with the Masaryk family and observing the desperate poverty in that city, that she finally declared herself a socialist. Like Thomas Masaryk, then professor of philosophy at Prague, Balch appreciated Marx's emphasis on the role of economic factors in history..11 But, even while Balch labeled herself a socialist she was not a Marxist.

At the start of a new appointment in 1913 as full professor and department chairman at Wellesley, Balch was at the peak of her academic career although she still privately questioned her usefulness to society in this employment. A year later the advent of World War I in August 1914, interrupted her college routine and by 1919 she had forged a unique public role in working for peace.

The eruption of the European war stunned Americans who believed in the world's progress judged by the United States' advance. The reform-minded, especially social workers, reacted to the crisis by calling meetings and forming groups to work for an early peace. Balch attended the meeting at the Henry Street Settlement in the fall of 1914, where the American Union Against Militarism was formed.

For Balch, pacifism was part of the creed taught by her minister, Charles Dole, an active pacifist during the Spanish-American War in 1898. In her present state of mind, Balch's socialist indoctrination prepared her to see World War I as a conflict between two imperialist nations. She did not hesitate when Jane Addams asked her to join the American delegation for the conference at the Hague called by a group of European women suffragist leaders from belligerent and neutral countries to consider the possibilities for peace. Addams knew how to appeal to Balch, and wrote to her: "Don't you think that there is a certain obligation on the part of women who have had the advantages of study and training to take this possible chance to help out?"[12] Balch agreed, for she already believed that the single professional woman should take risks for the public good.[13] Professor Balch received permission from Wellesley to leave her classes. Her journal, kept while on board the Noordam, showed that she had no illusions about what the women could accomplish: " . . . We just mean to do what we can and hope to stir little waves of thought and feeling that may multiply and expand [and] add our little momentum to the great whole that is rolling up against war."[14]

The meeting at the Hague, which led to the founding of the American Woman's Peace Party (with Jane Addams serving as president), launched the first stage of Balch's long involvement with peace work. Balch became one of the envoys chosen at the Hague to go that same spring and summer to seek the viewpoints of the Northern neutrals, the Scandinavian countries and Russia. Each discussion with these neutral powers reaffirmed her conviction that the United States could play a special role as mediator. President Woodrow Wilson, by receiving Balch, Addams, and other peace advocates in 1915 and 1916, strengthened this hope. But the events of the war, culminating in German submarine warfare, brought America closer to joining the Allies. In February 1917, the United States broke diplomatic relations with Germany. In those last desperate months, Balch and a minority of pacifists (many retreated) believed that every attempt to keep America out should still be tried. Such efforts as hers became increasingly controversial. Balch tried to influence public opinion using the press, lectures, and organization of parades and mass meetings. She was one of the founders of the Emergency Peace Federation which sought to reach "the people" and to keep pressure on the government to remain neutral. The Emergency Peace Federation, as described by Balch, included "labor men, plain people of all sorts, Grangers, religious pacifists, conscientious objectors to war, university men and women, from under-graduates to professors, city folk and country folk."[15] Activist leaders manipulated the EPF to oppose what they saw as further encroachments of militarism.

Oswald Garrison Villard, of the Nation magazine, financed the Emergency Peace Federation with the under-standing that Balch would steady the young radical women who ran the office, Lella Secor and Rebecca Shelley. Balch worked with an array of such impulsive, young people. Among them were two recent Bryn Mawr graduates, Frances Witherspoon and Tracy Mygatt, who founded the Bureau of Legal Advice, which offered legal services to conscientious objectors. They were joined also by Jessie Wallace Hughan, (founder of the War Resisters League). After the United States declared war, the Emergency Peace Federation disappeared into a new organ-ization, the People's Council of America; the name deliberately meant to evoke association with the 1917 Russian Revolution. Balch acted as liaison and inter-preter among diverse radical peace advocates and liberal and conservative pacifists. Thus she found herself explaining the views of Crystal Eastman, leader of the Woman's Peace Party, of New York to Jane Addams, president of the National Woman's Peace Party, among others.

Significantly of the older generation of women social reformers, Balch alone had tolerance for the new styles in reform of the younger generation. She lent her leadership and name, even to the most radical segments of the peace movement. Sometimes these young writers seemed and were uncontrollable. In the newsletter, Four Lights, sponsored by the New York Woman's Peace Party, flamboyant and subversive opinions were voiced. The publication welcomed the arrival of the Russian Revolution and scorned the participation of reformers in Herbert Hoover's food programs. Balch wrote occasionally for this publication in her own dignified style, and thus, her name became linked with the frenetic, irresponsible young writers. Balch's old friends and relatives disapproved of her activities but thought Balch heroic and only feared that she was being used.16

The Trustees of Wellesley College thought otherwise. During this five year appointment, Balch had taught very little. The Trustees had reluctantly permitted her leaves of absence in the springs of 1915 and 1916 for peace endeavors, and granted her a regular sabbatical in 1916-1917. It was mutually agreeable that she take another leave without pay in 1917-1918 during which time she supported herself through lectures and by editorial work for the Nation. Ordinarily her Wellesley reappointment would have been made in 1918; however, the Trustees deferred action.

Informally, Balch had received inquiries from individual Trustees, the last one asking whether she was a "Marxian Socialist", and what she thought of Bolshevism, or the Lawrence Strike of 1919. President Ellen Pendleton later acknowledged to Balch that there was unconscious prejudice on the part of conservative members of the Board. Balch understood what troubled the Trustees and did her utmost to explain her motivations. In a letter to Pendleton, March 30, 1918, she wrote: "I believe so deeply that the way of war is not the way of Christianity. I find it so impossible to reconcile war with the truths of Jesus' teaching, that even now I am obliged to give up the happiness of full and unquestioned cooperation where the responsibility of choice is mine."

Despite Balch's profoundly ethical letters of explanation to the Trustees as well as moving petitions from faculty members and a supporting statement from her department, on April 21, 1919, the Trustees let her appointment lapse. A close vote provided the genteel way of firing Professor Emily Balch. The Trustees' final statement (in the Minutes, not sent to Balch), claiming to uphold academic freedom, in reality emphasized the obligations of faculty members to "recognize their responsibilities for the good name of Wellesley and see that none of their acts and public utterances lack dignity or quiet judgment."[17]

For Balch the initial shock of rejection was profound. Until then, she had assumed that she would make the decision whether or not to return to her post at Wellesley College. As she knew the loss of her professorship had the makings of a significant academic civil liberties case, how do we assess her motives in not publicly protesting her dismissal? There were layers in her thinking and feelings about herself and her career which contributed to the complexity of Balch's reactions. Objectively Balch knew that Wellesley had betrayed academic freedom. Yet after she learned of her friends' concerted and visible efforts on her behalf, she did not want to embarrass or perhaps jeopardize their positions further. Characteristically, she did not want to be selfish in exploiting her grievances. In fact, Balch ignored the urgings of Charles Beard and others that she had an obligation to make a case.

I speculate that Balch put up no fight for her Wellesley post because for some time she had had serious misgivings about returning. She had been away from the college for the major portion of the five years. She received news of her dismissal when she was in Zurich, engrossed in the deliberations of the first post-war international peace conference of women. Another explanation might be that, given Balch's ethical standard for herself, she would choose to accept the penalty for standing up for what she believed. So it appeared to her colleague, Mary Calkins, professor of philosophy at Wellesley, who wrote "wistfully" to Balch: "You are living your faith."18

Throughout this intense period of Balch's work for peace from 1915 to 1919, she felt lonely and isolated. It was her religious justification that sustained her. Earlier in 1906, Balch had even envisaged leaving academia in order to form a religious group of which she would be the leader. (She had once discussed this idea with the Reverend Dole.) Her letters showed a constant concern with the spiritual implications of her work and during the war she joined the Fellowship of Reconciliation. Emily Greene Balch was finding her way to Quakerism; it was a long, quiet search, but from our historical perspective it was not a surprising move. In a letter to Jane Addams on February 21, 1921, Balch analyzed her decision. "I think you will be interested to know that I have applied for membership in the Society of Friends in London and have been admitted . . . I am not in the fervor of conversion but it is a warming and helpful thing to me to be in fellowship with the little Friends meeting that has been started in Geneva . . . Of course, going into something means in a sense going out from what is not in (or that is the danger)."19 What Balch did not say to Jane Addams was that she was "going out" of socialism. Did Balch herself make the connection?

Ironically, Balch, who had knowingly risked and lost her academic status by too close an association with radical socialists during the war, in 1921 no longer identified herself a socialist. Earlier, socialism had been an ideal by which to further democracy. Now she felt that socialism had become too narrow, too explicitly connected with Marxism. It was not that she was less concerned with economic issues, but Marx's theory of class struggle contrasted with Balch's purpose of transcending class, national, and racial barriers. Quakerism, not socialism, now gave Balch the space in which to remain open to different viewpoints and to expand her vision for the world.

Though pacifism is one expression of Quakerism, Balch did not become a Quaker solely because of this

Quaker belief. More fundamental for her, the Friends Meeting offered a form of worship that made possible "a beautiful type of communion between persons." The Quaker context of silence was particularly meaningful in enabling her to meet the variety of her public and personal concerns. She saw that the Quaker Business Meeting also afforded ways to exchange different views of a problem before reaching solutions. It was like the method of mediation Balch had always favored for political and social groups. In the last forty years of her long public career, Balch found in her Quaker membership, as she said, a "constant rebuke and challenge and support."20

At the same time Balch moved freely and securely to advance international peace among differing nations, groups, and individuals. As the first international paid secretary of the new Women's International League for Peace and Freedom in Geneva in 1919-1921, she set standards. Thereafter as a leader of the national American branch of the Women's International League for Peace and Freedom Balch had an organizational base through which she conducted many projects. Although she held no political office, as a representative of the Women's International League for Peace and Freedom, she used her scholarly expertise to investigate international problems. In the early 1920's when the League of Nations was young, Balch recommended constructive policies for its growth. In 1926, under the auspices of the WILPF, she made a study of Haiti and her recommendations were implemented by President Herbert Hoover. In the terrible crises of the 1930's--in Ethiopia, Manchuria, and Spain, Balch wrote proposals for

mediation.   Always,   she showed her belief in "effective
opposition by non-violent means."21

Indeed, the   Quakerly way permeated Balch's style
as a professional.   Characteristically, when a WILPF
committee was deadlocked or divided, she would leave the
room and by herself consider the arguments in silence
and return with a third position.   She transformed one
potentially violent scene when World War II veterans
started to disrupt a meeting.   She soon had policemen
and veterans sharing a discussion of their war experiences with members of the WILPF.22

To the end, Balch was firmly independent and
unpredictable in the resolution of   her own moral
conflicts.   Thus, during World War I Balch stood apart
from family and old friends in her advocacy of peace.
In World War II, Balch again differed from some Quakers
and WILPF members, this time supporting the United
States' intervention. To her   the threat of Hitler's
domination of Europe and Nazi treatment of Jews out-
weighed the ethic of non-participation.   Nor did she
resign from the Women's International League for Peace
and Freedom, even though she   frankly admitted that her
position on World War II was "neither very definite nor
very consistent."23

The award of the Nobel Peace Prize in 1946 gave
public recognition to Emily Greene Balch's commitments
of a lifetime.24 Her earlier professional endeavors in
Boston social service, the instruction of Wellesley
students, her probing of socialism, and her courageous,
deeply-lived activism in the   World Wars   were preparations for the later   expansive years.   Balch applied

what she had learned in each experience to the next in the public sphere. She sustained the same ethical and social values in all her thinking; that self-interest was not enough for individuals and societies. In the course of her career, gradually she learned how to come to terms with her identity as a single, educated, professional woman and she integrated her private religious quest with her public activism when she became a Quaker. At eighty-seven, Balch said; "When I grow old I hope I shall not become rigid in my thinking."[25] Emily Greene Balch was in no danger.

Notes

1Dorothy Detzer Denny to Barbara M. Solomon, January 27, 1979.

2Ibid.

3Edith Hamilton to Alice Hamilton, MMarch, 1950; courtesy of Barbara Sicherman.

4Mercedes Randall, Improper Bostonian: Emily Greene Balch, New York, 1964, p. 71.

5Emily Balch, quoted in M. Randall, p. 389.

6Emily G. Balch, Public Assistance of the Poor in France, published by the American Economics Association, 1893.

7Emily G. Balch, Manual for Use in Cases of Juvenile Offenders and other Minors in Massachusetts, Boston, 1895, Revised editions in 1903 and 1908.

8Emily G. Balch, quoted in M. Randall, Improper Bostonian: Emily Greene Balch, p. 86.

9Emily G. Balch, Our Slavic Fellow Citizens, New York, 1910. Barbara Miller Solomon, Ancestors and Immigrants, Cambridge, MA, 1956, especially chapter nine.

10See the illuminating essay by Dorothy Ross in Perspectives, "Socialism and American Liberalism: Academic Social Thought in the 1880's," Volume XI, 1977-78, p. 7-79.

11M. Randall, Improper Bostonian, p. 124.

12Jane Addams to Emily G. Balch, March 15, 1915.

13Emily G. Balch, "The Effects of War and Militarism on the Status of Women," Publications of the American

Sociological society, 1915, p. 47ff.

[14]Emily G. Balch, Journal on the Noordam, Balch Papers on microfilm at the Swarthmore Peace Collection.

[15]Emily G. Balch, MS. "Who's Who Among Pacifists: The Position of the Emergency Peace Federation," March 20, 1917. Balch Papers on microfilm at Swarthmore Peace Collection.

[16]Frank Balch to Emily G. Balch, April 7, 1915, Balch Papers, on microfilm, Swarthmore Peace Collection.

[17]Emily G. Balch to Ellen Pendleton, March 30, 1918, Balch Papers on microfilm. Wellesley College, Trustees Minutes, April 21, 1919, Wellesley College.

[18]Mary Calkins to Emily G. Balch, undated. Balch Papers on microfilm.

[19]Emily G. Balch to Jane Addams, February 21, 1921, M. Randall, p. 292.

[20]Emily G. Balch, quoted in M. Randall, p. 60, p. 48.

[21]Emily G. Balch, quoted in M. Randall, p. 334.

[22]Dorothy Detzer Denny to Barbara M. Solomon, January 27, 1979.

[23]Emily G. Balch, quoted in Lawrence S. Wittner, Rebels Against War: The American Peace Movement, 1941-1960, New York, 1969, p. 53.

[24]One of Balch's 35 sponsors, Professor Joseph P. Chamberlain of the Columbia Law School "had first admired Emily Balch in her Wellesley years as an influence on immigration problems, and he was deeply aware of the extent of her labors with rescuing European victims of Nazi tyranny," quoted from M. Randall, Improper Bostonian, p. 420.

[25]Emily G. Balch, quoted in Margaret Clapp to Pearl Buck, December 11, 1956, Wellesley College Archives, Wellesley college.

Other books useful for this paper include:

Mercedes M. Randall, ed., Beyond Nationalism The Social Thought of Emily Greene Balch, New York, 1972.*

John Herman Randall, Jr., Emily Greene Balch of New England, Citizen of the World, Columbia University, 1946.

Emily G. Balch, ed., Occupied Haiti, New York, 1927.

Blanche Wiesen Cook, ed. Crystal Eastman on Women and Revolution, New York, 1978.

Gertrude Bussey and Margaret Tims, Women's International League for Peace and Freedom, London, 1965.

*This book includes a complete bibliography of Balch's publications.

The Swarthmore Peace Collection, Swarthmore college is the main repository for Emily G. Balch's papers. The Wellesley College Archives, and the Schlesinger Library, Radcliffe College, also have material.

Dorothy Detzer Denny, Brand Blanshard, Blanche W. Cook, and Barbara Sicherman shared information with me.

Unpublished sources included:

Columbia Oral History, Interview with Frances Witherspoon and Tracy Mygatt, 1977.

Barbara Steinson, "Female Activism in world War I: The American Women's Peace, Suffrage, Preparedness, and Relief Movements 1914-1919," University of Michigan, 1977.

ALICE PAUL
Amelia R. Fry

This essay tells the story of Alice Paul's relentless pursuit of equal rights for men and women, a goal which broadened as she carried her pursuit of justice beyond the struggles for women's suffrage in England and America to include equal rights under the law, in the U.S. Constitution and worldwide. It is a story which is illuminated by the concept of human space as a way of conceiving of both mental and physical locality. We shall see how, after her initial phases of study and activism, Alice Paul defined with increasing precision her concern with the principle of gender equality. Her goal of equality under the law retained an essential narrowness in contrast to other reformers' engagement with multiple concerns, but the spheres in which she worked to apply this sharply-focused principle broadened beyond national politics to include the emerging and vast realm of international law.

This account of Paul's life and work space begins with her childhood confined to the homogeneous world of an important Quaker family in a New Jersey Quaker community and her education at Quaker schools from kindergarten through college and part of her graduate study. It traces her expanding cognitive realm and the similar growth in her sphere of influence as she became conscious of "the World's People" and the political arena, where she moved first into the British militants' struggle for suffrage and then as the non-violent leader for American women's enfranchisement, which was won in 1920.

The period following the suffrage campaign is the
focus of this paper, the first two decades of Alice
Paul's efforts to arouse her country's newly enfranchised women to make use of their political power to
place full gender equality in the constitution--the
Equal Rights Amendment. By the end of the Twenties, she
had expanded her legal training and her political
efforts to include all the Americas and the whole international scene. The Equal Rights Treaty, the Equal
Nationality Treaty, and the gender equality principle in
all international charters and agreements became the
vehicles that carried her vision.

The international phase of her career which follows
is told with particular attention to the establishment
in 1938 of the World Women's Party and its Headquarters
at Villa Bartholoni in Geneva, Switzerland; the account
culminates in this location where, until her return to
the United States in 1941, Alice Paul's work as a shaper
of human space took on a new, more physical, meaning.

Responding to the tragic plight of refugees fleeing
for their lives from the Nazi threat, she used her space
at the Villa to shelter many stateless feminist leaders.
The "room of her own" which these women lacked under
Hitler's genocidal regime was acutely literal. For
them, as in the book of Job, (the male pronoun notwith-
standing) the loss of space was a definition of death:
"He shall return no more to his house, neither shall his
place know him any more." Paul's nurturing of these
women, and often of their families, in the extremity of
their need shows Paul's personal dimension of Quaker
resourcefulness and compassion that is also demonstrated
in her political and legal quest for equal rights.

Although her refugee operation was small compared to those run by the Quakers, Paul used her expanded range of influence to obtain the financial and diplomatic assistance these feminist leaders needed to find the space in which to begin their lives anew.

Her goal of complete legal equality for women of all nationalities remained definitive of her cognitive space, however, even in the desperate last months before she, too, fled a war-torn Europe. In her sojourn at the Villa, she showed a Quaker-like clarity and perseverance which was finally to be rewarded in the success of her postwar leadership in the feminist effort to include equal gender rights "for men and women" in most sections of the United Nation's founding Charter.

Who was Alice Paul? She was born in 1885 and grew up in the Quaker community of Moorestown, New Jersey, as the daughter of a successful Hicksite farmer and town banker. She attended the Friends' school through high school, then went four years to the Hicksite college that her grandparents had helped found, Swarthmore. The question is, Was she as archetypically Quaker as the purity of her Quaker-defined environment would suggest?

She verifies that as she grew up she came into contact with few who were not Quakers, and in fact few who were not white, Quaker, middle or upper-middle class. In her oral history interview, Paul said,

> I have practically no ancestor who wasn't a
> Quaker. I don't know whether I had ANY who
> wasn't a Quaker. My father and mother were,
> and their fathers and mothers were. . . . My

first Paul ancestor was imprisoned in England
as a Quaker and came to this country . . .
This little village was named after him, the
town of Paulsboro in New Jersey, which is now
quite a big place.

And later she explained,

. . . I never met anybody who wasn't a Quaker,
and I never heard of anybody who wasn't a
Quaker except that the maids we had were
always Irish Catholics, always; we never had
anybody but Irish Catholics. But I never met
anybody who wasn't a Quaker, and I don't know,
I suppose it was like all Quaker homes.
(Fry: Did you have a prohibition of anything,
that sprang from Quaker beliefs?) AP: What
kinds of things? (Fry: Let's see. Some
Quakers would prohibit music.) AP: O yes.
We never had any music at all. I never heard
anything musical in the beginning of my childhood. Later on when I went to Swarthmore was
the first time I heard, I guess, a hymn or
anything like that. . . . But I never heard a
hymn until I went to Swarthmore; (laughter) I
never knew there was such a thing as a hymn. .
. . You didn't regard it as oppressive, you
know; you didn't know there WAS such a thing.
You just knew all these gay maids we had were
going off to dances and had a different life
than we did. We just felt that was a part of
common people who did these things. (Fry:
The lower classes?) Paul: Yes, the lower
classes did these things (laughing).

We played tennis. (Our house had) a very
great lawn so we had a tennis court there.
And we played all the little things that
people play, checkers and such things. . . .
And I read endlessly, ceaselessly, almost
every book it seems! We had a Friends library
there in the meeting house, and I took out
every book in the library. Also a great part
of these books here (indicating several book-
cases) are those that I had in my home, that I
grew up with, any number of them. I remember
reading every single line of Dickens as a
child over and over and over again. It's a
wonder![1]

Once at Swarthmore, faced with a decision for a
major field, she shunned subjects in which she had
already read, like English and history, and she said she
thought,

The one thing I don't know anything about and
I never would read and can't understand or
comprehend or have any interest in [are] all
the things in the field of science. . . . So I
decided to make biology my major.

But in her last year she had Professor Robert
Brooks in economics and political science, "and immmed-
iately I seemed to have a great joy in them." She was
given a year's graduate fellowship for work and classes
in College Settlement and the School of Philanthropy in
New York--now a part of Columbia University. For the
first time, she was thrown into a space that included a
heterogeneous mix of non-Quakers, the most intensive

melting pot in America--New York's Lower East Side in 1905-06, the peak of immigration.

Her social work degree in hand, she continued her academic education and a number of social work assignments, one of the few occupations open to women. In the following year she won her master's degree at the University of Pennsylvania with a sociology major and minors in political science and economics, then in 1907 went to England.

Now her physical space expanded dramatically, with a fellowship to the Quaker's Woodbrooke Institute. There she took Woodbrooke's combined program of courses at the University of Birmingham (mainly economics), social work training, and work at The Summer Lane Settlement, also two or three times a week.

It was at the University of Birmingham that Alice's great decision was--not made, but came upon her. She went to one of the public meetings arranged by the head of the University, Sir Oliver Lodge. Alice tells about it:

> So I went to his public meeting--after school
> hours, you see. It was Christabel Pankhurst.
> I don't know that I'd ever heard her name
> before. . . . She was [militant suffrage
> leader] Mrs. Pankhurst's daughter. . . . She
> was a very young girl and a young lawyer. . .
> Quite entrancing and delightful person,
> really very beautiful I thought. So she
> started to speak. And the students started to

yell and shout, and I don't believe anybody heard <u>one</u> <u>single</u> <u>word</u> that Christabel said. So she kept on anyway for her whole speech. She was completely shouted down.

So I just became from that moment very anxious to help in this movement. . . . I thought, 'That's one group now that I want to throw in all the strength I can give to help.'[2]

There followed more social work assignments in London after her year at Woodbrooke ended. She enrolled at the London School of Economics. With a classmate she did some scut work for the Pankhurst movement, such as walking in a huge "procession" through London. On this occasion she formally joined the Pankhursts' Women's Social and Political Union. Throughout her ensuing militant adventures she learned not only how to speak outdoors on street corners, to sell <u>Votes</u> <u>for</u> <u>Women</u>, but also how to interrupt speeches of British party leaders with a cry, "Votes for Women!" Three times she was sent to prison, where she went on a hunger strike and was force-fed. In a short time she climbed to the inner circle as a young assistant to Mrs. Pankhurst.

In the meantime, at the London School of Economics, her own social thought began to gel, especially under the tutelage of Professor Westermark, pioneering Dutch anthropologist, whose book <u>The</u> <u>History</u> <u>of</u> <u>Human</u> <u>Marriage</u> was a landmark in the field, and also for Alice Paul. She became convinced that there were basic, female traits that show up in any culture, which distinguish women's goals and personalities from those of men.[3]

(This became a quite pertinent legal corollary to her ERA, in which, for her, "equality" did not mean "identicalness."

When Alice returned home in 1910--after turning down a paid position with Mrs. Pankhurst--she worked at first in the Philadelphia suffrage organization. The Philadelphia chapter president knew about Alice Paul's activist work for suffrage in England, and summoned the courage to risk putting Alice Paul on the program to tell them about the British campaign. All went well, but afterward the President said to Paul: "You know, when we asked you, we didn't know who you were or what sort of person you were, or whether you were fanatical or what you might be. . . . Now we see . . . and we'd like you to go on our street meeting committee."[4]

She enrolled at the University of Pennsylvania and in June, 1912, was awarded her Ph.D., with a dissertation entitled "The Legal Position of Women in Pennsylvania." Her cognitive and political space was expanding into the field of law. Later her physical space also grew when in that year she offered her services to Jane Addams to become the national Chair of the Congressional Committee of the National American Woman Suffrage Association (NAWSA). Addams brought the proposal before the board, it was approved, and Alice Paul was responsible for getting through Congress a woman's suffrage amendment to the federal Constitution. It was not a popular job. NAWSA's primary goal was to pass a suffrage referendum in each of the forty-eight states.

The suffrage movement was in the doldrums in 1912, having suffered several defeats in state-by-state referenda where, by definition, only males could vote on the issue. The day before Woodrow Wilson was inaugurated, Alice Paul organized a beautiful and massive suffrage parade that drew unruly crowds, disrupted Washington, and required the cavalry to control the mobs. Then she used the political power of the women who were enfranchised already in Western states as a level to hold the political party in power responsible (the Democrats until 1919) for not having passed the "Susan B. Anthony" (suffrage) amendment.[*] She formed a parallel organization, The Congressional Union, specifically for the campaign for the Amendment, but NAWSA would not admit it to auxiliary status, a decision that split off Paul's group and led to the formation of her National Woman's Party later. In 1917, the group began organizing silent picketers carrying eye-catching purple, white, and gold banners at the White House fence and signs demanding votes for women and often accusing Wilson of hypocrisy in his brave words about fighting for democracy. When mobs attacked the women, police arrested the suffragists. In prison they, Paul included, went on hunger strikes and were brutally force-fed.

[*]Suffrage Amendment (19th Amendment to the United States Constitution)

The right of citizens of the United States to vote shall not be denied or abridged by the United States or any State on account of sex.

Meanwhile, increasing numbers of women came to picket, to burn the president's words in "watch fires," to keep a bell tolling for freedom, and to go to jail. But Alice Paul's political gestalt was much broader than just drama and mob violence in Washington. With the deftness of a generalissimo she directed a gifted staff in Washington for lobbying, publicity, fund-raising, and an active but lean network of women in nearly every state. These were women who often had connections to power either through their husbands, their brothers, or their friends and who could talk to a Congressman or a party chieftain with more chance of being listened to than the average woman. Paul's purposes were accomplished: Wilson and his staff, in spite of World War I, felt the stress of increasing public outcry over the treatment of the suffragists and their cause, all the while the front pages of the press keeping suffrage as a mainstream issue before the American people.

Although Alice Paul's tactics are called "militant," she did not like to so label them as such in her later life. She felt that, unlike the British sufragettes, the NWP actions were non-violent, and the civil disobedience was partly caused by the definitions of their picketing ("Obstructing traffic") in the courts.

She told the picketers to be well-dressed, she coached them to be genteel. No screaming, no conversing with bystanders, and no "unladylike" behavior was allowed; there was already too much criticism of her tactics and more could damage the movement. Paul herself was incurably shy, but the speakers she fielded were eloquent and impassioned. Her lobbyists were well-prepped and professional, and women attorneys--rare as they were--circulated in and out of headquarters writing defenses of the suffrage amendment where needed and providing legal opinions of hearings. Always, there was money to be raised. Alice Paul was a major success in organizing fund raisers for small donations and large: she sought out women who could easily foot the bill for anything from rental of a hall to purchasing a mansion for headquarters. Mrs. Alva Vanderbilt Belmont was NWP's major angel.

Although Alice Paul's operations covered the continent from ocean to ocean (this was symbolized by an intrepid automobile campaign from San Francisco to Washington in 1915--before roads were passable), although her domain was as large as any American political figure of the day, and even though she was in sympathy with the many progressive social reforms, she held the NWP to a one-issue goal: gender equality in the body politic. Not child labor laws. Not welfare for the needy. Not protections for only women in the industrial workplace. Not even the Quaker ideal of world peace when her nation was mired in an ill-begotten world war. There was no stocking-knitting at her headquarters. She simply refused to allow the war to change anything--perhaps obeying a major Quaker tenet of refusal to be a part of great evil. Her "Silent sentinels" kept their vigil at the White House for suffrage.

From 1916 to 1920, NAWSA, from which Paul's group had split, also threw its weight behind the federal amendment--but distanced itself from the militant NWP by criticizing it publicly, doing war work, and, behind the scenes, negotiating with President Wilson for his postwar support.

Alice Paul remembers how her lobbyists had managed to persuade a congressional committee to remove a time limit clause on ratification during one of the amendment's final hearings. In the light of the recent struggle over the ERA time limit, it is interesting to note that when the deadline was removed from the suffrage amendment, much of the opposition gave up.

In August, 1920, American women had the vote. Alice Paul was exhausted. Her lieutenants were exhausted. She went the final mile--raising money to pay off the Woman's Party debt--then launched bills in several states to replace statutes that discriminated against women. As she led her NWP toward the larger horizons of total equality under the law, she developed a "blanket equality" bill for the states, then another federal amendment. Taking law courses early mornings and at night, she got three degrees in jurisprudence, saw the ERA working through to a version which was finally submitted for the first time to Congress in 1923, then with a battery of women attorneys, made a complete survey of all laws affecting women and the family in every state, to demonstrate the need for a federal amendment.

The idea was to use the power that women now held with the ballot to obtain across-the-board equal rights. The same concept that Lucretia Mott, Martha Wright, Jane Hunt, and Elizabeth Cady Stanton had formulated three-quarters of a century before in their Declaration of Principles.

But from the beginning of the NWP's moves toward an ERA, other reformers viewed the amendment as an anomaly, or a selfish goal, or a block against labor protections. Paul witnessed "the new women" joining movements for maternity care reform, consumer's protection, peace, child labor laws, or education of women on public issues (the domain of the new League of Women Voters). Paul argued that those would naturally follow once women's power was secure under an ERA.*

*Equal Rights Amendment (proposed for U.S. Constitution)

   I. Equality of rights under the law shall not be denied or abridged by the United States or by any State on account of sex.

   II. The congress shall have the power to enforce, by appropriate legislation, the provisions of this article.

Protective labor legislation was the biggest reform
that kept liberals from backing the ERA, from the 20s
to 1972; the main women's organizations and labor unions
feared a federal amendment requiring gender equality
would kill the hard-won legislation (minimum wage,
maximum hours, no night work, lifting limitations--all
for women only) to which many of the leaders had devoted
their lives. A wide coalition of enemies of the ERA was
formed, one that would take decades to neutralize and
convert. But Alice Paul saw to it that the ERA was
introduced into Congress in each session until, with the
tremendous wave of enthusiasm from the new feminists of
the 60s, it passed from Congress to the states for
ratification in 1972. Paul died in 1977, and ratification ended in failure, three states short, in 1982.
Another bill, still Alice Paul's wording, was immediately submitted to start the Congressional battles again.

Also in the 1920s, Alice Paul and members of the
National Women's Party realized that the time was ripe
to extend the principle of equal rights to the world. A
strategy was envisioned of working to spread the gender
equality movement over all the Americas by treaty, and
then in Europe. (At the time, Alice Paul's research
indicated that domestic law in the United States had to
follow any treaties that country ratified.) To this end
Mrs. Belmont, in Paris, took over the job of visiting
and writing letters to 45 "foremost feminists"
representing 26 nations. These women were to serve on a
new International Advisory Council for the National
Woman's Party. Attempts were then made to contact other
women's groups to propose discussion of an equal rights
proposal and to create an organizational network of
feminist groups in several countries.

A first defeat came early in Paris in 1925 at the parliamentary hands of the International Woman Suffrage Alliance, which ironically Susan B. Anthony had helped establish long years before. Although many on its board endorsed the National Woman's Party's equal rights proposal and their affiliation with the International Alliance, the final vote killed The National Woman's Party affiliation when Carrie Chapman Catt (former head of NAWSA during suffrage days) threatened to pull out if protective labor legislation for women should be thus threatened by an NWP membership. The battle was lost.

Others rallied to NWP's aid, and the National Women's Party joined the Open Door Council the following year, a British equal rights group which also opposed protective legislation for women only. In the meantime representatives from three more countries had joined the National Woman's Party "International Advisory Committee." This affiliation increased the influence of Alice Paul and gave the National Woman's Party access to international governmental organizations before whom Alice Paul could present resolutions for women's rights in industry and government.

1928 was a good year. First, Alice Paul sent party members in January to the major event in hemispheric diplomacy, the Sixth Pan-American Conference in Havana. The mission was to place women's issues on the agenda by bringing pressure on delegates to introduce and support an equal rights treaty which, at least in the United States, would bind a signatory nation to making it federal domestic policy. And although the motion was defeated that year, the National Woman's Party's members helped to get a majority vote to establish the Inter-

American Commission of Women (IACW), which, for
starters, would compile a survey of each nation's laws
for nationality requirements for women and men and
report to the next Pan-American conference five years
hence. Alice Paul headed the survey committee and
produced a large report, one which the foremost international law authority, James Brown Scott, called "Alice
Paul's Golden Book." The new Inter-American Commission
of Women selected members from seven nations, and
National Woman's Party's Doris Stevens was chosen to
chair it.

After a prodigious amount of work through research
and hearings, the result was a legal digest of
nationality laws among the Pan-American nations and
proposed remedies for the wide variation in these laws.
The compendium became a ground of common, if rare,
agreement between the National Woman's Party, the
National League of Women Voters, and the International
Alliance of Women for Suffrage and Equal Citizenship,
even though it did not produce anything so drastic as an
endorsement for the Equal Rights Amendment by the latter
groups. In June the National Woman's Party sent
delegates to the Open Door Council meeting in Berlin,
which declared that women in industry should have equal
rights with men and not be bound by industry's
regulations for women only. Further, they drew up a
Charter of Economic Rights for Working Women, and an
Open Door Manifesto that demanded free access to any job
of a woman's choosing, equal opportunity in advancement,
equal pay for equal work, right to be employed while
pregnant as long as a woman feels like it, the right to
return to work after a pregnancy, and the right to work
at night. Nor did that conclude the conference. The

Council also began the establishment of an office for an
Open Door International in Geneva, where it would
monitor all the proceedings of the League of Nations and
the International Labor Office.

During the decade of 1927 to 1937, Alice Paul and
the International Advisory Committee of the National
Woman's Party carried forward the work for equal rights
for women on the following fronts:

(1) Working with the Inter-American Commission of
Women to see that an Equal Rights Treaty*was submitted
to the 1933 Pan American Conference. Four nations
signed it, and all--including the United States
delegation -- signed the Equal Nationality Treaty. The
two treaties were also submitted to the Assembly of the
League of Nations. Counter proposals embodying discrim-
inations against women were rife, and Paul led the women
to lobby against them. (2) Pressuring two U.S.
Presidents (Hoover and Roosevelt) and the U.S. Congress
to assure that the United States would participate in
the World Court only if nationality provisions
discriminatory to women were supplanted by an international legal code which did not contain inequalities
based on sex, the so-called equality reservation clause.

*Equal Rights Treaty (proposed by Equal Rights
International).

The contrasting states agree that upon ratification
of this treaty men and women shall have equal rights
throughout the territory subject to their respective
jurisdictions.

(3) Persuading League of Nations delgates to introduce the equal rights and equal nationality rights treaties for discussion, and fighting discriminatory (and no-night-work-for-women) resolutions at the International Labor Office (ILO). (4) Consulting with experts in international law and organizing a series of conferences to determine the best way to gain complete equality for women. This resulted in the formation of the Equal Rights International, a coalition that helped the W.W.P.'s drive for the Equal Rights Treaty. (5) Working for the League of Nations' legitimization of the Women's Consultative Committee on Nationality in the League of Nations and producing a massive study on the discriminatory effect on women of nationality laws of all member nations, which Alice Paul headed. She also prepared an agenda of four issues which this Consultative Committee should consider in an attempt to modernize the League Covenant: equality in nationality laws; suffrage rights for women in all countries; equality in political, civil, and economic rights; inclusion of women in all League Council and Assembly delegations. By 1937 the Legal Committee of the League had studied these issues, set up a committee of experts (five men, four women) to research the status of women and recommend action on the Equal Rights Treaty and other Covenant proposals.

The Equal Rights Treaty finally reached the stage of discussion at the League, but the threat of another world war intervened. One might ask why Alice Paul, as she surveyed the world scene in 1937, did not decide to stop her annual commutes to Europe, contract her spatial boundaries, and stay in the more manageable American scene where her network and Quaker pacifism could

prepare a base from which to work for international
equality after world turmoil settled down.   That would
make sense, had she not been Alice Paul.   She probably
was   fueled by the sheer momentum of her years of
Sisyphus-like struggles at the League and the ILO.   She
also loathed to restrict her work to the   U.S. Congress
and its constituencies as even more confining than work
within the affiliation framework at Geneva.

Being Alice Paul, she continued her lobbying in
Switzerland, initiated another organization, The World
Women's Party, based on the model of the National
Woman's Party, and focused on equal rights in
international laws and treaties as its primary emphasis.
By late in 1938, the World Women's Party was approved by
the NWP and officially incorporated.   Alice Paul leased,
at a bargain rate, from the City of Geneva, the palatial
post-Renaissance mansion, Villa Bartholoni, which was
strategically near the League of Nations and the ILO,
the better to be a setting for meetings and for entertaining diplomats. The building's   architecture emanates
charm, graciousness, and stability.   The International
Red Cross headquarters shared the spacious sweep of
lakeside gardens and grass.

In an elaborate ceremony broadcast by NBC in the
States, attended by international celebrities and filled
with music and dance, the Women's World Party
headquarters was officially opened.   The date was August
18, 1939.   Thirteen days later Hitler invaded Poland,
and two days after that France declared war.

Soon the character of the Villa Bartholoni changed
as it became a refuge for European feminist women and

their families fleeing the Nazis.   In the correspondence
of Alice Paul and others which was sent to N.W.P.'s
Washington headquarters, one sees a picture of the
activities of Alice Paul at the Villa: letter by
letter, the sequences of escape and resettlement play
out.   Alice Paul, caught up in procedures for resettling
refugees, had to find sponsors to guarantee financial
support in the USA for these feminist leaders, talented
and cultured, from Austria, Poland, Germany, and other
countries.   There were long scenarios of cables,
telephone calls to the American consul general at
Zurich, and even visits to that harassed and reluctant
official.   Always the U.S. State Department required
more and more data on the financial holdings of the
sponsors, new reasons for <u>why</u> the sponsor was motivated
to bring a person to the United States, and more copies
of the affidavit of assistance (photocopying could have
speeded up the process by months).   One reads the fran-
tic cables insisting another copy had long ago been sent
from a U.S. sponsor across wartorn Europe, only to
arrive after a visa for the refugee had been turned down
at Zurich.   Drawing on the resources of the informal
women's international network was crucial, as the
following quotation from a letter to Alice Paul from
Dorothy Detzer of the Women's International League for
Peace and Freedom (WILPF) verifies.   Mrs. Detzer said
she had talked to Eleanor Roosevelt about the problems
of the refugees and "the attitude of our Zurich
consulate, and I am hoping that after bringing as much
pressure as [you] can in various places, some of those
people may be changed there."

It looks as if Paul was busy stretching the anemic
budget when she wasn't ringing the consul general's

phone. In letters to the United States soliciting money for a refugee fund, Alice reminded donors that "nearly everyone at the Villa is waiting for the means to go to America." But banks in Geneva refused to take checks on U.S. banks. Paul's hope to supplement U.S. funds with contributions from well-to-do Europeans was shattered when money could not be sent out of many of the European countries. On October 26, 1939--only two months after the Villa was opened--Alice Paul wrote to Mrs. Amy Ransome, the treasurer of NWP, that of the $4,000 left in the National Woman's Party account in Washington, Mrs. Ransome is to send half now to run the villa and all its programs for as long as possible that winter, and to keep the other $2,000 in Washington as a reserve to pay next year's rent. They had bought enough coal for a month. Alice adds in her own hand at the bottom, ". . . I don't know how long we can keep open but I am hopeful," and notes the lack of reserve in their budget was ominous.

Deep in the first winter, on January 23, 1940, Mrs. Detzer writes to NWP Washington headquarters that her organization, WILPF, cannot pay for anything more either, since their own load of refugees is getting so difficult to carry. The next month Alice Paul writes to NWP officer Anita Politzer to help finance the Geneva work. They now need $2,000 raised by April to pay next year's rent and $500 a month for costs of their work. The actual amounts collected for Alice Paul's budget are low indeed. Donations of $15 and $25 were the objects of high gratitude and Amy Ransome, Treasurer, in the World Women's Party Progress Report of December 1940, said she had deposited a total of $1,038 since March-- nine months.

Although this period was before Hitler's grim dictum of the "Final solution" to systematically exterminate Jews, at least one refugee from a concentration camp had become a resident at the Villa. When Alice Paul opened the Villa and had it operating, approximately 100,000 Jews had fled Germany, and thousands were streaming out of Eastern Europe. Huge refugee centers processing numbers that dwarfed Alice Paul's efforts were working frantically in Geneva, Vienna, Zurich, and other cities--many operated by her fellow Quakers.

The Third Reich was levying an atonement fine of 25% of any property and money of Jews trying to leave the country in 1939; there was an emigration tax of 5%, a tax on all possessions--100% to 500% of value. Any remaining money one possessed was transferable at only a 6% exchange rate; soon no money at all could be taken across a border so that emigrants who had not left Germany during the early phase of Nazi rule usually arrived penniless in a foreign country. Total annihilation may not yet have become formalized policy, but it was implied increasingly in one government directive after another, and often was applied to any liberal and labor activists regardless of their heritage. They were forbidden to use motor vehicles, segregated in air raid shelters, discriminated against in food rationing on a starvation basis, denied clothing and thread rationing cards, and limited in shopping hours. Once in Switzerland, refugees were permitted only a very limited tenure by that government--and certainly prohibited from any employment.

That was what people had been through who made it.
to Switzerland and the World Women's Party at Villa
Bartholoni.   Imagine the refugee, typically a former
feminist leader not unknown to others there, entering
between the high arches that punctuated the front of the
villa, carrying in her arms all she owned.   Meeting
Alice Paul, she would probably be led into the drawing
room.   She may have had a child or her husband with her.
She probably could not acclimate herself to the carved
ceilings, the broad bands of mural designs around the
wall panels, the rich marble fireplace, and Persian rug
and the furniture that had been rounded up by Alice
Paul's chairmen of furnishings, donated by some of the
elite of Europe.   By contrast, a refugee could understand a coal supply that was usually barely sufficient,
only one paid employee--a handyman who also cooked
breakfast--and why everyone had to work.   One of the
women at the Villa, acting as a secretary, wrote to NWP
treasurer Amy Ransome in California on September 27,
1940, "Our house is full up just now; even the attic
rooms, intended to be storage rooms only, are occupied.
All those living with us have been, in their own
countries, worthy contributors to the women's movement
and we hope it will be possible for them to go to
America.   Their individual fates have been so terrible
and their work in our cause so distinguished, that they
are certainly entitled to all energy we are able to put
into their salvation."

Alice Paul was intent on preserving the women's
movement by keeping its leaders alive until after the
war.   In the midst of this refugee operation, she
persisted in periodically calling meetings of the far-

flung World Women's Party council. She eventually got results--even when travel and mails were uncertain. For instance, a meeting was called for June 12, 1940, with the council of the Equal Rights International, but was apologetically postponed "owing to the sudden invasion of the Low Countries by Germany, which prevented the chairman and honorary secretary from travelling to Geneva." The meeting was held a week later by the council members of the two organizations already in Geneva. They assigned Alice Paul and Louise Van Eeghan the job of drafting a new constitution that would be suitable for the amalgamation of both organizations, the ERI and the WWP, and a meeting of the WWP Council was scheduled for August to confirm this action. Again the women could not get there.

Paul tried again. November 12, 1940, she sent a cable to Ransome: "I am remaining another month. Please send check air mail for $200. Situation tragic and desperate for many of our women. The plan is for meeting of our European officers here the first week in December." In addition, Paul had obtained endorsements from several international organizations for an equality of rights statement to be included in the League's new Covenant ("Members of the League of Nations should not abridge or deny the right to vote in their respective country on the ground of sex, and no distinction based on sex in their law and practice regarding nationality. . ."). It also added a call for equal rights in "all other fields," and "there should be both men and women, with full voting powers, all delegations to the Council and Assembly of the League and to Conferences under the auspices of the League."

That the statements were being sponsored at the League Assembly by fifteen nations (Czechoslovakia, China, Latvia, Turkey, New Zealand, Haiti, Cuba, Albania, Finland, Colombia, USSR, Bolivia, Ecuador, Yugoslavia, and Bulgaria) was cause for hope that a starting power base for gender equality would exist after the war. She also was continuing efforts to get the hated Hague nationality resolution reconsidered so the gender-discriminatory clauses could be removed.

Alice Paul also saw to it that the women in Geneva continued to monitor the ILO proceedings and pressed for equality in labor regulations, such as the highly restrictive legislation on the indigenous women workers. In 1940 the ILO abandoned its Geneva headquarters and moved to Montreal, but Paul was not so easily put off; for her, the "women's work" must continue as long as possible.

Even in September 1940 the World Women's Party had announced, ". . . The European Committee of The World Women's Party will assume the responsibilities for the work in Europe [at the ILO and League] after the return to the United States of Alice Paul. Miss Paul will now direct her attention to the creation of another Continental Committee [from Washington headquarters] with its own shape and form but with the same living spirit of campaigning for world-wide equality for women."

Alice Paul did not leave that month, nor the next nor the next. She did continue to rally support, inside and outside the League, for the equal rights provisions

in the new covenant; and always there were messages to
relay between potential sponsors of the stateless women
and the hard-pressed consulate officials who seemed to
be becoming more hard-shelled. After the December
council meeting, Alice received a letter from treasurer
Ransome in Washington (December 17, 1940). "The news
today was that all of France may be occupied but
Railroad Belgaarde to Geneva is now open. . . . so
travel to Southern France is possible and so to Lisbon."

But Paul had several cases of refugees in critical
stages at that moment with final resettlement looking
possible in the United States or perhaps Argentina. The
meeting had not yet been held to amalgamate Equal Rights
International (ERI) with the World Women's Party (WWP).
Paul continued working in Geneva through December,
January, and February. After the council members of the
WWP and the ERI miraculously met February 28, 1941, at
the Villa and amalgamated into the World Women's Party
for Equal Rights, Alice Paul left, leaving instructions
to burn all records she left behind, lest they fall into
the hands of the Nazi SS present in Switzerland.
Details of the closing, packing, and storing were dele-
gated to various local members and those refugees still
waiting. On March 4, 1941, Alice left by train to cross
southern France. The Spanish border was difficult,
where a train change had to be made, and usually
required a hefty bribe from refugees, but she made it to
Protugal, where she stayed two weeks awaiting passage.
She finally achieved passage for the two-week trip
across the submarine-infested Atlantic in the Portuguese
ship Carvalha Araujo (a converted ferry boat, Paul
said)[5] with 232 other passengers, most of them German

Jewish refugees. The April 3 <u>New</u> <u>York</u> <u>Times</u> carries a picture of a tired, determined, and stiff-lipped Paul.

She was interviewed at the dock. Other passengers arriving on other ships that week had told of daily attacks from the air on the convoys,6 and reporters no doubt hoped that similar war adventures would be recounted by this women chairman of some equal rights club. Instead she was characteristically focused on her theme.

"This world crisis came about without women having anything to do with it," she said. "If the women of the world had not been excluded from world affairs, things today might have been different. This war is a man-made war. We have got our world organization well under way and now we are organizing in Asia. What we plan to do is to have [some say] when peace is discussed. Women must never again be excluded from the affairs of the world. There can be no democracy without women participating. . . ."7 Three days later Alice Paul was the honored guest at the NWP headquarters in Washington and 400 people came, including many senators and congressmen.

Alice Paul and other American women of the World Women's Party hoped to return to Switzerland after the war and reopen the WWP in Geneva, but the establishment of the United Nations in New York changed that plan.

Her commitment to the refugees remained strong, and she continued to direct much of it even after returning to the United States--finding the USA sponsors for refugees, getting visas, badgering State Department officials in Washington and Zurich.

What had the sojourn in Villa Bartholoni accomplished? It had saved the lives of some outstanding feminists of Europe. It had been the scene of last intense lobbying of the League and the ILO. The League had actually discussed the Equal Rights Treaty in the Assembly. But her work with the League had no lasting results in international legal codes. The war killed that. But it was an excellent prep course for her much more successful efforts at war's end. The World Women's Party for Equal Rights continued. At Lake Success and in San Francisco she and a band of feminists haunted United Nations delegates and committees with the result that equal rights is included in the preamble to the U.N. Charter and in several other articles throughout the document. Later, after much difficulty, gender equality became a part of the U.N. Human Rights Covenant.

These documents made little impact on U.S. domestic law, but abroad they did serve as the model for the constitutions of emerging nations. Forty years later women delegates from Third World countries to the Nairobi conference at the end of the United Nations Decade for Women were astonished to learn that women's equality was not a part of the constitution in the United States, but few knew about Alice Paul or appreciated the irony.

Notes

1"Alice Paul, Conversations with Alice Paul," an oral history interview conducted by Amelia R. Fry. The Bancroft Library, University of California, Berkely, California, 1972-73. pp. 1-15. Hereafter "AP OHI."

2"AP OHI," P. 32.

3"AP OHI," p. 42.

4"AP OHI," p. 60.

5Paul to Fry, pre-interview conference, 1972.

6New York Times, April 1, 1941 - The arrival of the freighter Blommersdijk is one example of that week.

7World Telegram, April 3, 1941.

BIBLIOGRAPHIC ESSAY
Amelia R. Fry

The major source on Alice Paul's life is her oral history, recorded in 1972 and 1973: "Conversations with Alice Paul: Woman Suffrage and the Equal Rights Amendment," an interview conducted by Amelia R. Fry, The Bancroft Library, the University of California, Berkeley. It contains a preface and interview history, appendices and is 670 pages. This is available as a manuscript in several research libraries in the United States, England, and Australia.

The World Women's Party main sources are the microfilm edition of the World Women's Party Papers, 1912-1972, the New York Times/Microfilm Corporation of America, series vii, reels 173-178; the appropriate volumes of the NWP organ, Equal Rights, also in the microfilms of the NWP papers; and in the archives of the committee papers of the League of Nations, available only in the League of Nations Archives, the United Nations, Geneva, Switzerland. This paper utilized all of these sources for the section on the World Women's Party.

Three secondary sources remain as classics on the suffrage phase of Alice Paul's life; they are:

Eleanor Flexner, Century of Struggle (New York, 1970)--originally published by Harvard University Press, Cambridge, 1959.

Inez Haynes Irwin, The Story of Alice Paul and the National Woman's Party, 1920 edition reprinted 1977 by Denlinger's Publishers, Ltd., Fairfax, Virginia 22030 (p.o. box 76) and available for purchase at the headquarters of the National Woman's Party, 144 Constitution Ave. N.E., Washington, DC 20002.

Doris Stevens, Jailed for Freedom, the Story of the Militant American Suffragist Movement, originally published in 1920 also, reprinted in paperback in 1976 by Schocken Books (New York) as part of the series, Studies in the Life of Women, general editor Gerda Lerner, and with an Introduction by Janice Law Trecker.

The latter two books were written by women who were a part of the National Woman's Party struggle. Paul says in her oral history that Irwin includes some journalistic imagination in her account; however, it, like Steven's book, contains quotations from original reports and interviews with the women which are not easily available, if at all, anywhere else.

A series of oral histories of other leaders of the National Woman's Party were also produced by the same Regional Oral History Office of the Bancroft Library at Berkeley, and the transcripts may also be ordered by other research libraries at cost. They are:

BARY, Helen Valeska. Labor Administration and Social Security: A Woman's Life. 1974.

MATTHEWS, Burnita Shelton. <u>Pathfinder</u> <u>in</u> <u>the</u> <u>Legal</u> <u>Aspects</u> <u>of</u> <u>Women</u>. 1975.

PAUL, Alice. <u>Conversations</u> <u>with</u> <u>Alice</u> <u>Paul:</u> <u>An</u> <u>Autobiography</u>. 1975.

RANKIN, Jeannette. <u>Activist</u> <u>for</u> <u>World</u> <u>Peace,</u> <u>Women's</u> <u>Rights,</u> <u>and</u> <u>Democratic</u> <u>Government</u>. 1974.

REYHER, Rebecca Hourwich. <u>Working</u> <u>for</u> <u>Women's</u> <u>Equality</u>. 1978.

<u>The</u> <u>Suffragists:</u> <u>From</u> <u>Tea-Parties</u> <u>to</u> <u>Prison</u>. 1975. Sylvie Thygeson, "In the Parlor" Jessie Haver Butler, "On the Platform" Miriam Allen deFord, "In the Streets" Laura Ellsworth Seiler,"On the Soapbox" Ernestine Kettler, "Behind Bars"

VERNON, Mabel. <u>The</u> <u>Suffrage</u> <u>Campaign,</u> <u>Peace</u> <u>and</u> <u>International</u> <u>Relations</u>. 1975.

WOOD, Sara Bard Field. <u>Poet</u> <u>&</u> <u>Suffragist</u>. 1979.

APPENDIX I
Time Line of American Female
Public Friends, 1650-1950
Carol Stoneburner

1647 - George Fox found Light Within, began to preach.1

1652 - George Fox on Pendle Hill--saw a vision of "a
       great people to be gathered"--beginning of Quaker
       Movement.

1656 - George Fox encouraged a group of women to
       establish "Box Meeting" to provide for the poor
       and needy.

     - George Fox established Two Weeks Meeting for (1)
       women to visit sick and prisoners (2) to look
       after the poor, widowed and orphaned.
     - George Fox, The Woman Learning in Silence, or The
       Mystery of Woman's Subjection to Her Husband, as
       also, The Daughters Prophesying When in the Lord
       hath, and is Fulfilling that he spoke by the
       prophet Joel, I will pour my spirit unto All
       Flesh.

     - Elizabeth Harris traveled to Maryland to preach.

     - Sarah Gibbons, Mary Wetherhead, Dorothy Waugh,
       Mary Pierce, and four men traveled from England
       to Boston. They were imprisoned and taken back
       to England.

1656 - Quaker missionaries from England, Ann Austin,
1657   mother of five children, and Mary Fisher went to
       Massachusetts. They were whipped and driven out
       of Boston. Later they went to Barbados and had a
       successful mission. Mary Fisher also visited The
       Sultan of Turkey.

1657 – Mary Dyer returned to Boston, Massachusetts, from England. She was banished from Massachusetts Colony again. (In 1638 she had supported Anne Hutchinson, in Massachusetts, when she was accused of Antinomian heresy. She and her husband were banished from Massachusetts. From 1652–1657 they were in England and became Quakers.)

– Sarah Gibbons, Mary Wetherhead, Dorothy Waugh, and Mary Clark joined seven men on Woodhouse, a small ship, and came to Long Island, New York, and Rhode Island.

– Quakers visited New Netherlands and Lady Deborah Moody was converted. On Long Island she helped start a Friend's Meeting in her home.

1660 – Mary Dyer returned to Boston where she was hanged.

– Elizabeth Hooten had a grant of land from King of England to open a house in Massachusetts Bay Colony.

– Elizabeth Hooten, Joan Brocksoppe, Mary Malluis, Catherine Chattam, and 23 other men and women were released from Boston jails and left for England; order of King of England.

– Virginia legislated imprisonment and expulsion for Quaker ministers.

1661 – London Yearly Meeting established--an outgrowth of the first meeting of national scope in Skipton.2

– Yearly Meeting Newport, Rhode Island, becomes New England Yearly Meeting.

– George Fox--published <u>Concerning</u> <u>Sons</u> <u>and</u> <u>Daughters,</u> <u>and</u> <u>Prophetesses</u> <u>Speaking</u> <u>and</u> <u>Prophesying</u> <u>in</u> <u>the</u> <u>Law</u> <u>and</u> <u>the</u> <u>Gospel</u>.

- Isabel Spring--abused an officer who came to
her house to suppress a Quaker Meeting (in
Virginia)--given 20 lashes on her bare back and
kept in the sheriff's custody until she begged
forgiveness.

1662 - Oath of allegiance in Virginia was to be administered to persons attending Quaker assemblies--
seven women were arrested and imprisoned for
refusing to take the oath and denounce heresy of
Quakerism.

- Mary Tomkins and Alice Ambrose visited Virginia
and "had good service for the Lord." They were
pilloried, given 32 lashes, their goods seized,
and expelled from the colony.

1662 - Cart and Whip Act established in Massachusetts
1667   Bay Colony--stripped to the waist, tied to the
tail of carts, and whipped through towns, ten
lashes in each, until they were out of the
province (men, women, and children). Ann
Coleman, Mary Tomkins, Alice Ambrose, Elizabeth
Hooten, Catherine Chattam, Deborah Wilson,
Margaret Smith, and Margaret Brewster were some
of the women suffering this fate, and worse, in
Massachusetts.

1663 - Mary Tomkins and Alice Ambrose were missionaries
off the Cliffs of the Cheasapeake in Maryland
(better received).

1666 - Margaret Fell--Women's Speaking Justified,
Proved, and Allowed of by the Scriptures, all
such as Speak in the Spirit and Power of the Lord
Jesus (while in prison in England).

1668 - George Fox established monthly and quarterly
meetings for business for men in England.

- George Fox established two schools, one at Waltham Abbey for boys and one at Shaklewell for girls.

1671 - George Fox (in England) established regular monthly and quarterly meetings for business meetings for women. Opposition came from John Story and John Wilkinson.

- Elizabeth Hooten, Elizabeth Miars accompanied George Fox and ten other men to Barbados. Elizabeth Hooten died there.

1672 - Baltimore Yearly Meeting--Men's and Women's meetings were established.

- Meeting of ten to supervise publications set up by George Fox in England.

1674 - Epistle from the Women Friends in London to the Women Friends in the County, also Elsewhere, about the Service of a Women's Meeting.

1676 - Fox's Epistle--"Encouragement to all the Women's Meetings in the World."

- Sarah Fell--epistle to "Women's Meeting Everywhere"--clerk of Lancashire Quarterly Meeting for Women.

1679 - Women at Maryland Half Year's Meeting a "serious consideration concerning Children's going to school."

- Dublin, Ireland, Yearly Meeting for Women established.

1681 - September 10 - Philadelphia Yearly Meeting of Women, Burlington, New Jersey established.

1685 - Mary Fisher (now married to John Crosse) emigrated to South Carolina where she was a minister.

1686 - Philadelphia Yearly Meeting established.

1689 - Friends Public School established. Keith as headmaster.

1691 - Quaker Period of Quietism.
1827

1691 - Truth Vindicated by Elizabeth Bathhurst.

   - Women Friends of Maryland--parents should not bequeath any money to children who marry out of meeting.

1696 - New York (Long Island) Yearly Meeting established..

1698 - North Carolina Yearly Meeting established.

1699 - First Epistle by Women's Philadelphia Yearly Meeting to women Friends' in London.

1699 - Hannah Penn, second wife of William Penn visited
1701   Philadelphia (from England).

1700 - "Queries" added to "Advices" in New England.

1701 - Mary Starbuck converted to Quakerism on Nantucket. Established Friends Meeting in her home. Much of the population on the island converted to Quakerism.

   - Elizabeth Haddon left England, went to New Jersey to help the Indians, and established a home in the wilderness for traveling ministers. Five hundred acres in Gloucester County, N.J. becomes the village of Haddonfield.

1701 - Elizabeth Haddon Estaugh had a skill in herbs
1762   and physic, making a healing salve.

1705 - Philadelphia Yearly Meeting annual collection through women's monthly and quarterly business meeting of fund or "stock" established.

1712 - Sybilla Master notified her meeting that she intended to go to London to secure patents on two of her inventions: (1) for cleaning and curing Indian corn used for cornmeal and patent medicine, (2) a new way of working and staining in straw the plat and leaf of palmetto tree. Both inventions were in her husband's name and marketed in the United States.

1712? - Elizabeth Haddon Estaugh--clerk of Haddonfield
1762   and Newton Monthly Women's Meeting for 50 years.

1713 - Mary Hayes and her husband--ministers from Anituga to Albermarle, North Carolina.

1717 - Yearly Meeting at Newport spoke against slavery; members were censured in 1727 if they continued to own slaves.

1722 - Jane Lenn (Hoskins) and Elizabeth Lewis were
1725   missionaries who went to England through Maryland, Virginia, and North Carolina, then to Barbados and New England.

1723 - Suzanna Morris and Ann Roberts--ministers from Pennsylvania to Albemarle, North Carolina.

1726 - Jane Lenn (Hoskins) with Abigail Bowles-- revisited Quakers in southern Colonies.

1735 - Elizabeth Ashbridge made first contact with Friends in Boston Meeting which led her to become Friends minister.

1737 - "Birthright Membership" begins in England.

1738 - First Book of Discipline in England.

1739 - Rebecca Jones--Minister.
1818

1744 - Jane Lenn (Hoskins) and Margaret Churchman--
revisited southern colonies (from England).
"Life of that Faithful Servant of Christ," Jane
Hoskins, Minister of the Gospel" Friends Library
I.

1747 - Sophia Hume (granddaughter of Mary Fisher)
returned from London to preach and call for
repentance in Charleston, South Carolina.

1748 - Sophia Hume published an Exhortation to the
Inhabitants of the Province of South Carolina in
Philadelphia. She also preached in Philadelphia
in 1748-1748 and returned to England. Preached
against luxury, sectarian strictness.

1750 - Elizabeth Nixon of North Carolina and Mary Weston
of London were ministers to Charleston Meetings.

1750's - Abigail Pike, Hannah Ballinger, and Rachel
Wright--all visited Friends in Eastern North
Carolina and Virginia.

1753 - Mary Peisley (Neale) from Ireland, and Catherine
Payton from England were in Charleston and other
parts of the southern colonies.

1754 - Hannah Jenkins Barnard--minister in 1754 --

    - In the first meeting of New Garden, North Carol-
    ina Monthly Meeting there was a minute for Hannah
    Ballinger to "travel in truth's service --

1756 - Quakers relinquished control of Pennsylvania
legislature; end of the "Holy Experiment."

1758 - John Woolman persuaded Philadelphia Yearly
Meeting to condemn slaveholding by Friends.

1759 - "The Journal of Elizabeth Sandwich Drinker"--
1807   example of philadelphia Quaker women during
Quietist Period--at center of Quakerism in

Philadelphia at that period--husband, business man.

1763 - Sophia Hume--published A Caution to Such as Observes Days and Times--denouncing religious festivals.

1766 - Lydia Barrington Darragh advertised the opening of a mortuary establishment to "make Grave Clothes and lay out the Dead, in the Neatest Manna" (Pennsylvania Gazette, December 4). She was already a midwife.

1767 - Sophia Hume returned to Charleston, South Carolina, where she preached at large public meetings. The meeting was almost gone before she returned to revive it.

1768 - Mary Stedham and Rachel Wright from Bush River in South Carolina were recorded as ministering in Charleston.

- New York Yearly Meeting--Query against owning slaves established.

1769 - Rachel Wilson (preacher from England) with Sary Jamney visited in Maryland, Virginia, North Carolina, and Charleston.

1771 - Suzanna Wright (Pennsylvania) raised silk worms and won ten prizes in Philadelphia for largest number of cocoons raised by individual as part of non-importation movement. Also, she was active in medical folklore and dispensing herbal medicine, etc.

1772 - Maryland Yearly Meeting discouraged slaveholding.

- Maryland and North Carolina Yearly Meeting Minute Quakers who owned slaves must be "discontinued."

1773 - Sarah and Mehitabel Jenkins from New England visited and ministered in Charleston.

1774 - Elizabeth Robinson from England and Ruth Holland
       from Maryland ministered in Charleston.

1776 - Charity Cook (daughter of Rachel Wright) and Mary
1787   Pearson of North Carolina traveled to Georgia
       and later to more meetings in Virginia, North
       Carolina, South Carolina, and Georgia.

1776 - Philadelphia Women's Meeting made it a disownable
       offense to keep slaves.

1777 - Lydia Darragh is said to have warned Washington
       about a surprise attack by the British who had
       requisited a room in her house for a council
       meeting.

1782 - Charity Cook and Mary Pearson (North Carolina)
       traveled in New England.

     - Jemima Wilkinson (dismissed by Society of Friends
       for attending New Light Baptist Meeting and
       using her title of Public Universal Friends)
       began traveling and preaching in Philadelphia,
       Rhode Island, Massachusetts, and Connecticut.
       1784--published The Universal Friends Advice to
       Those of the Same Religious Society and founded
       the Universal Friends--plain language and
       clothes, opposition to war and violence--
       opposition to slavery--celibacy. 1788--settled
       Jerusalem township in New York state for her home
       and society (near Keuka Lake)

1784 - Rebecca Jones (teacher and preacher) traveled to
       London in ministry. She was instrumental in
       persuading London Yearly Meeting to start a
       Women's Yearly Meeting. Traveled in England,
       Scotland, Wales,and Ireland (1,578 meetings for
       worship and discipline and 1,120 meetings with
       Friends in the station of servants, apprentices,
       laborers, and family visits)--pioneer in the
       Evangelical Movement in Quakerism.

- London Yearly Meeting for Women established.

- Philadelphia women appointed communication with men in assisting care and oversight of free Negroes.

1790 - Ann Jessup of New Garden, North Carolina, went to minister in England and Scotland for three years. She brought back seeds, shrubs, and cuttings. Laster employed Abijah Pinson to graft and plant an orchard for her. Many graftings were taken from orchards by Friends migrating West.

1784 - English Women Ministers Mary Dudley, Sarah R.
1788   Gruff, Hannah Cathrall, Mary Peisley, Christiana Hustler, Margaret Routh, and Esther Tuke.

1790 - Rebecca Jones influential in establishing Westtown (patterned on Ackworth in Yorkshire) outside Philadelphia in 1799.

1795 - Philadelphia woman appointed committee on feasibility of boarding school.

1796 - Charity Cook of South Carolina, Suzannah Wright, and Hollingsworth traveled to Pennsylvania, New York, New England, and then to England (Martha Routh) (1799) Germany (Charity Cook, Sarah Harrison and Mary Swett) (1798).

1799 - Mary Swett and Charity Cook in England.

1798 - Hannah Jenkins Barnard and Elizabeth Hosier
1800   Coggeshall from New York visited Friends Meetings in Scotland, England, and Ireland. Charged with heresy in London Yearly Meeting.

1799 - Westtown Boarding School opened (co-educational).

- Beginning of Quaker migration to Northwest Territory.

1800 - Charity Cook and Sarah Stephenson in Ireland

1801   returned home to husband and children five and a
        half years after leaving Bush River Meeting,
        South Carolina.

1801 - Hannah Jenkins Barnard published "An Appeal to
        the Society of Friends, on the Primitive
        Simplicity of the Christian Principle and
        Disapline"--when she was eldered by English
        Quakers for views very similar to those later
        preached by Elias Hicks.

1804 - "A Narrative of the Proceedings in America, of
        the Society called Quakers in the Case of Hannah
        Barnard" (attributed to Thomas Foster).

     - Philadelphia Yearly Meeting assisted establishing
        an Indian school at Tuesassa.

1809 - Wilmington School for Girls was established
        (became Hicksite).

1812 - Ohio Yearly Meeting established at Short Creek--
        west of Alleghenies.

1813 - In England, Elizabeth Fry starts prison reform
        work.

1814 - Deborah Logan started transcribing the
        correspondence between William Penn and her
        husband's grandfather, James Logan, and presented
        it to American Philosophical Society (a valuable
        collection for Pennsylvania history).

1818 - Lucretia Mott's first ministry. She was recorded
        in ministry in 1821 and continued this ministry
        all of her life.

     - First Friends Sunday Schools in U.S. started by
        Levi Coffin in Deep River, North Carolina.

1819 - Founding of Fair Hill Boarding School, Sandy
        Springs, Maryland (became Hicksite).

1821 - Indiana Yearly Meeting started at Whitewater.

1825 - Free produce movement--boycott of goods produced
1863   by slave labor. Some leaders were: Levi Coffin
       (North Carolina, Indiana), Lucretia Mott and
       Sarah Pugh (Philadelphia).

1820's - Sarah Mapps Douglas opened school for Negro
         children in Philadelphia.

1825 - Rebecca Webb Pennock Lukens took control of
       Brandywine Iron Works (after husband's death)
       which she managed successfully until 1850's

1826 - "Mixed Sunday Schools" established at Honey
       Creek, Indiana.

1827 - The Great Schism--Hicksite and Orthodox branches
       of Quakerism split in Philadelphia, then in New
       York, Baltimore, Ohio and Indiana. In 1834
       Genesee Yearly Meeting in New York state and in
       1875 Illinois Yearly Meeting also were
       established as Hicksite Yearly Meetings (with
       accompanying Quarterly and Monthly Meetings).
       Orthodox Yearly Meetings were in Philadelphia,
       Baltimore, Ohio, Indiana, New York, New England,
       North and South Carolina, Virginia, and Georgia.

     - The Friend--Orthodox periodical published.

     - The Congregational or Progressive Friends (a more
       liberaloff-shoot of Hicksite Quakers) were
       established in Western New York, Ohio, Michigan,
       and with one meeting in Iowa, Indiana and
       Pennsylvania (Longwood).

     - Deborah Logan became the first woman member
       (Honorary) of the Historical Society of
       Philadelphia for her extensive work in
       Pennsylvania history.

1828 - Friends Select School (Philadelphia) established (Orthodox).

1829 - Elizabeth Margaret Chandler superintendent of "The
1834 Ladies Repository" of the Genius of Universal Emancipation--first anti-slavery newspaper edited by Benjamin Lundy and assisted by William Lloyd Garrison.

1830 - English Friend Hannah Chapman Gurney Backhouse (1787-1850) traveled in America with Elizabeth Kirkbridge trying to heal Hicksite/Orthodox schism. Traveled in Pennsylvania, New England, Canada, North and South Carolina, Indiana and Ohio.

1830 - Hannah Backhouse and Joseph John Gurney (English
1838 Friends) traveled in America encouraging the establishment of Bible Societies.

1832 - Elizabeth Margaret Chandler helped establish the first Anti-Slavery Society in Michigan.

1833 - Lucretia Mott and Sarah Pugh attended the American Anti-Slavery Society in Philadelphia. Lucretia Mott spoke, but no women were members.

   - Lucretia Mott and Sarah Pugh helped organize the Philadelphia Female Anti-Slavery Society; also involved were: Sarah Mapps Douglas, her mother, and Sarah and Angelina Grimke. Sarah Pugh presided and they met in her home for many years.

   - Prudence Crandall established a boarding school and teaching training school for Negro girls in Canterbury, Connecticut. They were driven out of town in 1834.

   - Sybil Jones recorded as a minister.

- Philadelphia Yearly Meeting (Hicksite) established the Committee of Religious Concern for the
Right Education of Children--led to Hicksite
schools--elementary, and later secondary (George
School) and collegiate (Swarthmore). There were
Women's and Men's Representatives to this yearly
meeting committee. Both schools were to be co-
educational.

- Indiana, Ohio and Baltimore Yearly Meeting
established schools for western tribes of Seneca
Indians in Kansas; literary and manual education
included.

1834 - Hannah Backhouse published the pamphlet,
Scripture Questions for the Use of Schools (for
Orthodox).

- Abby Kelley Foster helped establish the Lynn,
Massachusetts Female Anti-Slavery Society.

1835 - Belvedere Academy at Rich Spring, North Carolina
(Orthodox) established.

- Westchester Graded School in Pennsylvania
(Hicksite) established.

- Elizabeth Buffum Chace helped found the Fall
River, Massachusetts Female Anti-Slavery Society
(her father was first president of New England
Anti-Slavery Society in 1832).

1835 - Elizabeth Gurney (English Friend) traveled in
1855 evangelical ministry and spelling out of Quaker
doctrine (Orthodox).

1836 - The Poetical Works of Elizabeth Margaret Chandler
(with a "Memoir of Her Life and Character" by
Benjamen Lundy) and her Essays, Philanthropic and
Moral were both published.

1837 - Angelina Grimke, An Appeal to the Christian Women
of the South, published by the American Anti-

Slavery Society. A letter from Angelina Grimke speaking out against slavery (as a southern woman--now living in Philadelphia) was published in the Liberator.

- Sarah Grimke was rebuked by Quaker elders for attempting to speak at an Orthodox meeting about slavery. She then wrote Epistle to the Clergy of the Southern States for the American Anti-Slavery Society.

- Sarah Mapps Douglas, Sarah and Angelina Grimke protested to English Quakers the separate seating of the Douglass family and other Negroes at Arch St. Meeting (Orthodox).

1837 - Lucretia Mott organized the first Woman's Anti-Slavery Convention in New York City, Abby Kelley Foster, Angelina and Sarah Grimke spoke.

- Angelina Grimke published Appeal to the Women of the Nominally Free States.

- Congregational Ministerial Association of Massachusetts issued a "Pastoral Letter" attacking Angelina Grimke for unwomanly behavior and speaking at "promiscuous (mixed sex) audiences."

- New Garden Boarding School (co-educational) established by North Carolina Yearly Meeting-- becomes Guilford College in 1888 (Orthodox).

- Friends Boarding School (co-educational) of Ohio Yearly Meeting was established at Mt. Pleasant (Orthodox).

1838 - Philadelphia Female Anti-Slavery Society financially supported school for Negro children run by Sarah Mapps Douglas.

- Angeline Grimke testified before the Massachusetts Legislature on Anti-Slavery petitions (first woman to testify).

- Angelina Grimke' wrote a series of letters about women's right to speak in The Liberator.

- Sarah Grimke' published Letters on the Equality of the Sexes and the Condition of Women.

- Angelina Grimke' married Theodore Weld (a Presbyterian Anti-Slavery Agent)--both Angelina and Sarah were disowned by Orthodox Quakers. The Douglass family attended the wedding with many other anti-slavery leaders. This racial mixing was publicized in the newspapers. Angelina Weld spoke two days later at the Philadelphia Anti-Slavery Convention at the new Pennsylvania Hall. Lucretia Mott presided and Abby Kelley Foster spoke--Pennsylvania Hall was burned down as was the Shelter for Colored Orphans. (The Mott house narrowly missed destruction by the mob.)

- Abby Kelley Foster and William Lloyd Garrison helped found the New England Non-Resistant Society.

- Union Normal Institute (near High Point, North Carolina) was founded by Orthodox Quakers and Methodists.

- Sharon Female Seminary in Darby, Pennsylvania (Hicksite) established.

- Freeman Institute of Massachusetts was organized--Lydia Pinkhem was secretary.

- Hicksite's established periodical, Friends Intelligencer.

1839 - Sarah Grimke' and Angelina Weld compiled American Slavery As It Is and Testimony of a Thousand Witnesses.

- Abby Kelley Foster began career as the Anti-Slavery lecturer and agitator--traveled extensively (1842-1867) under the banner of "No Union with Slaveholders"--supported by Garrison.

- Executive Committee of the Pennsylvania Anti-Slavery had Mary Greer, Abby Kimber, Sarah Pugh, Margaret Jones Burleigh, Lucretia Mott and six male members.

1840 - At the Convention of American Anti-Slavery Society the appointment of Abby Kelley to a committee was opposed because of her sex. The association split over this issue. W. L. Garrison founded the American Anti-Slavery Association. Arthur and Lewis Tappan founded the Liberty Party.

- Indiana Yearly Meeting opposed Anti-Slavery and Free Produce discussion

- Lucretia Mott and Sarah Pugh and several American women were refused acceptance as delegates at the World's Anti-Slavery Society in England. The American delegation was angered. Lucretia Mott (who was a delegate) met Elizabeth Cady Stanton (Henry Stanton, her husband was also a delegate).

- Sybil Jones traveled in preaching ministry with her husband Eli, to Nova Scotia and New Brunswick. They held family meetings, evangelical meetings and gave aid to temperance causes.

1841 - Abby Kelley Foster resigned from the Society of Friends because of the weak stand against slavery.

1842 - Indiana Yearly Meeting of Anti-Slavery Friends established (2,000 members--disbanded and remerged in 1857).

1842 - Female Manual Labor School at Cattaragus, New

1849   York for Seneca Indians, established (Hicksite).

- Abigail Hopper Gibbons resigned from Society of Friends when her husband and father were read out of meeting for Anti-Slavery activity.

1843 - Elizabeth Kirkbride Gurney and her husband, Joseph John Gurney, traveled in ministry in France. They were accompanied by Elizabeth Gurney Fry and they preached and spoke for the abolition of slavery and investigated prisons. They met with King Louis Philippe and his wife and urged them to free the slaves in The French West Indies.

- Maria Mitchell requested and received disownment by Quaker Meeting because of religious doubts.

- Eliza Farnham argued against political rights for women in Brother Jonathan, edited by John Neal.

- Elizabeth Buffam Chace resigned from the Society of Friends because of its opposition to abolition.

1844 - Friends Academy at Richmond, Indiana, established (Hicksite).

- The Friends Intelligencer - Hicksite periodical established.

- Eliza Farnham became matron of Women's Division of Sing-Sing prison (New York).

1845 - Bloomingdale (Indiana) Academy--Agricultural and Manual labor school established.

- Salem Seminary, Iowa, established.

- Wilburite-Gurneyite "separation" in New England.

- Yearly Meetings in South Carolina, Georgia and Virginia laid down.

- Friends Central School in Philadelphia established (Hicksite).

- Sybil and Eli Jones made an extensive preaching trip to Ohio, Indiana, Maryland and North Carolina because he was concerned over the plight of Negroes (Orthodox).

- Abigail Gibbons helped found the Prison Association of New York and worked in it until her death in 1877--special concern for Randall's Island Asylum.

- Abby Kelley Foster involved with W. L. Garrison's Anti-Slavery Bugle published in Salem, Ohio.

1846 - Elizabeth Farnham published Rationale of Crime and Its Appropriate Treatment by English phrenologist Marmaduke Blake Sampson.

1847 - Friends Boarding School, Richmond, Indiana (later to become Earlham College)--(Orthodox)--influenced by Elizabeth and Joseph John Gurney (English Friends). The college was named after Gurney estate in England.

- October 1, 1847 - Maria Mitchell discovered a Comet from her father's observatory on Nantucket Island. She was awarded a gold medal by the King of Denmark and the comet was named for her.

- Gurneyite Friends start publication--Friends Review.

1848 - Elizabeth Farnham was forced to resign as prison matron because of her attempts at prison reform.

- First Woman's Rights Convention--Seneca Falls, New York. Lucretia Mott, Martha Wright, Mary Ann

McClintock, Jane Hunt (all part of Progressive Friends Meeting) and Elizabeth Cady Stanton called the meeting. "The Declaration of Sentiments" proposed and approved in July meeting.

- September--Second Woman's Rights Convention held in Rochester, New York.

- Susan B. Anthony's first speech at a Daughters of Temperance Convention. (Hicksite)--she started attending the Unitarian Church when there was opposition within Quakerism over an Anti-Slavery petition. She officially remained a Friend all of her life.

- Maria Mitchell was the first woman elected to the American Academy of Arts and Sciences. In 1849 she was appointed one of the original computers for American Ephemeries and Nautical Almanac.

1849 - Oak Grove Seminary, Vassaboro, Maine (Orthodox) founded.

1850   - Elizabeth Farnham lectured in California on such
1855   topics as spiritualism, female valor, prison reform--she was opposed to woman's suffrage.

1850 - Eliza Buffam Chace signed the call to the Worchester (Massachusetts) Woman's Rights Convention.

- Lucretia Mott wrote and published "Discourse on Woman."

- Female (later Woman's) Medical College of Pennsylvania founded by a group of Quakers--Ann Preston and Hannah Myers Longshore were among the first students.

- Raisin Valley Seminary, Michigan, established.

- Farmer Institute near Lafayette, Indiana, was founded.

- Maria Mitchell elected to American Association of Advancement of Science by Louis Agassiz.

1851 - Sarah Adamson (Dolley) graduated from Central Medical College (Syracuse/Rochester, New York).

- Hannah Longshore and Ann Preston graduated from Women's Medical College (under police guard to stop threat of violence).

- Amanda Way was one of the founders of the Indiana Woman's Rights Society.

- Eli and Sybil Jones sailed to Monrovia,Liberia (Africa) to encourage colonization and conversion of freed slaves.

- Sarah Pugh traveled in England and Europe speaking about Anti-Slavery.

1852 - Lucretia Mott was President of Woman's Rights Convention in Syracuse, New York. She attended and spoke at all the annual woman's rights conventions.

- Sybil and Eli Jones traveled in evangelical ministry to Great Britain, Ireland, Germany and Southern France.

- Susan B. Anthony was refused the right to speak at an Albany, New York, Temperance rally because of her sex. She helped form the Women's New York State Temperance Society with Elizabeth Cady Stanton.

- Hannah Longshore--demonstrator of anatomy at New England Female Medical College; then Female Medical College in Philadelphia, and in 1853 Female Department of Pennsylvania Medical University.

1853 - Susan B. Anthony helped form the New York City Working Women's Association (to form unions for higher wages and shorter hours).

- Dr. Hannah Myers Longshore started private medical practice--held a series of lectures on medical education for women--presided over by Lucretia Mott--in practice until 1892.

- Women delegates refused recognition at World's Temperance Convention in New York City. Susan B. Anthony helped organize the Whole World Temperance Convention--also in New York City-- this year she attended her first Woman's Rights Convention (she would attend these meetings for the next 50 years).

- Influenced by Elizabeth Fry in England, Elizabeth Comstock of Michigan developed a ministry in which she traveled and worked for abolition, peace, temperance and women's rights--visiting prisons, asylums and hospitals as a form of "home mission."

- Ann Preston (after a year of graduate school) became the Professor of Physiology and Hygiene at Women's Medical College.

1854 - Darby Friends School (Lansdowne Friends School) (Orthodox) established.

- Amanda Way organized a "Woman's Temperance Army" in Winchester, Indiana (anticipating later Woman's Crusades to close saloons).

- Susan B. Anthony organized country canvass for petitions on woman's suffrage and improvement of New York Married Woman's Property Law (one enacted in 1860).

1853 - Abigail Gibbons worked with Catherine M. Sedgewick and Sarah Doremus on Women's Prison Association and Home.

1855 - Mary Thomas was President of Indiana Woman's
1856   Rights Society (American Woman's Suffrage
Association).

1855 - Ann Jeanes and sister Mary founded Home for
Destitute Colored Children in Philadelphia
(Hicksite).

1855 - Elizabeth Gurney traveled in Ministry in England,
1858   Switzerland, France, Italy, and Germany.

1856 - Emily Howland assisted Myrtilla Miner at her
Washington, D.C. School for free Negro girls
(Hicksite).

- Susan B. Anthony became an agent for American
Anti-Slavery Society--traveling and speaking
extensively.

1857 - Mary Thomas (Indiana) was editor of The Lily
(Woman's Right's paper begun by Amelia Bloomer).

- Friendsville Academy, Tennessee was started
(Orthodox).

- Western Yearly Meeting established (included
Central Indiana, Michigan and Illinois)
(Orthodox).

1859 - Mary Thomas read a petition to Indiana General
Assembly calling for Married Women's Property Law
and Woman's Suffrage Amendments to the State
Constitution.

- Earlhan College becomes a (co-educational)
collegiate institution in Richmond, Indiana
(Orthodox).

- Abigail Gibbons became President of German
Industrial School.

1860 - North Carolina Men's and Women's Yearly Meeting
met jointly and offered a prayer that God "would
turn the hearts of rulers and people, to
righteousness, to justice and mercy; and that
present forms of Civil Government with its
attendant blessings, may be preserved in peace,
and all be overruled to His glory."

- New York State passed a Married Woman's Property
Law which allowed women to retain their earnings
and sue in court. (Susan B. Anthony and
Elizabeth Cady Stanton were leaders in this
effort).

- Anna Dickinson made her first speech at Pennsylvania Anti-Slavery Society--she was encouraged by
Dr. Hannah Longshore and Lucretia Mott.

- Sybil Jones visited Quakers in the South.

1861 - Elizabeth Comstock given an omnibus pass by
President Lincoln to all Union hospitals. She
was also given a pass by Secretary of War,
Stanton, to visit prison camps in Virginia. She
also traveled widely to minister to refugee
slaves.

- "The Rights and Wrongs of Women"--lecture given
at Philadelphia concert Hall by Anna Dickinson--
part of a lecture series planned by W. L.
Garrison.

- Elizabeth Farnham--Matron of Stockton Insane
Asylum.

- Philadelphia Woman's Hospital founded--Dr.
Emmaline Cleveland and Dr. Ann Preston on the
faculty. Also included a training school for
nurses.

- Lucy McKim visited the Sea Islands with her
father, who was General Secretary of the Port

Royal Relief Committee, and started a collection "Songs of the Freedmen of Port Royal"--words and music.

- Friends Seminary established in New York City (Hicksite).

- Union High School, Westfield, Indiana, started.

1861 - Ellen Collins Chairman of the Committee on
1864   supplies the Woman's Central Association of Relief, the New York branch of the United States Sanitary Commission.

- Amanda Way was nurse at battlefields and hospitals throughout the war.

1862 - Women's Loyal National League organized to petition Congress for an Amendment for Emancipation of slaves. Susan B. Anthony, Elizabeth Cady Stanton and Eliza Farnham were leaders--collected hundreds of thousands of signatures.

- "Women's Aid" of Philadelphia Yearly Meeting to work with refugee slaves--co-operated with National Freedmen's Relief Association.

- Elizabeth Comstock addressed the Michigan State Senate. She often brought together groups of lawmakers to consider social issues. She had appointments with Governor John Palmer of Illinois about pardons for several prisoners and other leaders on similar issues.

1863 - Irene and Elkanah Beard and Lizzie Bond from Indiana Yearly Meeting went to Young's Point to establish camp and school, and to Vicksburg to help start Freedman's Home and Orphanage. They worked to get seed and farm implements for freed slaves.

- Emily Howland (New York State) taught at Freedman's campus outside of Washington, D.C.

- Eliza Farnham went to Gettysburg to nurse the wounded--Abigail Gibbons and her daughter, Sarah, went to Washington to visit in army camps and hospitals.

- Iowa Yearly Meeting established (Orthodox).

1864 - Elizabeth Gurney, Elizabeth Comstock and other Friends had an appointment (in form of a prayer meeting) with President Lincoln to emancipate the slaves.

- Eliza Farnham published Woman and Her Era--a treatise arguing the superiority of women--she had used these ideas in the 1858 Woman's Rights Convention in New York City.

- Swarthmore College (co-educational) chartered in 1864--started in 1869--Lucretia Mott was among the founders (Hicksite).

- Abigail Gibbons organized the Labor and Aid society to help returning soldiers find work.

1865 - Ellen Collins worked in New York--National
1870   Freedmen's Relief Association--ion the cause of Negro education.

- Maria Mitchell joined faculty of Vassar College at its opening and an observatory with a 12 inch telescope was built for her. She taught at Vassar until 1888.

- Elizabeth Buffam Chace was Vice-President of American Anti-Slavery Society while it turned to problems of freed slaves--Sarah Pugh, Lucretia Mott, and etc. were likewise involved during these years. In Philadelphia Lucretia Mott and others established The Friends Association for the Aid and Elevation of the Freedman.

1866 – Ann Preston became the first woman Dean of Women's Medical College (continued until her death in 1871).

– America Equal Rights Association established-- Lucretia Mott, (President), and Susan B. Anthony were among the founders.

– Pennsylvania Peace Society formed with James Mott as President--Lucretia active.

1867 – Free Religious Association started--Ralph Waldo Emerson, Lucretia Mott, and Elizabeth Buffam Chace were among the founders--composed of Christians and Jews for religious reform.

– Peace Association of Friends in America is organized.

– Sybil and Eil Jones went on trip to Holy Land (Palestine and Syria). At Ramallah, Palestine they started a school for girls. Also one at Brumamma in Syria. The funds for their efforts were raised by Women's Foreign Missionary Society--through the leadership of Hannah J. Bailey in Maine. (In 1888 these schools were taken over by English Friends.)

– Lucy McKim Garrison, Charles Pickard Ware and William Francis Allen published Slave Songs of the United States.

– Dr. Mary Frame Thomas was a physician and one of the founders for the Home for Friendless Girls in Richmond, Indiana (half-sister to D. Hannah Myers Longshore)--both pioneer women doctors.

– Emily Howland (New York) persuaded her father to buy a 400 acre tract at Heathsville, Virginia, to settle the former slaves. She assisted and taught school there until her mother's illness called her home.

- Canada Yearly Meeting (Orthodox) established.

1868 - When students from the Women's Medical College were allowed clinical practice at the Pennsylvania hospital, there was a protest about immodest behavior of women as doctors. Ann Preston responded with a strong statement for the right of women to be students and doctors as long as there were to be patients--Anna E. Broomal was one of these students.

- Elizabeth Buffam Chace attended the organization of the New England Suffrage Association and established one in Rhode Island where she was President from 1870-1890--Part of the American Woman Suffrage Association.

- Susan B. Anthony and E. C. Stanton started The Revolution supported by George Francis Train.

- Susan B. Anthony helped start the Working Women's Association--she was delegate to National Labor Union and called for an eight hour day and equal pay for equal work for women--also women's suffrage.

- American and National Woman Suffrage Conventions split--Susan B. Anthony was Vice-President at Large of the National Woman Suffrage (1869).

- Iowa Yearly Meeting Missionary Association formed.

1860's - (late) - Mary Mendenhall Hobbs reported on the ravages of war for Quakers in North Carolina, "Conditions in Carolina at Close of the Civil War" in Autobiography of Allen Jay.

- Anna Dickinson on the lyceum circuit--championed Negro rights, emancipation of women (social and economic as well as political). She was against double moral standards, large corporations and Mormonism.

1860's - Emily Howland provided philanthropy for 30
  1929   schoolsfor southern Negroes (including Tuskegge
          Institute), The National Woman Suffrage Associa-
          tion, temperance and peace movements.

1869 - Maria Mitchell was first woman elected to
       American Philosophical Society. She was also an
       officer in 1873 of American Social Science
       Association.

1870 - Indiana Foreign Missionary Society - supported
       work in Mexico and Mataneos.

     - Irena and Elkanah Beard were missionaries to
       India (Hoshaugatad and Bhopal).

     - Sage College at Cornell University open to women
       by Quaker and founder Ezra Cornell. He was
       partly influenced in this move by Emily Howland,
       who for many years gave interest free loans to
       poor women students there. M. C. Carey Thomas
       and Florence Kelley were two Quaker women who
       attended.

     - Women Ministers in revivals in Iowa and Kansas
       were Elizabeth Comstock, Laura Haviland, Sybil
       Jones, Sarah Smith, and Caroline Talbot.

1871 - Amanda Way read a "Memorial" to Indiana State
       Legislature requesting a Woman Suffrage Amendment
       to Indiana Constitution--soon after became a
       local preacher in Methodist Episcopal Church--
       itinerant in Indiana and Kansas.

1871 - Anna Elizabeth Broomall studied in hospitals in
  1875   Vienna and Paris after graduating from Women's
         Medical College in Philadelphia.

1872 - Kansas Yearly Meeting started.

     - Susan B. Anthony was arrested for trying to vote
       in Presidential election under 14th Amendment.

She was fined--refused to pay--then disappointed that it was not carried to a higher court.

- Elizabeth Buffam Chace spoke at International Congress on the Prevention and Repression of Crime in London.

1873 - Sarah Pugh helped form the Moral Education Society in Philadelphia to gather petitions against the licensing of prostitution.

- Abby Kelley and Stephen Foster refused to pay property taxes on the basis of "no taxation without representation." Their house was sold at auction and bought by friends, then returned to them.

- Maria Mitchell was a founder of the Association for the Advancement of Women.

1873-75 - Hannah Whitall Smith and her husband, Robert Smith, were preachers in the interdenominational "Higher Life"--evangelical holiness movement in England.

1873 - Abigail Gibbons was a founder of the New York Diet Association for dispensing of food to ailing poor.

1874 - American Women's Christian Temperance Union founded. Hannah Bailey of Maine was early President of WCTU. Later state presidents who were Quakers are: Mary J. Weaver, Hannah Whitall Smith, Mary Whitall Thomas, Mary C. Woody, Sarah J. Hoge, Margaret Hillis and Esther Pugh.

- Mary H. Rogers gave leadership to revivals in Cotton Wood Quarter, Kansas.

1875 - Dr. Anna Elizabeth Broomall became Professor of Obstetrics at Woman's Medical College until 1903--very low mortality rate at Maternity Hospital during her supervision.

- Illinois Yearly Meeting founded.

- Introduction of the "pastoral system" in the mid-west.

- Dr. Clara Marshall graduated from Woman's Medical College and was demonstrator of Materia Medica and practical pharmacy while she was enrolled in Philadelphia College of Pharmacy. She became Professor of Materia Medica and Therapeutics at 1905 Women Medical College (Remained in that position until 1905).

- Lydia Pinkham's Vegetable Compound formula introduced to the market for tired women.

- Hannah Whitall Smith published The Christian's Secret of a Happy Life.

1876 - "Woman's Declaration of 1876" on the civil and political rights of women--presented by Susan B. Anthony at the fourth of July ceremonies at the Centennial Exposition in Philadelphia.

1876 - "Department of Advice"--an advice by mail service
1885   started by Lydia Pinkham on good diet, exercise, and cleanliness. She also wrote a booklet on sex and reproduction.

- Dr. Mary Thomas, the first woman regularly admitted to the Indiana State Medical Society, was elected President of Wayne County, Indiana Medical Society in 1887.

- Ellen Collins became visitor of public charitable institutions. Reports on Almshouses, hospitals and asylums provided data for Josephine Shaw Lowell's work on the State Board of Charities.

1877 - Helen Magill (White) was the first American woman to receive a Ph.D. in the U. S. (Boston University). She married Andrew White, President of Cornell, who was interested in women's education but opposed to suffrage.

- Founding of the New Century Club in Philadelphia--Dr. Clara Marshall one of the founders.

- Hicksite women won an equal role (to men) in Philadelphia Yearly Meeting.

1877 - Dr. Eliza Marie Mosher (trained at New England
1880   Hospital for women and children which opened in 1869) became physician and then Superintendent of Massachusetts Reformatory Prison for Women.

1878 - First Woman's Suffrage Amendment to the United States Constitution was introduced in Congress. Same amendment (often called the Susan B. Anthony Amendment) was introduced every year till it was passed in 1920.

- Dr. Anna Broomall proposed for membership in Philadelphia Obstetrical Society (not granted until 1982).

1879- Elizabeth Comstock was secretary of the Kansas
1881   Freedmen's Relief Association.

1879 - Dr. Sarah Read Adamson Dolley (inspired by Quaker Graceanna Lewis of the Academy of Natural Science in Philadelphia) organized the Rochester, New York Society of Natural Sciences.

1880 - Ellen Collins, influenced by English philanthropist Octavia Hill, worked with experiments in low income rentals in the lower East Side.

1880 - Dr. Mary Frame Thomas presided at the American Woman Suffrage Association.

- Amanda Way returned to Quakerism after the General conference of Methodist Episcopal Church discontinued licensing women as local preachers.

She became a Friends minister in Whittier, California Monthly Meeting.

1880 - Rachel Foster Avery was the Corresponding
1901   Secretary of the National Woman Suffrage Association--a great assistant to Susan B. Anthony and a gifted organizer.

1880 - Anna Botsford Comstock illustrated Report of the Entomologist and in 1888, An Introduction to Entomology, written by her husband, John Henry Comstock (Anna educated at Cornell University). (Hicksite)

1881 - Women's Foreign Missionary Society formed in Indiana--(outside the Yearly Meeting)--led by Armstrong Cox.

- Helen Jackson published A Century of Dishonor on plight of the Indians.

- 1st Volume (of 6) of The History of Women Suffrage published by Susan B. Anthony, E. C. Stanton and Matilda Joslyn Gage. Other volumes published in 1882, 1886, 1903, and 1922 ed. by Ida Husted Harper.

- Missionaries to Jamaica--Jesse and Elizabeth Townsend.

1882 - Philadelphia Women Friends Missionary Society (Orthodox) established.

- Mary Carey Thomas received Ph.D from University of Zurick (first foreigner and first woman) in English Philology.

- Dr. Clara Marshall first woman appointed to staff of Philadelphia Hospital as demonstrator in Obstetrics.

- Emily Howland financed Sherwood Select School (founded by Quakers in 1871) and was its patron until 1927 when it became a public school.

- Hannah Bailey became treasurer of the newly formed Women's Foreign Missionary Society of New England Yearly Meeting.

- Florence Kelley started evening classes for working girls at Women's New Century Club in Philadelphia.

- Helen Jackson and Abbot Kinney were commissioned to review the needs of Mission Indians of the West Coast--report made in 1883.

1883 - Hannah Whitall Smith became the first secretary of the WCTU National Evangelistic Department.

- Elizabeth Buffam Chace agitated for Women's College to be affiliated with Brown University-- established in 1897.

- Dr. Anna Broomall appointed gynecologist to the Friends Asylum for the Insane in Frankfort, Pennsylvania. She saw that her medical students were placed in similar positions in asylums and prisons.

- Gurneyite women Friends begin a mission effort in Japan.

1883 - Hannah Bailey and Lillian M. N. Stevens worked
1915   for a state reformatory for women. Hannah Bailey was twice the delegate from Maine at National Conference of Charities and Corrections.

- Hannah also edited Pacific Banner (for adults) and Acorn (for children) as part of WCTU peace campaign.

1883 - Helen Magil (White) was principal of Howard
1887   Collegiate Institute at West Bridgewater, Massachusetts.

1883 - Helen Jackson wrote <u>Ramona</u> to bring "the Indian
1884   question" to the public as Harriet B. Stowe had
        done for the slaves in <u>Uncle</u> <u>Tom's</u> <u>Cabin</u>.

1884 - Bryn Mawr College opened for women--sponsored by
       Orthodox Friends (as a sister institution to
       Haverford College for men). M. C. Thomas was the
       first Dean.

1885 - Women Friends in Missionary Society in
       Philadelphia met with Japanese Women to form a
       school in Japan (Orthodox--but outside Yearly
       Meeting)--opened in 1887.

     - M. Carey Thomas, Mary Gwinn, and Mary E. Garrett
       founded Bryn Mawr School for Girls in Baltimore
       (preparatory school)

1886 - Dr. Clara Marshall first woman to secure staff
       appointment in a state institution. She was
       Attending Physician of Girl's Division of
       Philadelphia House of Refuge.

     - Anna Thomas published <u>The</u> <u>Sacrificer</u> <u>and</u> <u>The</u> <u>Non-</u>
       <u>Sacrificer</u>--drawing on scriptures of Judaism,
       Christianity, Hinduism and Buddhism--stressing
       direct Communion with a just and loving God.

     - Dr. Sarah Dolley and other women doctors in
       Rochester, New York, organized the Provident
       Dispensary Association (for medical and surgical
       care of needy women and men) when women were not
       allowed on the staff of local hospitals.

1887 - Florence Kelley's translation of Friedrick
       Engels' <u>The</u> <u>Condition</u> <u>of</u> <u>the</u> <u>Working</u> <u>Class</u> <u>in</u>
       <u>England</u> <u>in</u> <u>1844</u> was published with assistance of
       Rachel Foster Avery by New York Socialists.

     - Bertha Ballard Home for Girls established by
       Indianapolis Association of Quaker Women.

- Mary Wright Plummer was one of the first students at the School for Library Economy at Columbia College, New York City.

- Hannah Bailey became the Superintendent of the Department of Peace and Arbitration of National WCTU--later had same position in World WCTU.

1888 - International Council of Women was formed by Susan B. Anthony, Rachel Avery, and Mary Wright Sewall and others.

- Dr. Clara Marshall became Dean of Women's Medical College.

- Anna Comstock initiated in Sigma X--National Honor Society of Sciences--one of the first women.

- Guilford College in Greensboro, North Carolina (Orthodox). Co-educational college growing out of New Garden Boarding School.

- Dr. Eliza M. Mosher founded medical training course at the Union Missionary Institute in Brooklyn.

1889 - M. Carey Thomas and other feminists presented an endowment to Johns Hopkins University Medical School contingent upon admitting women students. It was accepted and women were admitted.

- Florence Kelley published Our Toiling Children.

- Jane Addams and Ellen Starr opened Hull House in Chicago (Quakers Florence Kelley, Edith and Grace Abbott were among early residents).

1890 - Hadley Industrial Home established.

- Dr. Anna Broomall toured the Orient and India, lecturing and visiting former students who were medical missionaries and inspecting medical facilities.

- Quaker women met from various Yearly Meetings at Glen Falls, New York, to form what is now the United Society of Friends Women. It has since held a major convention every three years. See Looking Back and Over the Trail by Eliza Armstrong Cox and Growth Development Service Unlimited for further history.

- Merger of National and American Woman Suffrage Association--Susan B. Anthony, Vice-President at large and President in 1892.

1891 - Florence Kelley resident at Hull House in Chicago
1899 (from Northwestern University). Took law degree and passed bar in 1894.

1890's - Hannah Bailey led the WCTU to petition Congress to use arbitration in international disputes.

1891 - Hannah Bailey was President of Maine Woman
1897 Suffrage Association.

- Whittier College in Whittier, California established. (Co-educational)

1892 - Florence Kelley investigated "sweating system" in garment industry--lobbied the Illinois legislature in 1893 to pass the Factory Art-- limiting hours of work for women and prohibiting child labor. This Factory Act, a form of protective legislation, was struck down in 1895.

- Walter and Emma B. Malone founded the Cleveland Bible Institute in Ohio.

1893 - Lucretia Longshore Blackenburg, daughter of
1908 Hannah Longshore, was President of Pennsylvania Woman's Suffrage Association.

1893 - Woman's Congress of the World's Columbian Exposition in Chicago.

- Oregon Yearly Meeting established (Orthodox).

- Anna and Irving Kelsey Missionaries to Mexico.

1894 - M. Carey Thomas became President of Bryn Mawr
College (until 1922).

- Mary Wright Plummer was named Head Librarian at
Free Library of Pratt Institute in Brooklyn and
was in charge of the Library School. She
published Hints to Small Libraries.

- George School--Pennsylvania Yearly Meeting
Boarding School established (Hicksite).

- Wilmington Yearly Meeting (Orthodox) established.

1895 - Anna Comstock named to Committee for the
Promotion of Agriculture (became a major project
on teaching of nature at Cornell University).
She was the first woman of Cornell faculty from
1899-1922.

1896 - Dr. Eliza M. Mosher became Dean of Women and
Professor of Hygiene (first woman faculty member)
at University of Michigan.

- Anna Jeanes gave $200,000 to establish eight
Quarterly Meeting homes for elderly Friends and
others (Hicksite).

1894 - Florence Kelley became General Secretary to
1932 National Consumer's League--"proposed to use
consumer pressure to assure that goods were
manufactured and sold under proper working
conditions." Lived at Henry St. Settlement in
New York City--organized 60 Consumer Leagues in
20 states and two international conferences.

- Helen Marot published A Handbook of Labor
Literature and she undertook an investigation of
tailoring trades in Philadelphia for the United
States Industrial Commission.

- Susan B. Anthony helped found the International Council of Women--headed United States delegation.

1891 - Mary and Emma Garrett established Pennsylvania Home for Training in Speech of Deaf Children Before They Are of School Age (Bala Home). Mary was principal from 1893-1923.

1897 - Lutie Stearns (1887 graduate of Milwaukee State Normal School) was the first paid staff of the Wisconsin Free Library Commission (assisted in establishing one hundred free libraries and 1,480 traveling libraries).

- Committee on Peace and Arbitration was established by Philadelphia Yearly Meeting (Hicksite).

1900 - Susan B. Anthony helped in the process of getting the University of Rochester to admit women students.

- Mary Vaux (Walcott) - was the first woman to climb Mount Stephen in British Columbia. Mount Mary Vaux (elevation 10,881 feet) in that province was named for her.

- "Blessed Art Thou Among Women" - a photographic cycle on motherhood by Gertrude Käsebier was published.

- Hicksite branch of Quakerism forms Friends General Conference.

1901 - Mary Garrett joined Philadelphia Juvenile Court and Probation Association to work for a juvenile court and probation system for Pennsylvania.

- Gertrude Käsebier had a photographic essay of Native Americans (featuring Buffalo Bill's Wild West troupe) in Everybody's Magazine. This exhibit is now in the anthropology archives of

Smithsonian Institute.

- A peace conference (sponsored by Orthodox and Hicksites--General Conference) was held in Philadelphia.

1902 - Helen Marot investigated child labor situation for the Neighborhood Workers of New York City. This led to the formation of the New York Child Labor Committee. Florence Kelley was also involved with others in this work.

- Emily Greene Balch was co-founder of Women's Trade Union League.

- Gertrude Käsebier was a founder and fellow of Photo-Secession--an organization of pictorial photographers led by Alfred Stieglitz.

- Jane Addams' Democracy and Social Ethics published.

- Five Years Meeting, a joining together of Orthodox and Gurneyite Friends, was established.

1903 - The lobbying of the New York Child Labor Committee assisted in passage of the New York State Compulsory Education Act.

- Woodbrooke Settlement (adult school near Birmingham, England) was established.

1904 - National Child Labor Committee established. Florence Kelley worked with Lillian Wald for this project.

- International Woman Suffrage Alliance was established in Berlin, Germany. Susan B. Anthony was a major founder and was declared "Susan B. Anthony of the World" at this meeting. Rachel Avery, also a founder, was elected Secretary from 1904-1909.

1904 - Dr. Clara Marshall worked to establish a teaching
1907   hospital at the Woman's Medical College in
        Philadelphia.

1905 - Florence Kelley's <u>Some</u> <u>Ethical</u> <u>Gains</u> <u>Through</u>
       <u>Legislation</u> published.

     - Anna Thomas Jeanes published a book of poems,
       <u>Fancy's</u> <u>Flight</u>, which stressed unity of all
       faiths and the importance of mysticism.

1905 - Dr. Eliza M. Mosher as a member of the American
1928   Women's Hospitals Committee sent women doctors
       overseas to assist post-war relief work.

1906 - Mary Garrett became Chairman of Legislation of
       the National Congress of Mothers to bring about
       legislative reform through juvenile courts,
       child labor laws, and uniform marriage and
       divorce codes.

     - Helen Marot became executive secretary of Women's
       Trade Union League of New York. She held this
       position until 1913.

1906 - Martha Platt Falconer was Superintendent of the
1919   House of Refugee (Girl's Division) in
       Philadelphia. This later became Sleighton Farm
       for delinquent girls.

1907 - Dr. Sarah Dolley became President of the Women's
       Medical Society of the State of New York
       (formerly the Blackwell Society).

     - Anna Thomas Jeanes gave a million dollars for the
       Rural Negro Fund (salaries for teachers and
       improvement of buildings and courses of study in
       Negro schools).

     - Rachel Avery elected 1st Vice-President of

National American Women's Suffrage Association.

1908 - Supreme Court case Muller vs. Oregon established constitutionality of protective legislation limiting hours of working women (based on brief of Louis Brandeis) assisted by Florence Kelley of consumer's League.

- M. Carey Thomas was elected first president of National College Woman's Equal Suffrage League.

1908 - Rachel Avery became President of Pennsylvania
1910 Woman Suffrage Association and won endorsement of suffrage by state Federation of Labor.

1908 - Lucretia Longshore Blankenburg was an officer in
1914 General Federation of Women's Clubs and worked for endorsement of woman suffrage. That endorsement came in 1914.

- Grace Abbott became head of Immigrants Protective League.

- Nebraska Yearly Meeting established (Orthodox).

1909 - Florence Kelley was one of the founders of the National Association for the Advancement of Colored People (NAACP).

- Jane Addams was first woman president of the National Conference of Charities and Correction (later the National Conference of Social Work).

- Hannah Clothier Hull represented Philadelphia Yearly Meeting (Hicksite) at Peace Conference.

1909 - Helen Marot assisted Women's Trade Union League
1910 support of formation of International Ladies Garment Workers' Union.

1909 - Anna Pratt was secretary of the Bureau of
1916 Associated Relief in Elmira, New York, and was instrumental in bringing charity organization

techniques to local philanthropy.

1910 - Edith Abbott's Women in Industry was published.

- Emily Greene Balch's Our Slavic Fellow Citizens was published.

1910 - Florence Kelley was Vice-President of National
1920 American Woman Suffrage Association for several years.

1910 - Grace Abbott assisted in the Chicago Garment
1911 Worker's strike.

1911 - Jane Addams was 1st Vice-President of National American Woman Suffrage Association and she was first head of National Federation of Settlements.

- Anna Comstock wrote The Handbook of Nature (translated in 8 languages with 24 editions).

1911 - Florence Kelley worked with Louis Brandeis on
1913 brief for minimum wage legislation.

1912 - Dr. Eliza M. Mosher published a book on hygiene, Health and Happiness: A Message for Girls.

- Mary Wright Plummer was involved in formation of Association of American Library Schools (an accrediting agency).

- Edith Abbott and Sophonista Breckinridge publish-ed The Delinquent Child and the Home.

- Children's Bureau of the federal government was approved. Florence Kelley was one of its strong advocates.

1913 - Grace Abbott worked in successful Illinois Woman's Suffrage Campaign.

- Alice Paul chaired and established the Congressional Union of the National American Suffrage Association. This was a more militant group focused on a national suffrage amendment rather than a state by state approach. This group organized parades and pickets, were arrested and had hunger strikes in jail. They put pressure on President Woodrow Wilson to endorse woman's suffrage.

1914 - Helen Marot published a tract, American Labor Unions.

- both Philadelphia Yearly Meetings (Hicksite and Orthodox) protested to President Wilson concerning U.S. troops in Mexico.

1914 - Agnes Tierney worked in Philadelphia Yearly
1918 Meeting (Orthodox) on peace issues.

1915 - The American Women's Peace Party was founded with Jane Addams as President.

- International Congress of Women was held at The Hague--Jane Addams, Grace Abbott, and Emily Greene Balch were part of U.S. delegation.

- Women's International League for Peace and Freedom (WILPF) established. Jane Addams was elected president. Florence Kelley and Emily Greene Balch were founding members.

- Grace Abbott wrote The Immigrant in Massachusetts for Massachusetts legislature.

- Edith Abbott published The Real Jail Problem.

- Harriet Wiseman Elliott was lecturer in Equal Suffrage League of North Carolina.

1915 - Lutie Stearns was a lecturer throughout U.S. for
1932 woman suffrage, child labor legislation, prohibition, and world peace.

- Congressional Union split from the National American Women's Suffrage Association and Alice Paul helped found the National Women's Party.

1916 - Florence Kelley, through the National Consumer's League, backed the Keating-Owen Child Labor Act.

- Emily Greene Balch attended the International Committee of Mediation in Stockholm.

1917 - Grace Abbott published The Immigrant and the Community and became head of Child Labor Division of Federal Children's Bureau.

- Edith Abbott and Sophonisba Breckinridge published Truancy and Non Attendance in the Chicago Schools.

- American Friends Service Committee was formed by Orthodox Friends.

- Emily Greene Balch helped establish the Emergency Peace Federation and the Collegiate Anti-Militarism Committee.

- Helen Marot's Creative Impulse in Industry was published.

1917 - Anna Comstock was editor of Nature-Study Review.
1923

1918 - U.S. Supreme Court found Keating-Owen Act unconstitutional.

1919 - Emily Greene Balch became the paid secretary of the WILPF and she continued in this role for several years. Her teaching contract at Wellesley College was not renewed because of her pacifism. She also attended the International Congress of Women in Zurick (Congress took a critical position on the Versailles Treaty).

- Esther Smith (Orthodox) worked on issue of black

lynchings in the South and helped establish a Committee on Race Relations in Philadelphia Yearly Meeting.

1920 - 19th Amendment to the U. S. Constitution was ratified. This woman's suffrage amendment was often referred to as the Susan B. Anthony amendment.

- Emily Green Balch and Jane Addams help found the American Union Against Militarism (predecessor of American Civil Liberties Union).

- Anna Beach Pratt became Executive of the new White-Williams Foundation in Philadelphia. This foundation introduced the study of social work into public education and did consultant work as social work programs began to develop in higher education.

- Rachel DuBois worked with Young Friends on the creation of a Quaker Committee on Race Relations. A conference was held in Greensboro, North Carolina.

- World Conference of Friends in London, England.

1920   - American Friends Service Committee program for
1922   feeding German children after World War I. Carolena M. Wood was active in this work and interpreting it to Quakers in America.

1921 - Philadelphia Yearly Meeting (Orthodox) established the Mission Board.

- Bryn Mawr Summer School for Women Working in Industry starts.

1921 - Grace Abbott was head of the Children's Bureau and 1934 administers the Sheppard-Towner Act (programs to combat infant and maternal disease and mortality--this bill was rescinded by Congress in 1929). She was unofficial delegate

to League of Nations Advisory Committee on
Traffic in Women and Children.

1922 - Alice Paul convened a meeting of the National
Women's Party at Seneca Falls, New York, and a
"Declaration of Principles" is endorsed. This
meeting approved the first draft of the proposed
Equal Rights Amendment to U.S. Constitution. It
was called the Lucretia Mott Amendment.

- Jane Addams, Emily Greene Balch, and Rachel
DuBois attended the International Conference of
Women at The Hague, The Netherlands.

- Rachel DuBois attended an international
conference of trade unionists in Europe. She
also toured the A.F.S.C. German feeding program.

- Rachel DuBois established a Junior International
League for Peace and Freedom for high school and
college students.

- Auto Peace Tour (Rachel DuBois one of three
organizers) was sponsored by the National Council
for Prevention of War, Fellowship of Reconciliation and Carnegie Peace Institute. Speakers
traveled from city to city across the U.S. advocating peace.

1923 - Equal Rights Amendment introduced in U.S.
Congress supported by Alice Paul and opposed by
Florence Kelley (because of her advocacy of
protective legislation for women and children).

- Orthodox men and women in Philadelphia Yearly
Meeting began to meet together. There was a
Women's Clerk of Women's Yearly Meeting (a
formality) until 1929.

1924 - Jane Rushmore was chosen Clerk of Philadelphia
Yearly Meeting (Hicksite) as Men's and Women's
Meetings were merged.
- Edith Abbott became Dean of School of Social

Service Administration of University of Chicago.

- German child-feeding program resumed.

1924 - Hannah Clothier Hull was elected Presidentof
1939   American Women's International League of Peace
       and Freedom.

1924 - Rachel DuBois helped establish the Unified
       Assembly Program for high schools. This was a
       series on the contribution of ethnic groups to
       America and was prepared for high school assembly
       programs to combat racism. Used in Englewood,
       N.J., Washington, D.C., and New York City.

1924 - Martha Platt Falconer became Executive Secretary
1927   of Federation of Protestant Welfare Agencies in
       New York City.

1925 - Harriett Wiseman Elliott attended the Conference
       on the Cause and Cure of War led by Carrie
       Chapman Catt.

     - Mary Vaux Wallcott's five volume North American
       Wild Flowers (400 watercolor drawings and
       descriptions) was published by Smithsonian
       Institution. In 1926 she became an early woman
       member of Society of Geographers.

1927 - Emily Green Balch published Occupied Haiti.

1927 - Mary Vaux Wallcott was appointed to the U.S.
1932   Board of Indian Commissioners (appointed by
       Presidents Coolidge and Hoover).

1928 - Jeanes Hospital was established as a general
       hospital for cancerous, nervous and disabling
       ailments in Fox Chase, Pennsylvania, from the
       bequest of Anna Thomas Jeanes.

- Martha Platt Falconer was delegate to the International Conference of Social Work in Paris. She also took a tour of prisons and reformatories in England and Europe.

- Alice Paul and other National Women's Party members attended the Open Door Council in Berlin where a statement in support of equal rights for women in industry was adopted as part of the "Charter of Economic Rights for Working Women" and the "Open Door Manifesto." An Open Door International was established to monitor Women's concerns at League of Nations and the International Labor Organization (I.L.O.).

- Alice Paul and other N.W.P. members lobbied the Sixth Pan-American Conference in Havana for the creation of Inter-American Commission of Women (IACW) which was to prepare a digest of nationality laws and their effect on women. A NWP member was chosen chairperson of the IACW and this group was invited to the Conference on the Codification of International Law.

1929 - The lobbying of the National Women's Party and the Inter-American Commission of Women assured the introduction of the Equal Rights Treaty in the Assembly of the League of Nations. Alice Paul wrote this statement for the treaty: "The Contracting States agree that upon the ratification of this treaty men and women shall have equal rights throughout the territory subject to their respective jurisdictions." It was defeated but continued to be introduced while the League existed. Alice Paul prepared a massive study of women and nationality laws.

1930 - Pendle Hill, adult Quaker learning center, was established at Wallingford, Pennsylvania. Anna Brinton and her husband, Howard, were leader/directors. She was very active in A.F.S.C.

1930 - Rachel DuBois' Service Bureau (intercultural
1938   program for young people and an outgrowth of the
        Unified Assembly Program) was sponsored by the
        American Jewish Committee. It became part of the
        Progressive Education Association as Commission
        on Intercultural Education.

1931 - Jane Addams was first woman to be awarded Nobel
        Peace Prize.

      - Anna Beach Pratt was a delegate to White House
        Conference on Child Welfare.

1932 - Lutie Stearns wrote a column on reform issues for
1935   the Sunday Milwaukee Journal.

1933 - Grace Abbott organized Child Health Recovery
        Conference. From 1934-1939 she was editor of
        Social Service Review. From 1934-35 she was a
        member of President Franklin Delano Roosevelt's
        Council on Economic Security and she helped draft
        the Social Security Act.

1935 - Harriett Wiseman Elliott was Dean of Women at
1947   Woman's College of the University of North
        Carolina (at Greensboro). She was also active in
        many facts of the New Deal (including the White
        House Conference on Children in Democracy).

1935 - Alice Shaffer's The History and Administration of
        the Indiana Poor Law was published. She had
        studied with Grace and Edith Abbott and
        Sophonisba Breckenridge at the University of
        Chicago.

1937 - Friends World Committee for Consultation
        established in Washington, D.C.

1938 - Grace Abbott published two volume The Child and
        the State. This helped bring about a partial ban
        on child labor in the Fair Labor Standards Act

but was not the amendment against child labor she advocated.

- Alice Paul founded a new lobbying organization, the World Women's Party, and opens its headquarters at the Villa Bartholoni, Geneva, Switzerland, across from the League of Nations and the I.L.O. This became a refuge for emigrants from Germany, Poland, etc.

1939 - Alice Shaffer was loaned by the A.F.S.C. to the
1940   Committee for Refugees in Berlin to help evacuate Jewish children. She becomes a director of the Quaker International Center in Berlin which cared for persons whom the Nazis had designated Jews but who had no religious affiliation.

1939 - American and British Friends carried on war
1946   relief in Europe and Asia.

1939 - Rachel DuBois persuaded the United States Commission on Education to sponsor a series of 26 radio programs on intercultural education called "Americans All--Immigrants All."

1940 - Rachel DuBois initiated a program of Group Conversations (to bring persons of different racial and ethnic backgrounds into conversations in their homes). She wrote Get Together, America to explain and promote this movement.

- Harriet Wiseman Elliott and Eleanor Roosevelt preside at Washington Conference on Unemployment among Young Women. Elliott was appointed by President F. D. Roosevelt as Consumer Commissioner of the National Defense Advisory Commission (an adjunct of the National Defense Council).

1941 - Alice Shaffer became Chief of the Social Branch
1947   of the Division of International Labor, Social and Health Affairs (of U.S. Department of State) and was a consultant on child welfare in Central South America countries for the Children's Bureau

of U.S. Department of Labor.

1941 - Alice Paul helped establish the World Women's Party for Equal Rights and the Equal Rights International.

1941 - Alice Paul and others lobbied the developing
1945 United Nations to include principles of equality for women into the preamble to the U.N. Charter, in articles throughout the document and in the U.N. Human Rights Covenant.

1943 - Friends Committee on National Legislation established in Washington, D.C.

1945 - "The Preamble" of The Charter of the United Nations included the principle of equal rights for men and women. (Part of the credit for this inclusion goes to Alice Paul and others in the World Women's Party.

1945 - Rachel DuBois published Build Together, America and established the Workshop for Cultural Democracy (intercultural education and race relations).

- Harriet Elliott was appointed advisor for State Department at London Educational Conference sponsored by United Nations Educational, Scientific and Cultural Organization.

1946 - Emily Greene Balch was awarded the Nobel Peace Prize for her work in W.I.L.P.F.

1946 - Elizabeth Grey Vining was tutor to the Crown
1950 Prince of Japan.

1947 - American Friends Service Committee and Friends Service Council (Great Britain) awarded Nobel Peace Prize.

1949 - Alice Shaffer became part of the UNICEF staff and begins 23 years of work for children in Central America and Brazil.

1950 - Rachel DuBois published Neighbors in Action.

Notes

[1]Included in this time-line are some dates of events in the history of the Society of Friends which are of particular significance to women.

[2]The dates for the establishment of Yearly Meetings in the American colonies and nation are given. It is important to remember that accompanying (often preceding as well) the formation of these state-wide Quaker meetings are numerous local or Monthly Meetings and regional or Quarterly Meetings. At each level there were separate Men's and Women's Meetings for Business and leadership possibilities for many men and women.

[3]Yearly Meeting schools are included because most of them were co-educational and thus had female students, teachers and administrations. There were also many local Quaker schools which feed into the yearly meeting schools.

REFERENCES

Included in the sources for Time-Line are papers from
the collection, American Quaker Women as Shapers of
Human Space. Other references are:

Bacon, Margaret. "A Widening Path: Women in Philadel-
phia Yearly Meeting Move Toward Equality, 1681-1929,"
Friends in the Delaware Valley, John M. Moore, ed.,
Friends Historical Association, 1981.

Brinton, Howard H. Friends for 300 Years: The History
and Beliefs of the Society of Friends since George Fox
Started the Quaker Movement. Harper and Brothers, 1952.

Curtis, Barbara. "Appendices" in Friends in the
Delaware Valley.

Elliott, Errol T. Quakers on the American Frontier.
Friends United Press, 1969.

James, Edward and Janet, eds. The Dictionary of Notable
American Women: 1607-1950. Cambridge, Massachusetts,
Belknap Press of Harvard University Press, 1971.

Jones, Rufus M. The Quakers in the American Colonies.
London: Macmillan, 1923.

Kenworthy, Leonard. Living in the Light: Some Quaker
Pioneers of the 20th Century in the U.S.A. Kennett
Square, Pa.: Friends General Conference and Quaker
Publications, 1984.

Russell, Elbert. The History of Quakerism, New York: 1942.

Selleck, George A. Quakers in Boston: 1656-1964 Cambridge, Mass.: Friends Meeting, 1976.

Spruill, Julia Cherry. Women's Life and Work in the Southern Colonies. Chapel Hill: The University of North Carolina Press, 1938.

West, Jessamyn, ed. "A Quaker Chronology" in The Quaker Reader, New York: Viking Press, 1962.

APPENDIX II

A Listing of Notable Women who were Friends
(or of Friendly Connection)
and are included in
THE DICTIONARY OF NOTABLE AMERICAN WOMEN 1607-1950
E. & A. James, Eds.
prepared by Edwin B. Bronner, Haverford College

Abbott, Grace 1878-1939**
Social Worker
NAW 1:2-4

Anthony, Susan Brownell 1820-1906*
Reformer
NAW 1:51-57

Avery, Rachel G. Foster 1858-1919*
Suffragist
NAW 1:71-72

Bailey, Hannah Clark Johnston
1839-1923*
Reformer
NAW 1:83-85

Barnard, Hannah Jenkins 1754?-1825*
Minister
NAW 1:88-90

Blankenburg, Lucretia Longshore
1845-1937*
Reformer
NAW 1:170-71

Broomall, Anna Elizabeth 1847-1931*
Obstetrician; medical educator
NAW 1:246-47

Butler, Phoebe Anne (Moses)
1860-1926**
see **Oakley, Annie**

*Found in DQB
**Insufficient evidence to be included in
DQB at this time
(Dictionary of Quaker Biography
Manuscripts--Haverford Library)

Chace, Elizabeth (Buffum) 1806-1899*
Reformer
NAW 1:317-19

Chandler, Elizabeth Margaret 1807-1834*
Abolitionist; author
NAW 1:319-20

Claypoole, Elizabeth (Griscom) Ross
Ashburn 1752-1836*
see **Ross, Betsy**

Collins, Ellen 1828-1912*
Philanthropist; reformer
NAW 1:360-62

Comstock, Anna (Botsford) 1854-1930**
Naturalist
NAW 1:366-69

Comstock, Elizabeth Leslie (Rous)
1815-1891*
Minister; reformer
NAW 1:369-70

Crandall, Prudence 1803-1890*
Abolitionist; teacher
NAW 1:399-401
(see **Philleo, Prudence (Crandall)**
in DQB)

Darragh, Lydia (Barrington) 1729-1789*
Nurse; midwife
NAW 1:434-35

Dickinson, Anna Elizabeth 1842-1932*
Lecturer
NAW 1:475-76

Jeanes, Anna Thomas 1822-1907*
Philanthropist
NAW 2:270-71

Jones, Jane Elizabeth (Hitchcock)
1813-1896**
Lecturer
NAW 2:285-86

Jones, Rebecca 1739-1818*
Minister
NAW 2:290-01

Jones, Sybil (Jones) 1808-1873*
Minister
NAW 2:291-93

Kasebier, Gertrude (Stanton)
1852-1934**
Photographer
NAW 2:308-09

Kelley, Florence Molthrop 1859-1932*
Social reformer
NAW 2:316-19

Ladd, Catherine Everit (Macy)
1863-1945*
see Ladd, Kate (Macy) 1863-1945*

Ladd, Kate (Macy) 1863-1945
Philanthropist
NAW 2:352-54

Logan, Deborah (Norris) 1761-1839*
Collector of historical records'
writer
NAW 2:418-19

Longshore, Hannah E. (Meyers)
1819-1901*
Physician
NAW 2:426-28

Lukens, Rebecca Webb (Pennock)
1794-1854*
Entrepreneur
NAW 2:442-43

Madison, Dolley (Payne) Todd
1768-1849*
Wife of Pres. James Madison
NAW 2:483-85

Marot, Helen 1865-1940*
Reformer; writer
NAW 2:499-501

Marshall, Clara 1847-1931*
Physician
NAW 2:501-02

Masters, Sybilla (Righton) d. 1720*
Inventor
NAW 2:508-09

Mitchell, Maria 1818-1889
Astronomer
NAW 2:554-56

Moody, Lady Deborah (Dunch)
d. 1650?*
Colonist
NAW 2:569-70

Moore, Clara Sophia (Jessup)
1824-1899**
Author; writer on etiquette
NAW 2:573-74

Mosher, Eliza Maria 1846-1928*
Physician
NAW 2:587-89

Mott, Lucretia (Coffin) 1793-1880*
Minister; abolitionist
NAW 2:592-95

Nichols, Mary Sargeant (Neal) Gove
1810-1884*
Reformer; writer
NAW 2:627-29

Oakley, Annie 1860-1926**
Sharpshooter
NAW 2:644-46

Penn, Hannah (Callowhill) 1671-1726*
Second wife of William Penn
NAW 3:47-48

Philleo, Prudence (Crandall) 1803-1890*
see Crandall, Prudence 1803-1890

Pinkham, Lydia (Estes) 1819-1883*
Patent medicine proprietor
NAW 3:71-72

Plummer, Mary Wright 1856-1916*
Librarian
NAW 3:77-78

Pratt, Anna Beach 1867-1932*
Social worker
NAW 3:93-95

Preston, Ann 1813-1972*
Physician
NAW 3:96-97

Pugh, Sarah 1800-1884*
Teacher; abolitionist
NAW 3:104-05

Ross, Betsy 1752-1836
*Legendary maker of first
Stars and Stripes*
NAW 3:198-99

Schofield, Martha 1839-1916*
Educator
NAW 3:239-40

Slocum, Frances 1773-1847*
Indian captive
NAW 3:298-99

Smith, Hannah (Whitall) 1832-1911*
Religious author; evangelist
NAW 3:313-16

Starbuck, Mary (Coffyn)
1644/45 OS-1717OS*
Minister
NAW 3:347-49

Stearns, Lutie Eugenia 1866-1943*
Librarian; lecturer; reformer
NAW 3:353-54

Stephens, Alice (Barber) 1858-1932*
Illustrator
NAW 3:359-60

Thomas, Martha Carey 1857-1935
Educator; feminist
NAW 3:446-50

Thomas, Mary Frame (Myers)
1816-1888*
Physician; suffragist
NAW 3:450-51

Walcott, Mary Morris (Vaux)
1860-1940*
Artist; naturalist
NAW 3:525-26

Way, Amanda M. 1828-1914*
Reformer; preacher
NAW 3:552-53

White, Anna 1831-1910*
Reformer
NAW 3:583-84

White, Helen (Magill) 1853-1944*
*Educator; first American woman
to earn Ph.D*
NAW 3:588-89

Wilkinson, Jemima 1752-1819*
Religious leader
NAW 3:609-10

Wischnewetzky, Florence Molthrop
(Kelley) 1859-1932*
see Kelley, Florence Molthrop
1859-1932

Wright, Martha (Coffin) Pelham
1806-1875*
Women's rights leader
NAW 3:684-85

Wright, Patience (Lovell) 1725-1786*
Sculptor in wax
NAW 3:685-87

APPENDIX III
Carol Stoneburner, Ruth Fulp
and Charlotte Simkin Lewis

Comparison of 85 Quaker Women and a Sample Group of Non-Quaker Women
as described in
THE DICTIONARY OF NOTABLE AMERICAN WOMEN 1607-1950
Analysis done by Carol Stoneburner, Charlotte Simkin Lewis and Ruth Fulp at Guilford College. List of Quaker women included in DICTIONARY OF NOTABLE AMERICAN WOMEN was done at Haverford College. Six and three tenths percent of women included in Dictionary were Quaker (higher than proportion of Quakers to the population at any time in U.S. history.)

	Quaker	Non-Quaker
Quaker or religious education	33	12
Level of education: Elementary (E)	5	7
Secondary or		
Seminary (S)	25	41
College (C)	9	19
Graduate or		
Professional (G)	14	5
Tutoring (T)	10	2
Single	28	30
Married (number of marriages in parentheses)	54 (61)	55 (74)
Divorced or separated	5	14
Widowed	22	27
Number of women who were mothers	42	37
Number of children (for whole group)	176	135
Employed (at some time during life)	40	59
Financially dependent	49	29
Public speaking, lecturing, etc.,	46	17
Civic activity	39	31
Writer	39	41
Belonged to women's clubs, networks, etc.	24	22
Involved in abolition or civil rights	30	5

*Family (parents and siblings) in		
abolition or civil rights	16	2
Involved in temperance	15	7
*Family involved in temperance	7	1
Women's rights	30	21
*Family involved in women's		
rights	11	1
Pacifist, involved in peace		
movement	14	4
*Family were pacifists	2	0
Co-worker with husband (in		
employment or in volunteer		
cause work)	26	5
Traveled extensively	46	38
Lived primarily in urban setting		
(U)	52	49
Lived primarily in town setting(T)	28	27
Lived primarily in rural setting(R)	13	8
Lived primarily in		
North Eastern U.S.A.	68	49
Lived primarily in south	6	11
Lived primarily in mid-west	8	14
Lived primarily in west	5	14
Negro women	1	2
Age at death (average)		
for the whole group)	74.4	69.1

*This is probably a very unreliable set of figures because it was not a standard question considered in all of the biographic descriptions.

FOR THE WOMEN WHO WERE QUAKERS:

25 converted to Quakerism ("Convinced Friends.")
9 were "Read out of Meeting" either for marrying a Non-Quaker at certain periods in history, or for taking a radical stand on Abolition or some other cause, or for "heresy."
14 left Quakerism--often in protest over some issue such as Abolition.
9 were noted as Hicksite Friends.
4 were listed as Orthodox Friends.
1 was listed as a Free Quaker.
1 was a New Light Quaker.
1 was a Guernite Friend.
1 was a Progressive Friend (branch of Hicksite Friends.)
1 was listed as an Evangelical Friend.

10 Quaker women were listed as Ministers (M.)
2 Quaker women were listed as Clerks (C.)

FOR THE NON—QUAKER WOMEN:

Their religious preferences were charted as follows:

	Parent's Religious Preference	Adult Religious Preference
Congregationalist (C)	10	7
Episcopalian (E)	10	18
Presbyterian (P)	5	8
Roman Catholic (RC)	3	3
Methodist (M)	5	6
Unitarian (U)	3	8
Baptist (B)	4	2
Dutch Reformed (DR)	1	
Jewish (J)	5	2
Mormon (Mor)	1	
Universalist (Univ)		
African Methodist (AME)		1
Christian Science (CS)		1

Comparison of vocational categories used by DICTIONARY OF NOTABLE
AMERICAN WOMEN

	Quaker	Non-Quaker
Reformer (includes women's rights, abolition, peace, civil rights, temperance, etc.)	25	13
Social worker, settlement house, social reformer	5	10
Science and medicine	11	5
Writers	8	24
Business or entrepreneur	2	3
Philanthropist	3	1
Religious leader or minister	14	7
Lecturers	3	4
Artists	5	4
Educators and scholars	10	15
Known primarily in relation as wife or child	3	5
Newspaper publishers, editors, etc.		7
Actress or singer		8
Colonist or frontierswoman	2	
Other	Maker of U.S. flag Indian captive Sharpshooter	Confederate spy Rev. war heroine Interpreter Benefactor of Jefferson Davis

In Volume III of DICTIONARY OF NOTABLE AMERICAN WOMEN there are classified listings of the women from the whole dictionary. Of particular interest to Quaker women are the following:

12 out of the 30 abolitionists are Quakers - 40%
11 out of the 60 feminists are Quakers - 18%
13 out of the 28 ministers and evangelists are Quakers - 48%
2 out of the 9 naturalists are Quakers - 22%
12 out of the 53 physicians are Quakers - 22%
3 out of the 16 prison reformers are Quakers - 18%
2 out of the 18 political advisers and appointees are Quakers - 11%
3 out of the 29 college administrators are Quakers - 10%
6 out of the 41 entrepreneurs are Quakers - 16%

In a comparison of the Quaker and non-Quaker women in reference to dates of activity, it seems clear that Quaker women were influencing the public scene earlier. There were 11 Quaker women active before 1800 as compared to 5 non-Quaker women. There were 34 Quaker women active in the 19th century as opposed to 21 non-Quaker women. During the 20th century there were 40 Quaker women active with 20 of these active in the 30's - 50's. There were 60 non-Quaker women active in the 20th century with 29 of them living into the 30's - 50's.

Several characteristics of the Quaker women seem to form a profile. By and large their marriages were more stable. There was a high level of partnership in their marriages. They had more children. It was not at all infrequent for some parts of these children's education to be carried out in the home, supervised by the mothers. They were much more financially dependent upon their husbands or families than the non-Quaker women, although almost half of them were employed at some time in their lives. There is also a clear picture of familial stability between the generations, with members often supporting the same causes and issues.

Quaker education plays an important part in the lives of at least a third of the Quaker women. Advanced degrees are much more prevalent among the Quaker women than the non-Quaker women. The relatively lower number of collegiate women in the Quaker group is partly attributed to the larger number of women who were living before the 1860's - 1880's when college education became much more extensive for women. The Quaker women after the turn of the century then have a much higher rate of graduate work following college. Involvement in science and in medicine were important parts of their educational pursuits.

Quaker women led much more public lives, even though the home and family were of more importance in their lives. They spoke and acted in public with much more frequency. They traveled more extensively and were parts of more groups, network causes, etc., which took their influence out of their own limited regional areas. They seemed to know a lot of people, either from traveling or entertaining them in their own homes.

Quaker women's influence in the Society of Friends was considerably more important than similar religious influence by non-Quaker women. Thirty five Quaker changed from the religious preference of their parents, as opposed to forty three non-Quaker women. Again there is some evidence of greater familial solidarity among the Quaker women and their families.

Proportionately Quaker women entered the public scene sooner than non-Quaker women in the history of this country. They also seem to move into a period in the 20th century when they lose in relative strength of presence to the non-Quaker women. Some of the reasons for this may relate to changing definition of "notable" which takes effect in the 20th century for women. Much more the emphasis is on professional competence and skill. With the continued emphasis on the family, fewer Quaker women who married were in positions which claimed attention. They may be changing with the recent generation of Quaker women who have combined home and career (pioneers in doing this) and who later in their lives (between 50 and 70 years of age) are becoming noted.

INDEX

World's Temperance Convention,
 NYC 434
Wright, James 153
Wright, Joel 253
Wright, John 153, 154
Wright, Martha (Coffin) 44,
 220n, 237, 269, 391, 431, 472
Wright, Patience (Lovell) 472
Wright, Rachel Wells 153, 154,
156, 419, 420, 421
Wright, Suzanna pref. 4, 420,
 422

Yearly Meetings:
 Baltimore 254-260, 416, 424,
  426
 Canada 440
 Dublin, Ireland 416
 Genesse 235, 239, 424
 Georgia 424, 431
 Illinois 424
 Indiana 424, 426, 437, 443
 Iowa 438, 440
 Kansas 441
 London, England 414, 421, 422
 Maryland 420
 Nebraska 454
 New England 414, 418, 424,
  446
 New York 277, 417, 420, 424
 North Carolina 279, 417, 419,
  424, 427, 436
 Philadelphia 221n, 256-260,
  284-285, 416, 417, 423,
  426, 437, 444, 451, 454,
  456, 457, 458, 459
 Progressive 238
 Ohio 423, 424, 426, 427
 Oregon 450
 South Carolina 424, 431
 Virginia 424, 431
 Western 435
 Wilmington 450
Young Friends 457
Young Women's Christian
 Association (YWCA) 286

STUDIES IN WOMEN AND RELIGION